Designing and Managing Programs

SAGE SOURCEBOOKS FOR
THE HUMAN SERVICES SERIES

Series Editors: ARMAND LAUFFER and CHARLES GARVIN

Recent Volumes in This Series

Designing and Managing Programs

An Effectiveness-Based Approach

Second Edition

Sage Sourcebooks for

the Human Services

Peter M. Kettner
Robert M. Moroney
Lawrence L. Martin

SAGE Publications
International Educational and Professional Publisher
Thousand Oaks   London   New Delhi

For information:

 SAGE Publications, Inc.
2455 Teller Road
Thousand Oaks, California 91320
E-mail: order@sagepub.com

SAGE Publications Ltd.
6 Bonhill Street
London EC2A 4PU
United Kingdom

SAGE Publications India Pvt. Ltd.
M-32 Market
Greater Kailash I
New Delhi 110 048 India

Printed in the United States of America

Library of Congress Cataloging-in-Publication Data

Kettner, Peter M., 1936–
    Designing and managing programs: An effectiveness-based
approach/Peter M. Kettner, Robert M. Moroney, and
Lawrence L. Martin.—2nd ed.
        p. cm.—(Sage sourcebooks for the human services; v. 11)
    Includes bibliographical references and index.
    ISBN 0-7619-1548-6 (cloth: acid-free paper)
    ISBN 0-7619-1549-4 (pbk.: acid-free paper)
        1. Social service—United States—Planning. 2. Social service—
United States—Evaluation. 3. Social service—United States—Finance.
I. Moroney, Robert M., 1936– II. Martin, Lawrence L. III. Title.
IV. Series: Sage sourcebooks for the human services series; v. 11.
    HV95 .K428 1999
    361'.0068'4—ddc21   98-25496

99 00 01 02 03 04 10 9 8 7 6 5 4 3 2

Acquiring Editor:	Jim Nageotte
Editorial Assistant:	Heidi Van Middlesworth
Production Editor:	Astrid Virding
Production Assistant:	Stephanie Allen
Typesetter	Marion Warren
Indexer:	Juniee Oneida

CONTENTS

Part IV. Calculating the Costs and Value of the Intervention

PREFACE

Since this book was first published in 1990, demand has remained fairly steady, so it is with a good deal of caution that we approach revisions, operating from the perspective that "if it ain't broke, don't fix it!" On the other hand, from our own use of the book as well as from feedback from colleagues and students, we are aware that some sections in the first edition could stand to be strengthened with better examples and more illustrations. In addition, some developments in the last few years have affected components of the program planning process such as program design and budgeting. We felt that if users of this book are finding that they are expected to meet new demands for accountability, then the design and budgeting changes should be incorporated into a second edition.

In the preface to our first edition, we noted that programs were an important unit of analysis in the field of social services because they have a tendency to take on lives of their own, regardless of changing social conditions and changing needs. Recent developments in terms of federal expectations for accountability, which we discuss, reinforce even more the importance of understanding what programs are intended to accomplish and measuring what they achieve.

Also in the preface to our first edition, we noted that the methods and techniques of effectiveness-based program planning were introduced and discussed from a theoretical perspective. To do otherwise, we said, would imply not only that the subject matter was atheoretical but that the professional practitioner was basically a technician. Programs without a sound theoretical base, we observed, are built on a flimsy, unsupported foundation. And because the theoretical underpinnings for sound program planning have not changed substantially over the past decade, we have left Chapters 2 through 5 relatively untouched in the second edition.

The overall model of effectiveness-based program planning remains intact. We have changed some of the terminology to fit with the terms more generally in use today. Instead of using the adjective *ultimate* to describe outcome objectives, outputs, and outcomes, we now use the adjective *final*. In addition, we have introduced the concept of quality measures and have suggested some techniques for defining and measuring quality.

Probably the major changes have been introduced in the chapters on budgeting and program evaluation. In the budgeting chapter, four cost allocation methodologies are presented. The chapter on evaluation has been retitled "Performance Measurement, Monitoring, and Program Evaluation." In this chapter, techniques for meeting new requirements for performance measurement are integrated into methods for program evaluation. A new appendix presents an example that will require users to incorporate all the techniques of performance measurement in the course of completing the nine-step process.

As with the first edition, we have attempted to produce a product that will be useful to both practitioners and students. We are aware that many are currently devoting a great deal of time and energy to designing programs and data collection systems that will be responsive to the new and continuing demands for accountability. We sincerely hope that this volume will support and strengthen their efforts.

Peter M. Kettner
Robert M. Moroney
Lawrence L. Martin

Part I

ASSESSING CURRENT PRACTICES

Chapter 1

CONTEMPORARY ISSUES
IN SOCIAL SERVICE PROGRAM
PLANNING AND ADMINISTRATION

THE ERA OF ACCOUNTABILITY

This book is about social service programs and the ways in which they can be planned to make them effective. In the following chapters, we will examine in great detail the many developmental phases a program must go through and the many elements that need to be included if it is to be considered "effectiveness based." Effectiveness is the theme throughout this book. It refers to the extent to which social programs and social services are successful in achieving positive changes in the lives of the clients they serve. The issue of effectiveness has been at the center of much controversy in the social work literature for more than two decades (see, e.g., Fischer, 1973; Rubin, 1985). The question addressed over the years has been, Do social services make a difference in the lives of clients?

When the first edition of this book was published in 1990, the demand for accountability and the need to demonstrate effectiveness were just emerging. As the decade of the 1990s unfolded, these concerns became part of a national debate, and funding agencies at all levels began to require that service providers develop mechanisms to respond to these issues. Rhetoric gave way to practice.

In their book *Reinventing Government,* Osborne and Gaebler (1992) discussed the advantages of market-oriented government as involving the changing of systems (government services, competition, customer choice, accountability for results and public interest). They noted, however, that markets can create inequitable outcomes (e.g., poor people with limited access to health care). Because of this, Osborne and Gaebler stressed the need to improve communities: "To complement the efficiency and effectiveness of market mechanisms, we need the warmth and caring of families, neighborhoods and communities. As entrepreneurial governments move away from administrative bureaucracies, they need to embrace both markets *and* communities" (p. 309).

Two significant attempts to move in this direction are the growth of purchase-of-service contracting (POSC) and managed care. The federal government first authorized state welfare departments to purchase services from other state agencies through amendments to the Social Security Act passed in 1962 (Pub. L. No. 87-543). Through the 1967 amendments to the Social Security Act (Pub. L. No. 90-248), Congress encouraged the states not only to expand purchase of services but to purchase these services from private agencies. Thirty years later, POSC not only has expanded but also has become the preferred vehicle for financing many of the human services, to the point that most private, not-for-profit agencies are dependent on these contracts for their survival (Eggers & Ng, 1993; McMurtry, Netting, & Kettner, 1990). Under this program, agencies agree to provide a specific number of units of services to designated client populations. State agencies, beyond deciding what services are to be delivered to whom, have the responsibility to monitor the contracts: That is, they are concerned that the services are actually delivered and that they meet quality standards.

Managed care is a more recent innovation in the human service field, emerging in the 1980s. Unlike POSC, with its emphasis on accountability and partnerships between the public and private sectors, managed care is beginning to turn the human service system around. The flexible system of block grants and POSC has been replaced by a highly structured and rigid set of policies and procedures that determine the type and amount of services that providers will be allowed to deliver. Managed care is basically concerned with cost containment, and the organizations that reimburse providers are in a position to determine how much they will pay and what standards will have to be met through an elaborate monitoring system.

Finally, the federal government, through the Government Performance and Results Act of 1993 (Pub. L. No. 103-62), will require government at all levels to establish performance measures for all federally funded programs under what will be known as Performance Partnership Grants (PPGs). The performance measurement movement is proposed as a management tool to be used, not primarily to determine cutbacks and contain costs, "but to clarify what we want to achieve, document the contribution we can make to achieving our goals, and document what we are getting for our investment" (U.S. Department of Health and Human Services, 1995, p. 19).

Each of these initiatives directly addresses the issues of effectiveness, efficiency, and planning in a different way, but all of them have similar intents. Social agencies are faced with the challenge of developing appropriate systems and processes if they want to remain viable over the next decade. Over the past 10 years, and since the publication of the first edition of this book, we have observed changes within many agencies that suggest such a transformation is not only possible but likely. Ten years ago, most midsize agencies either did not have personal computers or, if they did, used them primarily for fiscal purposes and word processing. Today, as you walk through these same agencies, there are computers in almost every office, and they are being used by management staff for planning and evaluation activities and by direct practitioners for the tracking of services provided and results achieved. The capability to be accountable—to develop and then evaluate programs—is available.

THE ISSUE OF EFFECTIVENESS

We have adopted the theme of effectiveness as a central concept in this book in the belief that it can become a major consideration in social service agency administration. Building on some of the concerns first expressed by Patti (1985), we attempt to take effectiveness-based planning to the next level by prescribing precisely what must be done in planning and administering programs so that they can be said to be effective.

The term *program* has been used in social services for decades, and in many ways it has been taken for granted. In this chapter, we illustrate, through the use of a series of questions addressed to the reader, that designing effective programs requires a careful, detailed thought process that begins with understanding a social problem and ends with analyzing data on effectiveness. Chapters 2 through 11 focus on the tasks to be accomplished and the elements to be considered and defined to create programs capable of demonstrating effectiveness.

The tasks and processes of program development proposed here are in no way simplistic or intended for the beginner. They require thoughtful study and analysis of the issues that confront program planners. The purpose of delving into the complexities of social problems and social service programs is to draw attention to the need to understand more about programs so that they can become more precisely focused on getting the kinds of results they are intended to produce. In short, this is all about clients and the changes that need to be achieved in their lives.

Perhaps in the same way that an understanding of the law is of critical importance to a practicing attorney or an understanding of the body to a physician, so an understanding of social problems and programs is central to the practice of social work. This understanding will require that old assumptions be challenged and new approaches to serving clients be implemented as we learn more about effectiveness. In a sense, we will be proposing that programs go through periodic checkups to determine their continuing effectiveness and relevance in a changing environment.

WHAT IS EFFECTIVENESS-BASED PROGRAM PLANNING?

The idea of conducting periodic checkups is, in essence, what effectiveness-based program planning is all about. Designing effective programs requires that social service professionals develop more thorough understandings about social problems, people in need, and social services than has been expected in the past. A commitment to effectiveness requires that we collect new kinds of data—data that will inform us about client conditions at entry into and exit from services so that we can learn more about our ability to have an impact on their problems. This approach, which we will refer to throughout this book as *effectiveness-based program planning,* will allow us to make changes in our programs so that we do more of the things that help and fewer of the things that do not. And, as you will see, it is designed to be useful for both direct service and management purposes.

Effectiveness-based program planning involves taking a program through a series of steps designed to produce a clear understanding of the problem to be addressed, to measure client problem type and sever- . ity at entry, to provide a relevant intervention, to measure client problem type and severity at exit, and to examine selected indicators in a follow-up study to determine long-range outcomes. The purpose of all these activities is to provide a basis for continual improvement of services to clients and to provide a common database for both clinical and administrative staff for analysis and decision making about program changes. This way, instead of asking clinicians to fill out forms useful only for completing management reports, clinical staff can record data useful for understanding the progress of their clients and, at the same time, provide data and information necessary to good program management.

USING EFFECTIVENESS PRINCIPLES TO UNDERSTAND EXISTING PROGRAMS

In the following chapters, we present a step-by-step process that will enable the reader to begin with a social or personal problem experienced by clients and end with a program designed to get results that can be documented. Before beginning these chapters, however, we propose that you take a few minutes to take stock of current agency practices in a social service agency with which you are familiar. This may be helpful in drawing a contrast between the way most social service programs are currently designed and the way they must be designed for effectiveness-based program planning.

The following assessment instrument is divided into sections on each of these topics:

- Defining programs
- Problem analysis
- Needs assessment
- Selecting a strategy and establishing objectives
- Program design
- Management information systems
- Budgeting
- Program evaluation

If you are interested simply in a quick overview of a program's strong and weak areas, you may wish to limit your assessment to checking yes and no answers. If, on the other hand, you wish to conduct a more in-depth assessment, use the instrument as a basis for interviewing key program staff and fill in their answers to the follow-up questions. The program planning model discussed is designed for those programs that provide a direct service to clients. It is not applicable for support programs such as fund-raising, lobbying, or advocacy.

Defining Programs

In this section, we explore the extent to which agency services are organized into programs. Some social service agencies may keep programs separate so that each is clearly identifiable in terms of staff, resources, clients, and services provided. Others may have so much overlap that it almost appears that the agency offers only one undifferentiated program to all clients, no matter what their problems or needs. The following two questions are intended to encourage you to think through where your agency stands on its definition and separation of programs.

1. Does your agency provide for clients a number of clearly
    defined and distinct programs (as opposed to providing
    undifferentiated casework services for all clients)?   Yes___ No___
2. If your agency does have separate programs, can you identify
    agency staff and resources that are allocated to each of your
    programs?   Yes___ No___

Count the number of yes answers, and calculate a subtotal for this section.

Subtotal ____/2 = ____%

If the answer to both of these questions is no, you may conclude your participation in this survey at this point or select another agency because the remaining sections focus on questions about programs.

Problem Analysis

In Chapter 2, we deal with the need for a thorough understanding of the social problem the program or service is expected to address. Historically, programs were sometimes built on emotional appeals around specific cases (e.g., orphaned children, the elderly poor) rather than on a clear analysis of data and an understanding of the history and development of the problem. If we are committed to getting the best possible results in the shortest possible time for clients, it is critical that we develop a graphic depiction of the type, size, and scope of the problem as well as its relevant historical highlights, theory, research findings, and etiology. For example, if a program is to be designed to treat drug users, we will clearly want to avoid planning the program with the assumption that drug users are all alike. We know, in fact, that they differ in many ways and therefore will want to develop a typology to discover how many of each type are in the community, where they live, and how severe their problems are. This approach provides a solid foundation on which to build an effective and precisely targeted program or intervention.

3. Thinking of one particular program or service, can you identify the problem(s) this program is intended to address, first in general terms and then in specific terms (e.g., inadequate housing; lack of housing for families with temporarily unemployed breadwinners)? Yes___ No___
   If yes, state it/them:

4. Can you define the target population(s) this program is intended to serve, first in general terms and then in specific terms (e.g., families without housing; families residing in Franklin County in need of temporary shelter for up to 90 days)? Yes___ No___
   If yes, define it/them:

5. Can you identify geographic boundaries for the population served by your program? Yes___ No___
   If yes, state them:

6. If necessary, could you provide a reasonably accurate estimate (based on reliable documentation) of the number of people within these boundaries who fit the description in Questions 3 and 4 for the problem(s) and target population(s) in both general and specific terms? Yes___ No___
   ,If yes, identify populations, and list estimates:

7. Can you identify data sources for the above statistics? Yes___ No___
   If yes, state them:

8. Can you define the commonly agreed-on understandings among staff who work in your program about the primary or most common causes of this problem and about cause-and-effect relationships? Do you think you could get at least 75% agreement? Yes___ No___
   If yes, list them:

Count the number of yes answers, and record a subtotal for this section.

Subtotal = _____/6 = _____%

Needs Assessment

When someone is experiencing a problem, that individual has a need. Sometimes the need is obvious: Someone who is homeless needs a home; someone who is unemployed needs a job. At other times, the need is more subtle and more difficult to meet—for example, the need for increased self-esteem or the need for a permanent and loving relationship with a nurturing parent substitute.

Accuracy and skill in matching needs to services come from solid, thorough work on problem analysis. Once you are comfortable that you have an understanding of need, it is time to turn to techniques of needs assessment. There are four different perspectives from which we look at need: normative need (as defined by experts in the field), perceived need (as seen by those experiencing the need), expressed need (as evidenced by those who seek out services), and relative need (needs and resources in one geographic area compared with needs and resources in another).

The following questions will give you an opportunity to explore your understanding of each of these perspectives on need and to think through the extent to which your programs have taken these perspectives into account.

9. Given the problem you identified in Question 3, is there
    agreement among your clinical staff about the major,
    predominant categories of needs of clients who come to you
    with these problems?   Yes____ No____
    If yes, list the categories of need:

10. Are there any standards that are used to establish normative
    need (a point or level defined by experts below which one is
    defined as being in need in this particular problem area: e.g.,
    a certain income level or a specified level of neglect)?   Yes____ No____
    If yes, identify the standards:

11. Can you define what consumers of your services (clients)
    perceive their needs to be?   Yes____ No____
    If yes, list the major categories of need:

12. Of those people who seek services from this program,
    do you know what percentage are served?   Yes____ No____
    If yes, state the percentage:

13. Do you know how the volume of services provided in your
community compares with the volume of these same services
provided in other communities in terms of percentage of needy
population served? (In other words, do you serve a larger or a
smaller percentage than other communities?)   Yes___ No___
If yes, cite some comparative data:

14. In relation to the needs identified in Questions 9 and 11,
do you know approximately how many people within
your geographical boundaries have these needs?   Yes___ No___
If yes, identify the numbers for each:

15. Do you know in what census tracts or zip codes
the highest levels of need are located?   Yes___ No___
If yes, list them:

Count the number of yes answers, and record a subtotal for this section.

Subtotal = ____/7 = ____%

Selecting a Strategy and Establishing Objectives

Once you have completed the problem analysis and the needs assessment, it is time to begin to think about a strategy for reducing or eliminating the problem by meeting the needs of people who have the problem. This involves a number of steps. When we reach this point in the program planning process, we are well grounded in history, theory, research, and etiology of the problem; therefore, we are in a position to propose an appropriate intervention. We then propose one or more program hypotheses—statements about what outcomes are expected if a person with the problems we have defined receives the service(s) we are about to design. Program hypotheses, then, provide a framework for the development of precisely stated goals, objectives, and activities.

The following questions should help in assessing your understanding of a program's underlying assumptions and expectations.

16. Can you spell out the underlying assumptions about your
client population and the expected effects of your program in
the form of a series of "if . . . then" statements (e.g., "If parents
learn good communication skills and if they use them with their
children, then they are less likely to resort to physical violence
with their children")?   Yes___ No___
If yes, state them:

17. Can you identify the following as they relate to your program?
    • An independent variable (services provided)   Yes___ No___
    • A dependent variable (expected ultimate or long-term
      results of services)   Yes___ No___
    • An intervening variable (intermediate or short-term
      results of services)   Yes___ No___
    If yes, state them:

18. Looking at the way you assess client need in your program,
    • Is the assessment quantified?   Yes___ No___
    • Does it permit you to categorize and compare clients at
      intake by type and severity of problem?   Yes___ No___
    If yes, identify the assessment instrument and list its categories:

19. Does your program have written objectives that specify
    expected outcomes for clients?   Yes___ No___
20. Is there evidence that your program staff attempt to move
    clients toward these outcomes?   Yes___ No___
    If yes, describe the evidence:

Count the number of yes answers, and record a subtotal for this section.

Subtotal = ____/8 = ____%

Program Design

It is one thing to understand a need; it is quite another matter to design an intervention that will meet that need. For many years, social service professionals have simply prescribed "casework" in response to almost every need. Advances in the field have made it clear that certain problems will respond better to certain more precise interventions than to a generalized casework approach. The purpose of the program design phase is to put together that service or combination of services that appears to have the best possible chance of achieving the program's objectives.

Program design involves careful consideration of the resources needed to address the needs of clients and attention to the ways in which these resources will be organized. It is a critical point in the planning and management of programs.

If we simply consolidate a great deal of program design under the heading of "casework," we leave decisions about client assessment, service provision, service completion, and outcome assessment to the professional judgment of each caseworker. When this happens, it becomes difficult, if not impossible, to examine program effectiveness and to modify program design in the interest of improving services to clients. On the other hand, bringing precision to each element of program design allows for constant examination and constructive program change as data and information about effectiveness become available to guide our refinements.

The following questions should help you in assessing the level of precision achieved in specifying the elements of your program design.

21. Does your program have identified problem or need categories
    that can be checked off at intake and used to help in
    understanding client needs in the aggregate?   Yes____ No____
    If yes, list the categories:

22. Does your program have some method for quantifying or
    scaling severity of problems?   Yes____ No____
    If yes, describe it:

23. Do you collect quantified data on the following?
    - Client demographics   Yes____ No____
    - Client social history data   Yes____ No____
    - Client problem type and severity   Yes____ No____

24. Do you itemize service tasks for each service you provide
    and record the amount of time or volume of each task
    provided for each client?   Yes____ No____
    If yes, list them:

25. Do you specify acceptable service methods for each type of
    service (e.g., one-to-one counseling, group treatment,
    classroom instruction)?   Yes____ No____
    If yes, list them:

26. Do you have some way of identifying those who complete
    your program and those who drop out so that you can do
    some analysis of these as separate populations?   Yes____ No____
    If yes, describe how they are tracked:

27. Do you quantify and measure results with clients using
    some sort of a pre-post measure?   Yes____ No____
    If yes, describe it:

28. Do you follow up with clients and collect data that indicate
    long-term effects of treatment?   Yes____ No____
    If yes, list the follow-up variables:

29. Do you have a formally defined unit of service that you
    use to measure the amount or volume of service provided
    by your program?   Yes____ No____
    If yes, describe it:

30. Do you have written standards to which you adhere
    that protect the quality of service provided to clients?   Yes____ No____
    If yes, cite them:

Count the number of yes answers, and record a subtotal for this section.

Subtotal = ____/12 = ____%

Management Information Systems

Once designed and implemented in accordance with the guidelines established for effectiveness-based program planning, program data can be collected, processed, and aggregated in a manner that informs both clinical staff and administrators. Programs can be said to meet objectives and to bring about positive changes in clients' lives only if the data generated from the program provision process can support such statements.

In contemporary social service agency management, the use of computers to build such a database is absolutely essential. Narrative case recording is useful for individual case analysis, planning, supervision, and documentation but is virtually useless for purposes of program management and administration. In effectiveness-based program planning, we propose a client data system that is capable of producing data and information about the progress of clients throughout each episode of service and the effects of these services at termination and follow-up. This information, we believe, should be used by all levels of staff, each from its own perspective.

The following questions may be useful in assessing the strengths and weaknesses of an existing management information system.

31. Do you have a computerized data collection and data-processing system that is used for client data? Yes___ No___
32. Which of the following data elements do you collect, enter, aggregate, and cross-tabulate to achieve a better understanding of your clients and their problems:
     - Client demographics Yes___ No___
     - Client social history data Yes___ No___
     - Client problem type Yes___ No___
     - Client problem severity Yes___ No___
     - Staff characteristics Yes___ No___
     - Material resources provided to clients Yes___ No___
     - Service type Yes___ No___
     - Service tasks Yes___ No___
     - Method of intervention Yes___ No___
     - Service completion Yes___ No___
     - Service quality Yes___ No___
     - Service outcome Yes___ No___
     - Long-term outcome Yes___ No___

33. Do you produce tables of aggregated data about clients and
    client services on a regular basis?   Yes____ No____
34. Which of the following groups use them?
    • Clinical/direct service staff   Yes____ No____
    • Supervisors   Yes____ No____
    • Program managers   Yes____ No____
    • Administrators   Yes____ No____
    • Board of directors or political body to whom
      the program is accountable   Yes____ No____
35. Do you regularly discuss what changes should be made to
    improve your program based on data produced by your
    management information system?   Yes____ No____

Count the number of yes answers, and record a subtotal for this section.

Subtotal = ____/21 = ____%

Budgeting

All programs and services depend on funding for their continuation. It is therefore in the interests of clients and staff to ensure that the best possible results are being achieved at the lowest possible cost. A well-designed budgeting system is capable of generating important and valuable information for use in making program changes in the interest of providing better quality services for clients at a lower cost. Unfortunately, many budgets in human service agencies reflect only categories for which dollars have been spent. In effectiveness-based program planning, we propose, instead of or in addition to those categories, methods for calculating costs for items such as provision of a unit of service (e.g., an hour of counseling), completion of the full complement of prescribed services by one client, achievement of a measurable outcome by one client, and achievement of a program objective.

For example, by costing out services, we may learn that it costs just $500 per trainee for a training program. However, if we also find that there is a 50% dropout rate, the cost then doubles to $1,000 per "graduate." These kinds of calculations help staff keep focused on using resources in a way that steers clients in the direction that offers them the best possible chance of success at the lowest cost. These types of calculations should ultimately lead to more cost-effective and cost-efficient operation of social service programs.

The following questions should help you in assessing the strengths and weaknesses of your current budgeting system.

36. Can you calculate the following from the budget data you
    collect?
    - Line items by program   Yes___ No___
    - Direct costs by program   Yes___ No___
    - Indirect costs by program   Yes___ No___
    - Total program costs   Yes___ No___
    - Cost per unit of service   Yes___ No___
    - Cost per service completion   Yes___ No___
    - Cost per client outcome   Yes___ No___

Count the number of yes answers, and record a subtotal for this section.

$$\text{Subtotal} = \underline{\hspace{1cm}}/7 = \underline{\hspace{1cm}}\%$$

Program Evaluation

One of the most exciting features of effectiveness-based program
planning is that it produces information that informs staff about how
successful the program was in relation to expectations as expressed in
objectives. How many abusing and neglecting parents completed parent
training? How many can demonstrate improved parenting skills? How
many have stopped abusing and neglecting and are progressing toward
more effective relationships with their children? This information can
bring together direct service staff, supervisors, managers, administrators, and board members around a common set of concerns and
interests. Surely it is more satisfying to be able to say, at the end of a
program year, "We helped 75% of our clients to master at least 10
techniques of effective parenting" than simply to be able to say, "We
provided services to 100 abusing and neglecting families."

In this section, we explore methods of evaluating social service
programs from several different perspectives.

37. Do you regularly use any of the following approaches in
    monitoring and evaluating your programs?
    - Assessment of the amount of staff time and resources
      used in direct client services   Yes___ No___
    - Assessment of costs and ways to reduce them without
      adversely affecting the quality of service   Yes___ No___
    - Assessment of the cost of outcomes and ways to reduce
      them without adversely affecting the quality of service Yes___ No___
    - Evaluation of outcomes achieved with clients and ways to
      improve them   Yes___ No___

- Assessment of the service provision process and the extent to which it fits the program design as originally intended   Yes___ No___
- Assessment of the contribution made by your program to the total community in terms of its impact on the social problem experienced by the community   Yes___ No___

Count the number of yes answers, and record a subtotal for this section.

$$\text{Subtotal} = \underline{\hspace{1cm}}/6 = \underline{\hspace{1cm}}\%$$

Total Score

Now count the total number of yes answers, record them, and calculate a total program assessment score.

$$\text{Total assessment score} = \underline{\hspace{1cm}}/69 = \underline{\hspace{1cm}}\%$$

If you have systematically completed this questionnaire, you should now have eight subscores and one overall score. Although this is not presented as a validated instrument for inquiry, it can, nevertheless, provide some clues as to where the major work should be done to achieve an effectiveness-based program planning system.

The following chapters are intended to explain each of the phases of effectiveness-based program planning. As you proceed through these chapters, we encourage you to think through and apply the concepts to the program you have assessed using the foregoing questionnaire. You will find that many of the concepts in the remaining chapters can be applied and a program converted to an effectiveness-based program planning system without incurring great financial cost to the agency. The primary costs are time, thoughtful analysis, and staff and executive commitment. Beyond these, the major costs come at the point of computerization and data entry. We are confident that when your conversion has been completed, the staff, the administrators, the board, and the ultimate beneficiaries, clients, will all feel it was worth the effort.

Part II

PROBLEM ANALYSIS/
NEEDS ASSESSMENT

Chapter 2

UNDERSTANDING SOCIAL PROBLEMS

Most social programs are justified on the basis of one intention: to address identified social problems, which become translated into the needs of a target or client population. Once implemented, programs often drift from their initial focus and are adjusted to meet the demands of agency and staff. Nevertheless, in their original design it is important that programs develop a clear focus on client need and that the extent to which it is met becomes the barometer for measurement of program integrity and effectiveness. This is the "bottom line" for social service programs because we cannot use profit or loss as a measure of success. Though considerations of profit and loss are important in business, in the social services we need to go beyond these and give primary consideration to meeting client need in a way that is cost-efficient and cost-effective. In the following pages, we explain how one develops an understanding of a social problem in a way that makes explicit the relationship between problem, client need, and program.

Problem analysis and needs assessment can be viewed as the first of a number of related activities that, in sum, constitute the planning process. Such a process, according to this perspective, would also include the formulation of a policy framework expressed in goals and objectives; the selection and implementation of a particular intervention or program; the calculation of resources needed to implement the program; and the management of monitoring, evaluation, and feedback procedures.

These activities often require the participation of many, including professionals familiar with the problem, administrators familiar with service capabilities, consumers or potential clients who have experienced the problem firsthand, and others knowledgeable and influential in this area of concern. We will frequently refer to this group as *program planners*. Most human service professionals, at one time or another during their careers, serve in the role of program planner. Perhaps in some large, well-funded agencies there are professionals specifically designated as planners. For the most part, however, planners in human service agencies are those involved in the direct provision of services, supervisors, or administrators who have a special assignment to develop a program plan and who draw on a variety of people for their special talents and perspectives.

An orderly, systematic approach to program planning suggests that planners begin by asking: What is the problem? What are its facets, and what are its causes? What are the characteristics of those who can be defined as having the problem? How many people are affected? Can they be located geographically? Effectiveness-based planning presumes that needs can be responded to if, and only if, such questions can be answered.

Pursuing answers to these questions appears at first glance to be both logical and necessary. In a typical agency, however, both the phases of the process and the questions asked are often likely to be ignored or treated in a perfunctory fashion. Why might this be so?

STATING PROBLEMS AS SOLUTIONS

The answer might be found in the following scenario. Whether it resembles your experience or not, it describes an all-too-common occurrence in many communities.

> A planning agency concerned with the problems and unmet needs of the aged (e.g., the area agency on aging) brings together representatives of all agencies offering services to the aged. The convener hopes that the process will not only identify these problems and needs but also provide the basis for establishing priorities and a blueprint for long-range planning. After introductions are made and the purpose of the meeting is stated, each participant is asked to share with the group his or her perceptions of problems, needs, and priorities.
>
> The first person, a supervisor for the local visiting nurse association, describes that agency's programs and the number of patients it serves and

concludes that, on the basis of these data, there is a pressing need for three more nurses to make home visits in the southern part of the county. The next person at the table, a social worker from the local senior center, speaks of the large numbers of aged who are coming for socialization services and meals and the problems many have in obtaining transportation. She concludes with a plea that priority be given to developing a specialized transportation service for the elderly and disabled. A third person, a dentist from the health department, describes the severe dental problems most elderly persons face and suggests that priority be given to setting up a dental clinic in the large senior housing complex in the center of the city. The next person, a representative from adult protective services, speaks of the tragedy of elder abuse and the need to establish a more comprehensive respite care system as a preventive measure. As the meeting progresses, a case for additional housing for the elderly is articulated by the representative of the housing authority, for increased employment opportunities by the representative of the local community action program, and for additional specialized counselors by the representative of the community mental health center. At the end of the process, the area agency representative thanks the members and promises to draft a report based on their "planning."

Many planning efforts are initiated with the implicit assumption that the problems are fully understood and their solutions known. In fact, the problems are frequently stated in terms of solutions, often qualified by the word *more,* as in "more physicians" (or nurses, social workers, counselors, day care facilities, hospital beds, or training slots). The common denominator to this approach, regardless of the problem in the community or the target population, is a strong belief that the major problem is basically a lack of resources. We know what to do and would be able to solve most, if not all, problems if we had sufficient resources.

The Limitations of This Approach

Additional resources are not necessarily always the solution. Times change, conditions change, people change, and problems change. The assumption that "business as usual" with additional resources is what is needed may well prove to be faulty. A fresh analysis of condition and problem may well lead to a number of different interventions or programs.

Commitment to business as usual is certainly understandable. As human service professionals, we have come to believe in the efficacy of our profession and therefore advocate for an increase in numbers. But these services tend to take on lives of their own, thereby reducing the potential for flexible approaches to problem solving and inhibiting efforts to initiate change through experimentation.

The emphasis on planning is too often on organizational survival or program maintenance and expansion. Administrators who are responsible for the management of programs often structure their agencies in such a way that the purpose of the organization becomes defined as the sum total of the services provided. Staff tend to view potential clients in terms of those services the staff are in a position to offer. The elderly, for example, are often grouped into those "needing" homemaker services, meals on wheels, institutional care, and other services. Likewise, persons who are mentally retarded may be seen as those who "require" institutional care, special education, training, and other services long after these approaches have outlived their relevance for selected groups.

Whatever the system, this labeling has the potential to begin at intake and to continue throughout the client's contact with the agency. All too often, services that were initially introduced as "possible" mechanisms to assist people in need quickly become the "only" way to do things. Services initially developed and seen as potentially beneficial for certain people with particular needs take on a life of their own and are rarely questioned. There is a universal tendency when we approach planning with a focus on the existing service delivery system to emphasize management aspects—the efficiency of our system. We rarely step back and examine the purposes of these services or question their effectiveness.

Looking only at existing programs and services serves to maintain the status quo, and the process generally discourages experimentation. Change, when it does occur, offers minor modifications to the existing system. The problem with the approach, however, is that although the system has grown exponentially over the past 30 to 35 years, and although expenditures have mushroomed, many of the social problems that these expenditures were to alleviate remain unchanged. The persistence of serious problems despite monumental financial efforts has brought renewed pressure for experimentation with new processes and changes in the existing system. The expectation that resources will continually expand to meet need as defined in the existing system is not realistic.

The critical considerations in developing an understanding of a social problem, then, are these:

- Problem analysis should be seen as the first of a series of related activities in the planning process.
- Problem analysis initially should focus on understanding the problem—not on generating the solutions.
- Problem analysis should involve a fresh look at issues, free of assumptions about services.

THE NEED FOR A NEW APPROACH

These pressures, in part, have stimulated a growing recognition that there must be a better way to understand and address problems. The need for data to justify predetermined service planning decisions is being replaced by a need for data that will lead to a clearer understanding of social problems and will help in identifying the most effective directions for planning decisions. This, in part, has been the impetus for developing a model for effectiveness-based program planning.

Current decision making is not, and probably will never be, a purely technical process removed from the political environment. This does not mean, however, that decisions should not be influenced by sound technical analysis. Attempts need to be introduced that establish more rational decision-making processes that take into account both the political and the technical.

The appropriate first activity, then, is problem analysis and the assessment of need. It is one that seeks to stimulate independence from the status quo by focusing on the problems and needs of people rather than on the existing network of human service programs. This activity begins with the recognition of a social condition.

IDENTIFYING A SOCIAL CONDITION

The temptation in problem analysis is to move directly to a definition of a problem. Premature definitions, however, can lead to premature conclusions about the nature of the problem. Instead, program planners should begin with an understanding of a condition: the facts, or a statistical representation of the phenomenon under study. The facts may tell us, for example, how many people are experiencing the condition, who they are, where they live, and for how many the condition is mild, moderate, or severe. This begins to present a profile or portrait of a condition. From there we can move to an understanding of a problem.

The concept "social problem" needs to be understood as relative, in that an individual brings a frame of reference, shaped by a value system, to a condition and labels a condition as a problem. Webster defines a problem as a "source of distress." A condition, on the other hand, can be defined as a social fact: that is, a datum that stands independently and is without value interpretation. An example may clarify this distinction. To report that a particular family's income is $16,000 for the year 1999 is to describe that family's income condition only. An income of $16,000 is a social fact and only a social fact. To label a family's income of $16,000 as a social problem requires bringing some frame of reference to that social fact.

DEFINING PROBLEMS

A problem that is inadequately defined is not likely to be solved. Conversely, a problem that is well defined may be dealt with successfully, assuming that adequate resources are made available and appropriate services are provided. Still, it must be understood that problem analysis is by nature more an art than a science. If it were a science, there would be only one approach to it, and no matter how many program planners were involved in this phase, collectively or individually, the analysis, grounded in objective methods, would always result in the same conclusion.

Although it involves a good deal of creative activity, problem analysis still has its foundation in an orderly approach based on proven principles. What we find, however, is that different program planners can assess the same situation and produce quite different analyses insofar as each shapes the problem in terms of his or her background, training, experience, and values.

Scientific objectivity in the analysis of a community's problems would be, in fact, an unrealistic and possibly undesirable goal. It would be unrealistic in the same way that social science has recognized that objectivity in science is not possible. It would be undesirable, moreover, in that existing attempts to translate this "scientific objectivity" tend to result in the application of dominant values under the guise of neutrality when labeling a situation as a "problem" (Moroney, 1986).

Social Problems and Standards

One way to move from fact to problem is to bring some standard to assess the individual situation. If the family with the $16,000 income in 1999 was made up four or more members, they would be defined as living below the federally defined poverty level with that income in that year. If, on the other hand, the family was made up of a parent and a child, or two parents and no children, their income of $16,000 in 1999 would place them above the poverty level. The fact of the income has not changed, only the size of the family, and thus the label that applies to that level of income. The standard by which we determine whether a particular family is poor, or living in poverty, is a judgment that there is a level of income under which a family of a particular size cannot meet basic needs.

A second way of looking at this labeling of an income level (a social fact) as constituting poverty (a social problem) was offered by Lourie (1964), who pointed out that an income below a certain level is a social problem because it is related to a number of other conditions that have been labeled as pathological, such as "high morbidity and mortality rates, poor housing, broken families, low education and high incidence of crime" (p. 205). Conditions become problems when they are judged by someone or some group to be negative, harmful, or pathological. Furthermore, whereas one individual or group may label a condition to be a social problem, another individual or group may argue the opposite. One group may describe the existing housing stock in a neighborhood as "substandard" because the social facts/conditions fall below the published standards (the federal definition of *substandard* relates to various aspects of plumbing, heating, electricity, and space as it relates to overcrowding). Another group may look on that same housing and draw a different conclusion; in fact, that housing may be viewed by the homeless as superior to their existing situation. A third group may feel that if the owners (assuming they are absentee landlords) were required to upgrade the housing, they might raise the rents to the point that some low-income families might find themselves forced to vacate.

Given varying perspectives on social conditions, therefore, it is critical that all views be taken into account during the planning process. To do otherwise opens up the possibility of an incomplete analysis and the probability of future political backlash during the implementation phase.

In summary, in problem analysis it is important to remember the following:

- The first point of focus is on conditions or social facts.
- Conditions become problems when they are judged to be negative, harmful, or pathological.
- It is important to know who is judging the condition as a problem and why.

FRAMEWORKS FOR PROBLEM ANALYSIS

Two frameworks offer a number of questions as guides in this phase of the planning process (Cohen, 1964; Morris & Zweig, 1966). In general, they deal with the nature of the situation, the social values being threatened, the extent to which the situation is recognized, the scale of the problem, and the etiology of the problem. These concerns can be reduced to the questions listed below, each of which is discussed in turn.

1. What is the nature of the situation or condition?

In pursuing an answer to this first question, program planners need to collect facts and impressions from as many different individuals and groups as possible—including service providers, community leaders, and those affected by the problem—to ensure that all perspectives are considered and that the problem is not labeled prematurely. If, for example, we are concerned with the increase in the incidence of teenage pregnancy, we will want to collect information not just from human service professionals but also from others who are affected—for example, parents, teens, teachers, and clergy.

2. How are the terms being defined?

One of the reasons that many planning efforts either terminate prematurely or result in ineffectual programs is that the problem is not clearly understood in the same way by all who participate in the planning. For example, the planning effort might be concerned with the problem of unemployment in the community. The term *unemployment,* however, may refer only to those actively looking for work or may include "discouraged jobseekers" and the "underemployed," those working part-time or fewer than 50 weeks each year. Common understandings must be achieved on all terms so that there is a shared definition of the problem and the target population.

3. What are the characteristics of those experiencing the condition?

This question closely follows the previous question. In answering it, we are able to describe those experiencing the problem in sociodemographic terms. Who are they, and what do they look like? If the planners are concerned with the homeless problem, for example, and have achieved agreement on their definitions, the next task will be to describe who the homeless are. In most communities, we are likely to find that many different subpopulations make up the homeless. They cannot be thought of as a single homogeneous group. A percentage are likely to be families with young children, another group will probably be severely mentally ill persons, and still another will be individuals with alcohol-related problems. Without these data, the planning effort is likely to produce programs that may be appropriate to only one or a few of the subgroups experiencing the problem of homelessness.

4. What is the scale and distribution of the condition?

This question addresses the need to estimate the numbers affected and the spatial distribution of the condition under study. These data provide two figures: (a) an estimate of the numbers, important for deriving some notion of the level of effort needed to deal with the condition; and (b) the distribution of the condition, whether concentrated in specific geographic areas or spread out. This might give program planners some beginning direction in terms of intervention strategies.

5. What social values are being threatened by the existence of the condition?

There is a need to explore, to the extent possible, how people in the community would respond to the presence of the condition if they knew that it existed. For example, how would the general community react if the situation involved the number of children being left alone during the day or after school by working parents who had no other alternatives? Would people be concerned with the safety of these children? Would they support the position that young children need supervision? Perspectives of community people, community leaders, the media, and various special interest groups are important for later use in determining whether this particular condition will be seen as a problem that should be addressed.

6. How widely is the condition recognized?

It is valuable to have some idea of potential community support for later action. Furthermore, if the situation is not widely recognized, there may be a need for community education before an intervention can be implemented. If the condition is known only to some professionals or agencies and those who have experienced it, it is unreasonable to expect the larger community to respond favorably to a request for support. The problems of homelessness and AIDS demonstrate this point. In the early 1980s, few people were concerned with these problems; many saw them as both small in scale and involving narrowly defined populations. Community action occurred only when the general public and community leaders became more aware of and knowledgeable about these conditions.

7. Who defines the condition as a problem?

A corollary of this is the question, Who would support and who would oppose resolution of the condition? It should be apparent that problem analysis in a planning context is different from problem analysis in a traditional research framework. It includes an analysis not only of who, what, and where but also of the political environment. This assessment of the readiness to deal with the problem and to commit resources to its resolution is an important part of problem analysis.

In any situation, there is likely to be one group of people who define the condition as a problem, another who have no opinion, and still another who oppose any resolution or change in the situation. When facing demands to improve substandard housing, for example, those opposing change may include landlords and others who are benefiting from the status quo. Whenever money is involved, which includes almost all areas of social services, there is likely to be competition for scarce resources and therefore opposition. Whatever the situation, it is critical to identify these possible opposing forces. To do otherwise could result in failure during later stages of the planning and implementation processes. Force field analysis offers one strategy to carry out this task (for discussions of this strategy, see Netting, Kettner, & McMurtry, 1998).

8. What is the etiology of the problem?

This question raises concerns that are the most critical part of these frameworks—the need to identify the cause(s) of the problem. Interventions that target the causes of the problem will result in positive out-comes; others may not.

Typically, etiology emerges from a review of the theoretical and research literature on the topic and from an understanding of the history and development of the problem. The epidemiological model can be helpful in determining etiology. An epidemiological approach hypothe-sizes the existence of causal chains and assumes that if a link in that chain can be altered or broken, the problem can be dealt with, at least with partial success.

Two classic examples are found in the literature on communicable diseases: response to a cholera outbreak in the 19th century and the antimalaria campaign of the 20th century. In the first case, the investi-gator noticed that those who contracted cholera were likely to have used water from a single source—the Broad Street pump. The epi-demic abated after the source was sealed and closed (MacMahon, Pugh, & Ipsen, 1960). In the second example, the researchers found that malaria existed only when three essentials were present—a human to contract the disease, a mosquito to carry the disease, and a swamp to breed the mosquitoes. Assuming a causal chain, efforts were initiated to eradicate the breeding grounds, and the incidence of malaria was dramatically reduced (MacMahon et al., 1960). More recently, epidemiological thinking has been helped us better understand current communicable and infectious diseases such as sexually transmitted diseases and AIDS.

Although the model has been less successful in dealing with multi-causal problems and problems that do not involve infection, it has great value as a framework for thinking about problems. Cloward, Ohlin, and Piven (1959) incorporated this approach in their proposal dealing with juvenile delinquency. They hypothesized that delinquent behavior re-sulted from "blocked opportunity" and that "blocks" included a nonre-sponsive educational system, an inaccessible health care system, discrimination, poverty, and substandard housing. Their intervention, then, focused on removing these blocks.

Some risks may have to be taken in speculating about etiology in multicausal social problems. The amount of knowledge and information program planners have about the problem will have a major influence on the accuracy and validity of their common understandings of cause and effect. Reaching agreement is extremely important in that it is around these common understandings of cause and effect that interven-tions are designed.

9. *Are there ethnic and gender considerations?*

Although not a part of the early analytical frameworks, this question has taken on a new significance in the past few years. As the bodies of literature on culture and gender grow, it is important that program planners be aware of the ways in which the problem and the proposed intervention will affect and be affected by ethnic and gender considerations.

Though the general intervention may be the same for many different groups, the way the intervention is packaged is shaped by these considerations. Several authors have developed feminist and ethnic-sensitive interventions (see, e.g., Cross, 1989; Morales & Salcido, 1989; Rauch, 1989; Solomon, 1989). Where programs will affect and be affected by these populations, this literature should be explored.

In summary, it should be apparent that problem analysis in a planning context is different from problem analysis in a traditional research framework. It includes not only an analysis of the who, what, and where issues but also an analysis of the political environment, an assessment of a community's readiness to deal with the problem, and a measure of the resources the community is willing to commit to its solution. Finally, it is critical that program planners understand history, theory, and research related to the problem so that cause-and-effect relationships can be hypothesized and areas of need for gender and ethnic sensitivity can be identified.

Chapter 3

NEEDS ASSESSMENT
Theoretical Considerations

THE CONCEPT OF NEED

To illustrate the concept of need and its application to human services, we present a brief, and not uncommon, scenario. A task force is
appointed to explore and to make recommendations about alarming
increases in reported drug use in a community. A study is undertaken,
and key community leaders share their perspectives with the task force.
The police chief believes that the community needs stronger law enforcement capability. A major corporation executive believes that there
is a need for widespread drug testing in places of employment. A social
service agency executive sees a need for more treatment and rehabilita-
tion of drug users. A legislator believes there is need for harsher
sentencing and more jail cells. Without some framework for understanding need, the task force will probably end up recommending a little
of each, or it may simply choose to define need as it is perceived by the
most powerful individuals and groups. Neither solution really pursues
a serious understanding of the concept of need.

In determining that individuals or groups have a need, it is important
to evaluate existing conditions against some societally established standards. If the community is at or above those standards, there is no need;
if it is below those standards, there is need. The difficulty comes in
defining the standards. They are often vague, elusive, and changing. We

discuss a number of perspectives on standards in subsequent sections of this chapter, but first we examine two theoretical perspectives on need.

THEORETICAL UNDERSTANDINGS OF NEED

Two theorists—Ponsioen and Maslow—have offered a number of useful insights on need. Ponsioen (1962) suggested that a society's (or community's) first responsibility is to meet the basic survival needs of its members, including biological, social, emotional, and spiritual needs. Although these needs may be defined differently over time, each society or community will identify a level below which no one should fall. Within this framework, social need exists when some groups do not have access to these "necessary" goods and/or services whereas others do. Need, in this sense, is relative, and the planning issue becomes one of distribution and redistribution.

Maslow (1954) took a slightly different approach: He argued the value of discussing need in hierarchical terms. Accordingly, people become aware of their needs in a prescribed manner—from the bottom up—and only when the more basic, or lower, needs have been satisfied can higher ones be attended to. More specifically, until physiological survival needs are met (e.g., food and shelter), a person cannot be overly concerned with safety and security. Achievement of this second level of need then allows attention to higher levels—the need for love and self-actualization.

Although this discussion of concepts may seem far removed from the practical problems of planning, it is in fact incorporated into much community and societal planning. For example, the British have developed their National Health Service with a keen understanding of Ponsioen's argument. Rather than spending their resources on developing the more sophisticated medical technologies and then making them available to patients, the official policy is to give priority to making primary medical care and health services available to the general population. It is only when this level of basic service is available to all that other forms of medical technology will be supported.

An example of how Maslow's hierarchical framework has been applied can be found in programs dealing with family violence. The first level of service provision is the shelter—a place a woman can turn to when she has been abused. Initially, basic *survival* needs are addressed—food, housing, and, if necessary, medical care for the woman and her children. Only when these have been addressed can the staff turn to the next level—*security* (although the shelter does provide safe housing, legal services are often needed for longer-term security). When these survival and security needs have been met, the staff can then turn to higher-level needs—helping the woman achieve a *sense of belonging* (the shelter actually creates a "community" of families and staff who are supportive of each other) and a sense of *self-esteem* (through participation in support groups) and finally *self-actualization* (self-reliance, autonomy, and self-governing) through finding meaningful employment, child care arrangements, child support, and permanent housing.

Despite the above applications, need as a concept remains somewhat vague, often buried in phrases so global that it has little value for placing boundaries on the planning task. Alternatively, it is at times employed so narrowly that specific services are mandated and analysis is unnecessary. Moreover, although the word *need* is used frequently by program planners and managers, it is rarely operationalized. All too often, the professional assumes that it is understood and therefore requires little elaboration, only to discover later that the program has targeted neither the "real" needs nor the "right" group. In the following sections, we explore the importance of the concept of need and argue from a number of perspectives that needs-based planning is not only possible but necessary for the design and implementation of effective human services.

NEEDS ASSESSMENT
AND THE PLANNING PROCESS

Once problems have been identified and defined, they have to be translated into needs (eventually the needs will be translated into services or other interventions) that are to be addressed through the planning process. As a concept, need is not only difficult to define but, once defined, difficult to measure. One of the first "official" definitions in the human services arena was introduced in 1974, when the federal government consolidated a number of social service programs through the creation of the social service block grant. The legislation, commonly referred to as Title XX or the Title XX Amendments to the Social Security Act (Pub. L. No. 93-647), required each state, as a condition of the receipt of funds, to initiate a planning process that included the assessment of need as the beginning point. The legislation defined a need as

> any identifiable condition which limits a person or individual, or a family member in meeting his or her full potential. Needs are usually expressed in social, economic or health related terms and are frequently qualitative statements. Need assessment refers to the aggregation of similar individual needs in quantified terms. (20 U.S.C. § 228.31)

Although need is defined globally and rather ambiguously in the regulations, Title XX did advance our thinking and practice by asserting that need has both *qualitative* and *quantitative* dimensions. The qualitative statement implicitly requires the labeling of the situation as a problem to be corrected or ameliorated. This, of course, was the major thrust of the previous chapter.

Quantification or tabulation of that problem represents the second dimension of need. Planning assumes that it is possible to identify similarities among people or groups of people who are experiencing problems and that these problems can be translated into needs that can be categorized and aggregated. In turn, once these aggregations have been tabulated, they can be further transposed into service budgets and appropriate service delivery structures. However, the ability to group or aggregate is a sine qua non for effective planning for the human services.

In summary, thus far we have tried to illustrate the following:

- Problems must be translated into needs.
- Need is a normative concept shaped by social, political, and economic environments.
- Theorists differ on the interpretation of the concept.
- Ponsioen defined need in terms of a level below which no one should fall.
- Maslow defined need in terms of a hierarchy in which higher-level considerations become needs only after lower-level needs are satisfied.
- Need has both quantitative and qualitative dimensions.

Understanding need requires that we address a number of key issues. The first is understanding what we mean by the term *need,* with specific emphasis on the complexity of need as a planning concept. The second is examining factors influencing need. The third involves exploring categories of need, and the fourth deals with general problems of reliability and validity of data used to determine need.

FACTORS INFLUENCING
THE DEFINITION OF NEED

At the beginning of this chapter, we introduced the idea that need involves statements of values and preferences and that these are influenced by existing social, political, and economic institutions. We expanded this argument by suggesting that Ponsioen and Maslow accepted this reality when they attempted to describe levels of need and the development of priorities. This position is built on a number of important assumptions.

The first assumption is that need itself is elastic and relative rather than static and absolute. If need were absolute, the planning task would be relatively straightforward. Once we had defined the need and quantified its scope, the primary task would be to develop a plan for services and programs to meet the defined need and then to acquire sufficient resources to implement the plan. Experience shows otherwise. At best, needs assessment assists the planner in estimating what the need is at that moment and what it may be at some time in the future if attitudes, expectations, conditions, and values do not change dramatically.

As attention is focused on a problem and services are provided, expectations are raised and demand increases. The homeless, for example, do not necessarily create a demand for housing in a community. Homelessness exists side by side with thousands of vacant houses. It is only when affordable housing becomes available and the means are found to enable the homeless to afford that housing that a demand is created for this limited type of home.

In short, expanding services tend to raise expectations in the target population. We now realize that many people who might need services seek them only when they believe there is a real possibility of actually receiving them. Planners, then, must begin with the assumption that need is elastic—that it is likely to change over time—and that this elasticity extends also to demand: That is, demand is likely to increase with increased service provision. This influence, furthermore, can have unintended consequences. For example, if we allocate a greater share of social welfare resources to institutional services at the expense of funding community services, people who are experiencing mental ill-ness may need to be institutionalized even if they are good candidates for community-based care.

A number of factors emerging from existing social, political, and economic considerations influence the phenomenon of elasticity. Three of these—the standard of living, the sociopolitical environment, and the availability of resources and technology—are discussed in turn below.

The first and most obvious factor is the *standard of living*. Housing without indoor plumbing or toilets, considered to be adequate in the past, would be classified as substandard today. The housing itself has not changed, but expectations have. An example of a similar shift is the official definition of poverty used in the United States. In the 1960s, the Social Security Administration developed a series of poverty profiles. These were based on particular standards that made allowances for different circumstances that families were experiencing. In all, 124 different types of families (e.g., large versus small, rural versus urban, young versus elderly) were identified. The poverty line was tied to the amount of money a family was thought to require to obtain basic necessities (this approximates Ponsioen's level below which no one would be allowed to fall and Maslow's first and possibly second levels). Allowing for inflation, the poverty line has been raised a number of times over the past 35 years. Whereas the poverty line for an urban family of four was $3,600 in the mid-1960s, in the late 1980s the line for that same family was over $11,000, and by the mid-1990s that family needed more than $15,000.

A second factor influencing the definition of need is the *socio-political environment*. Public attitudes and expectations are constantly shifting. A generation ago, for example, the notion of universal day care would have been rejected out of hand. It was expected that mothers would remain in the home to raise their children, entering the labor market only when this function was completed. Mothers who did work during this earlier period did so out of necessity, and many profession-als, including those at the Children's Bureau of the U.S. Department of Health, Education and Welfare, argued that this had a negative effect on the family and on child development outcomes. By the 1970s, attitudes had changed considerably, and as of today, little, if any, stigma is attached to placing a child in day care. In fact, some research actually suggests that for some children these arrangements can have a positive impact. As these sociopolitical attitudes have changed, the definition of need has changed.

A third factor influencing the definition of need is the *availability of resources and the existence of technology.* If people do not believe that the available resources are adequate to meet the particular social needs under consideration, it is unlikely that they will follow through on their concerns and take any significant action. For instance, before there were heart transplants and artificial hearts, there was no expectation of extended life for a person with a diseased heart. New technology in this arena created a demand. An example of how this affects social services can be seen in programs for the elderly. From 1935 to 1960, income maintenance programs represented the major national effort on behalf of this group. Since then, however, the move has been to develop and support programs that emphasize not the just the economic but also the social needs of the elderly. Examples of such programs include adult day care centers, foster grandparent programs, and special employment opportunities, as well as programs focusing on the physical needs of the elderly (e.g., meals on wheels, home care and homemaker services, and comprehensive health maintenance programs). Our knowledge about the aging process has changed, along with the resources and technology available to improve the quality of life for the aged. As resources and technology have changed, the definition of need has changed.

Need, therefore, is a concept deserving of careful analysis by those responsible for the planning of human services. As has been indicated, vague or implicit use of the term can lead to ill-conceived programs or inaccurate predictions. It is important to keep in mind that need is shaped by values and that it possesses an elasticity affected by changing standards of living, changing sociopolitical environments, and changing resources and technology. Bearing this in mind, we can now move on to a consideration of the categories of need: that is, the *what* of need mentioned earlier.

DIFFERENT PERSPECTIVES ON NEED

Conceptually, four distinct approaches to measurement of need can be identified: Need may be conceived of as normative, perceived, expressed, or relative (Bradshaw, 1972). (The issue of how to measure need is the focus of Chapter 4.) The categories are useful in that they offer different perspectives on need and different but complementary approaches to understanding the concept.

Normative Need

By definition, the term *normative* implies the existence of standards or norms. When we add the concept of need, we posit the existence of some standard or *criterion* established by custom, authority, or general consensus against which the quantity or quality of a situation or condition is measured. Program planners working within this framework do not collect new information but rely on existing data. Surveys from comparable communities or opinions from knowledgeable professionals can produce suggested targets, usually expressed as ratios against which existing levels of services are compared. If the actual ratio falls short of a particular standard, a need is said to exist. Examples of these ratios are the number of beds in hospitals or nursing homes that a particular community might need (often expressed as numbers per 1,000 population), the number of home-delivered meals per 100 elderly population, or the number of case managers for each 100 chronically mentally ill persons. The strength of this approach is that it allows program planners to generate objective targets. Its limitations are those discussed above: Need levels are likely to change as knowledge, technology, and values change.

Perceived Need

Need can also be defined in terms of what people *think* their needs are or *feel* their needs to be. Although the idea of felt need is important, it can be unstable. Depending on the current situation, people's expectations may fluctuate in that they are susceptible to change. Moreover, people who have a higher standard of living (by objective standards) may feel they need more than do those who are living in poverty. Program planners must be sensitive to what consumers state and, of equal importance, must be able to interpret this in the context of other perspectives on need.

In exploring need as perceived by the potential consumer of the service, program planners are provided information that will be useful in designing a more responsive service delivery system. A fine balance must be maintained, however, between the professional's judgment of client needs and potential consumers' perceptions of what those needs are. Consumers may express what in reality are symptoms of problems and not causes, and professionals may provide what they consider to be the client's "real" needs.

The major drawback of using perceived need in planning is that whereas with normative need a single standard exists, with perceived need the standard changes with each respondent. In addition, experience has demonstrated that in actively soliciting consumers' perceptions of their needs, program planners are likely to raise expectations in that they leave the impression that those needs will be met. This can raise levels of frustration and even alienate potential consumers if the services are not provided.

Expressed Need

Need can also be discussed in terms of whether it is met or unmet. Economists are most comfortable with this approach in that the critical variable is whether the individual actually *attempts to obtain a service* rather than whether or not some "expert" judges that the individual needs that service. Either way there is a drawback. On the one hand, there is evidence that a major deterrent to seeking a service is the absence of the service. On the other hand, individuals may not perceive or feel that they need a service and may not use it even if it is made available, despite what the experts say.

Relying on "demand statistics," program planners attempt to determine how many people actually have sought help. Of this group, a percentage have been successful (met need or demand), and a percentage have failed (unmet need or demand). The strength of this approach is that it focuses only on situations where people actually translate a feeling into action—and the unmet need/demand then becomes the basis of planning targets. The limitation of this approach is its lack of concern for overall community need, especially if program planners assume that all persons with needs seek appropriate help. In this instance, the standard (the level of met need or demand) is influenced by people asking for help, and not all people with well-documented needs actually seek services. In fact, community survey after community survey has provided sufficient data to demonstrate that "expressed need" or demand statistics represent only the tip of the need iceberg.

Relative Need

The definition of relative need does not begin with the assumption that there are existing standards or desirable levels of services that should be met. Relative need is measured as the gap between the level of services existing in one community and those existing in similar communities or geographic areas. The analysis must, of course, take into account differences in population as well as social pathology. Unlike a measure of normative need, which provides an absolute standard to work toward, programs based on relative need are concerned with equity. Given scarce resources, how are criteria best developed that give priority to population groups or geographic areas in "greater need" than other groups or areas? In some instances, this means that a poor community that already is receiving many resources may be favored over a more affluent community with fewer resources if it can be demonstrated that the relative unmet need is greater and that they are at higher risk.

To illustrate the different possible conceptions of need further, we present below an example showing how all four might be applied in a particular community.

An Application

The director of the Franklin County Department of Human Resources has been informed that the number of new cases of family violence, especially spouse abuse, has been increasing in the county over the past few months. After meeting with a number of community leaders, she establishes a task force to analyze the situation and recommend a course of action that would proactively address the community's "need." She has assigned one of the agency's professional staff members to assist the task force. After initial discussions, the task force decides to explore this need using the framework described above.

Normative Need

The staff member contacts the director of the National Coalition Against Domestic Violence as well as a number of people with the National Institute of Mental Health (both in Washington, D.C.) and finds that another state—New Jersey—has completed a similar planning exercise. The New Jersey plan includes guidelines for a comprehensive community service delivery system for women who have been abused. The staff member contacts the New Jersey Department of Human Services and requests any material that might be available on this issue; within a week she receives a copy of the New Jersey plan, *Physically Abused Women and Their Families: The Need for Community Services* (Department of Human Services, 1978).

At the next meeting of the task force, the staff member discusses her analysis of the New Jersey plan and its possible implications for Franklin County. First, the New Jersey planners, using a number of studies, estimate that 6.1% of all couples engage in serious violence in any given year. If this rate were applied to Franklin County, we would estimate that 6,100 women are being abused each year by their spouses (i.e., 6.1% of 100,000 couples). The New Jersey report also discusses various theories of causation found in the literature and the problems of and services needed by abused women and their children. Finally, the report outlines the components of a comprehensive system as developed in New Jersey system:

- Crisis intervention
- 24-hour hot line
- 24-hour crisis intervention unit
- Shelter
- Crisis counseling
- Crisis financial assistance
- Crisis transportation
- Crisis day care
- Crisis medical care
- Immediate police assistance
- Crisis legal assistance
- Ongoing services
- Information, referral, and advocacy
- Self-help groups
- Short- and long-term counseling
- Transitional housing
- Financial planning
- Training and employment
- Medical services
- Long-term child care
- Parent education
- Children's services
- Medical services
- Education
- Counseling
- Recreation

- Program development support
- Public/community education
- Training
- Coordination
- Preventive services
- Education in schools
- Law revision

If the task force concluded its efforts at this stage and recommended that Franklin County implement the above system for an anticipated 6,000 women each year for the near future (assuming that preventive efforts would reduce the numbers in the long term), the needs assessment would incorporate only the normative need approach.

Perceived Need

One of the task force members, a woman who has been abused and now serves as the president of Franklin County's major advocacy group, raises a number of questions at this point and suggests that, although the New Jersey program is an excellent beginning point, it may need to be modified to fit the particular needs of the area. She points out that because many women who are abused delay seeking help or do not seek help at all, the task force should attempt to identify specific reasons the abuse is occurring in the community and whether these barriers are related to cultural expectations and values, feelings of shame, embarrassment, powerlessness, or fear, or even previous negative experiences with human service agencies. This approach incorporates perceived need. In talking with women who have been abused, the task force will be able to design the program(s) so that clients' perceptions of what their needs are will be incorporated.

Expressed Need

At the next meeting, one of the members, an administrator from the Franklin County Mental Health Department, states that although he is in agreement with the strategy the task force has decided to use—that is, using the New Jersey plan and its estimates of the prevalence of spouse abuse (normative need) and undertaking a survey of women who have been abused (perceived need)—he suggests that the task force go beyond these two sources of information and collect data from the existing programs in the community. In this way, the task force will be able to assess the capacity of the existing system as well as to establish short- and long-term priorities. It is agreed that the programs will be asked to provide data on the numbers and characteristics of the women and children they served over the previous 12 months and the numbers and characteristics of those on their waiting lists. A survey of the major community programs in the county shows that 2,000 women (and their children) were provided services during the past year. Specific services (e.g., shelters, counseling, child care, employment) and utilization rates were documented. This suggests that approximately 4,000 women were not receiving services and were "in need." This approach incorporates expressed need in that it looks at demand for services.

Relative Need

At a later meeting, after the staff member has presented the results from the above data collection efforts, another member of the task force points out that she is concerned that whereas 94% of the women who received services or who were on waiting lists were White, 18% of the county population is Hispanic and 9% is African American. Moreover, in the task force's survey of women who have been abused, it was found that a significant number of the respondents were from these two minority groups. On the basis of these and similar findings, the task force recommends that immediate priority be given to the development of two new shelters that will be accessible to neighborhoods where there are large numbers of Hispanics and African Americans, that these shelters be staffed with workers sensitive to the needs of minority women, and that bilingual workers be placed where needed. This approach incorporates relative need by diverting resources to those with lower availability of resources.

NEED CATEGORIES AND
THE PLANNING PROCESS

It should be apparent that need cannot be measured adequately by selecting only one of these approaches. Because each is limited and provides insight into only one facet of the phenomenon, a serious exploration should account for all four dimensions.

Given that needs assessment is conceptually ambiguous, that need is elastic and subject to shifts in scale over time, and that most social service agencies are experiencing demand levels greater than the resources available at any one time, why should agencies and program planners spend scarce resources and energy on this activity? Despite these "realities," there are clear and compelling reasons for utilizing the needs assessment process. In practice, managers must constantly review the money and resources available to them and employ techniques that make the best use of this information. If they do not, they are likely to end up not knowing what the needs of their communities really are. The needs assessment process can feed a well-organized and pertinent flow of information into the overall management decision process. It can show what the actual demand on human service agencies is and what potential demand might be. It can provide useful information as long-term goals and capital budget programs are reviewed. Further, it can provide a useful early warning system regarding potential changes in demand. And once key data sources are identified and data collection systems are organized, all four perspectives on need can be incorporated in a low-cost and efficient manner. Without this information, managers are likely to find scarce resources being squandered on programs that may well serve to further the bureaucratic status quo rather than to address the concerns of the community.

Needs analysis, then, in both its qualitative and quantitative aspects, is an activity that begins with problem analysis as outlined in Chapter 2 and provides the agency with an idea of what is to be done and the size of the target group. Needs are then translated into measurable objectives, resources, and the criteria necessary for program evaluation.

DETERMINING WHO IS IN NEED

The concept of "at-risk" populations is fundamental to any discussion of needs assessment. It has been inherent in the development of such programs as those dealing with poverty, programs for the homeless, families at risk of abusing their children, and persons with AIDS. These activities are based on the principle of channeling resources to "high-risk areas" in which there are concentrations of "high-risk families and individuals." Needs assessment, then, consists of establishing standards of need and devising some methodology of counting the number of people in a given community who fall below the standard and therefore are in need. The methodology is discussed in Chapter 4.

It should be emphasized that to identify a group of people as vulnerable is not to argue that all members of that group have problems or that all members have similar problems. Rather, to identify such a group is only to document a high statistical correlation between that group's characteristics and specific types of problems. For example, to show a high correlation between advanced age and poverty, chronic illness, mental illness, and social isolation in a community does not mean that every person over 65 in that community is poor, ill, and unable to function socially. What it does mean is that an aged person is more likely to have one or more of these problems than is a younger person. Dangerous stereotyping can occur if we are not sensitive to these concerns. Many individuals have suffered discrimination in obtaining home mortgages, automobile insurance, or bank loans because they happen to live in neighborhoods that have been described as "high-crime areas," for example; assumptions about an area tend to attach to everyone from that area.

Two Major Problems:
Reliability and Availability of Data

There are two major problems in conducting a needs assessment. First, current methods are useful only for deriving estimates, and decision makers often prefer greater precision. They need to be informed that such expectations are perhaps both unnecessary and unrealistic and that estimates are of considerable value in providing targets. For example, a program planner may estimate that 10% of a state's elderly population of 100,000—that is, 10,000 people—may need homemaker services. The actual number may fall somewhere within the range of 9,000 to 11,000. With the introduction of various standards and criteria, the number of eligible elderly may be reduced to 7,000. Although exact numbers cannot be generated at a reasonable cost, targets can be established, and they can be modified later as additional data become available.

A second problem planners face in conducting needs assessment is that of data availability. For example, the analysis undertaken to estimate the number of elderly persons needing homemaker services requires considerable data—data that some would argue are not available in most situations. It may be pointed out that information does not exist or that even if it does, it is not easily accessible or usable in its present format. The existing database may be criticized also in that it is not specific to the particular planning issue—it does not contain the right kind of data. The response is often to delay needs assessment until "more appropriate" data are available. It is, however, unlikely that a perfect or ideal data set will ever become available. Program planners must accept these limitations and use existing data sources creatively. Although the data are imperfect, they can still be used to generate targets.

Following this line of argument, that existing data are better than no data, program planners often must identify surrogate measures of needs. The percentages of working mothers with children under 6 years old, single-parent families, and families with incomes below the poverty line have been used as indicators of day care need. Although it is reasonable to assume that these variables are highly correlated, they do not directly measure these needs. The problem is twofold: to identify appropriate surrogates (the theoretical requirement) and to develop the best possible argument that those surrogates are valid (the political argument).

The next chapter identifies a number of methodologies that have proven useful in identifying indicators of need and collecting data. In summary, this chapter has attempted to make the following points:

- There are four different conceptions of need: normative, perceived, expressed, and relative.
- All four should be considered in any assessment of need.
- Identifying at-risk populations is fundamental to any needs assessment.
- Reliability and availability of data are important considerations in needs assessment.

Chapter 4

NEEDS ASSESSMENT
Approaches to Measurement

The discussion of such concepts as at-risk populations, estimations of
need, and data availability in the previous chapter underscores the fact
that needs assessment is more than just the application of technique in
a predetermined cookbook fashion. Furthermore, just as we discussed
four different but complementary perspectives on need in Chapter 3
(normative, perceived, expressed, and relative), we find that there are
different methodologies available as we attempt to measure need. Each
of these, however, has its own strong and weak aspects, and program
planners need to be aware of these as they consider what resources are
available for the needs assessment, how soon the assessment has to be
completed, and how accurate or precise the assessment has to be. Five
methodologies are explored: (a) extrapolating from existing studies, (b)
using resource inventories, (c) using service statistics, (d) conducting a
social survey, and (e) holding a public forum.

EXTRAPOLATING FROM EXISTING STUDIES
(NORMATIVE NEED)

All too often, program planners assume that any attempt to assess
need must be based on primary data sources (i.e., data they themselves
collect). In doing so, they ignore the value of using secondary sources
(data collected by others in other geographical areas or for other purposes) and confuse specificity with accuracy—thinking, for example,
that because the study was not carried out in their county it cannot

accurately describe their situation. Not only can these studies be useful, they often provide the most efficient and effective strategy for assessing need when time and resources are a factor.

Furthermore, the number and subject matter of these studies cover most of the issues of concern to local communities. For example, the National Center for Health Statistics (NCHS) is one of four general-purpose statistical agencies of the federal government charged with collecting, compiling, analyzing, and publishing data for general use. (The other three are the Bureau of Labor Statistics, the Bureau of the Census, and the Department of Agriculture's Reporting Service.) Within the NCHS, the Health Interview Survey (HIS) is one of three major survey programs, the other two being the Health Examination Survey (HES) and the Health Records Survey (HRS). These surveys provide estimates of the prevalence of specific diseases and disability in the United States.

For example, national surveys have been carried out in this country and others that estimate a prevalence rate for the severely mentally retarded of 3 per 1,000 population, with more age-specific prevalence rates of 3.6 per 1,000 persons under 15 years of age and 2.2 per 1,000 persons aged 15 and over. Application is then fairly straightforward. Table 4.1 presents an example of a county's population distribution. The number of Franklin County's population under the age of 15 is 111,251. When we apply the prevalence rate of 3.6 per 1,000, we can conclude that the number of severely mentally retarded children is approximately 400 (111,241 × .0036). Similarly, the number of people in the county aged 15 and over is 388,540. When we apply the prevalence rate of 2.2 per 1,000, we can conclude that the number of severely mentally retarded people aged 15 and over is approximately 855 (388,540 × .0022). The total number across all ages would be approximately 1,255.

There are also special topic surveys covering such areas as child abuse (e.g., National Center for Child Abuse and Neglect, 1981), children (e.g., Hobbs, 1975), the elderly (e.g., Moroney, 1986), and mental illness (e.g., Gurin, 1960; Srole, Rennie, & Cumming, 1962). These prevalence rates can be useful for estimating need and for serving as benchmarks against which proposed targets can be measured.

Strengths and Limitations of Surveys

Two important qualifications need to be introduced at this point. First, it must be noted that the data from these surveys will not be specific to the geographic area of concern. Before the rates can be applied, differences in population characteristics must be weighted. For

Table 4.1

Age Distribution, Franklin County

Age	Male	Female	Total
0-4	17,896	17,072	34,968
5-9	18,891	18,025	36,916
10-14	20,273	19,364	39,367
15-19	20,103	19,338	39,441
20-24	17,411	17,124	34,535
25-29	15,641	15,811	31,452
30-34	16,951	17,304	34,225
35-39	19,061	19,835	38,914
40-44	19,448	20,343	39,791
45-49	17,630	18,463	36,093
50-54	15,544	16,429	31,973
55-59	11,834	12,824	24,658
60-64	8,876	10,120	18,996
65-69	7,639	9,553	17,192
70-74	6,402	8,935	15,337
Over 74	8,851	16,918	25,769
Total	242,451	257,348	499,799

example, most prevalence rates are age and sex specific: That is, different rates are given for different groupings. Functional status and ability are highly correlated with age: The elderly, for instance, are much more likely to be physically handicapped. Yet an overall rate for the population over 65 years of age can be misleading. Program planners need to apply differential rates—that is, rates for the "frail elderly" (those over 75 years of age) as well as rates for those 65 to 74 years of age, or the "young elderly" (see Table 4.2). This refinement will generate more sensitive and precise estimates.

The next task is to apply these rates to our own data (Table 4.1). Table 4.3 provides estimates only for the total handicapped as an example of how the rates might be applied to a local community.

A second caveat is related to the definitions behind the estimated rates. How is the condition operationally defined? For example, two national studies on the needs of the elderly carried out in the 1960s suggested different rates of "impairment" (not to be confused with the term *handicap* used above, which involves more severe restrictions on ability to function). The first survey reported that 37% of the elderly 75 years of age and older were limited in their normal activities (Harris,

Table 4.2

Impairment and Handicap, by Age (rates per 1,000)

Age	Very Severely Handicapped	Severely Handicapped	Appreciably Handicapped	Total
16-29	0.46	0.41	1.02	1.89
30-49	0.86	2.28	4.18	7.32
50-64	2.65	9.59	16.47	28.71
65-74	8.28	23.99	50.67	82.94
> 74	33.91	52.95	74.90	161.73
Total	3.47	7.68	13.37	24.52

SOURCE: Adapted from Harris (1971); see Moroney (1986) for a discussion of the methodology and definitions of terms.

Table 4.3

Estimates of Total Handicapped, Franklin County

Age	No.	Rate per 1,000	No. Handicapped
16-29	105,428	1.89	190
30-49	149,043	7.32	1,088
50-64	75,627	28.71	2,170
65-74	32,529	82.94	2,697
> 74	25,769	161.73	4,167
Total			10,312

1971), whereas the second reported that 62% were limited (Shanas, Townsend, & Streib, 1968).

Although both studies used the terms *impairment, capacity,* and *limitations,* the former actually used much more stringent measurements and tested actual ability rather than just asking respondents whether they could do something. In the latter study, the elderly were asked whether they were able to perform certain tasks. Apparently the elderly were able to do more than they thought they could or that they were willing to admit. On a theoretical level, neither study is more "correct" than the other. The program planner must choose the study that incorporates definitions that are the most meaningful for program development in his or her community. Given an environment of scarce resources, a home-based program might realistically expect to target the smaller number and, within this, a particular age group.

A complementary approach to the above also addresses the category of normative need and is based on professional or expert judgment. In the previous chapter, for example, we introduced the *New Jersey Plan for Physically Abused Women and their Families* (Department of Human Services, 1978). Rather than relying on the published document, we could have invited someone from the program to translate the New Jersey system to our community. His or her expertise would not be the processes of planning or administration, but would be in such specific substantive areas as family violence. Such specialists are likely to be most familiar with existing surveys and relevant research in their area of expertise and are usually in a position to propose specific strategies and suggest reasonable levels of service provision.

The strengths of expert judgment are numerous. Costs are likely to be reasonably low (consultant fees can be as low as $500 to $700 per day), and the time required is likely to be short. The planning effort will benefit in that parameters of need are established by recognized experts and the credibility of subsequent budgetary requests will be fairly high.

Although the limitations of using experts are considerable, they tend to be subtle. Professionals, even experts, are often biased and at times view problems through a form of tunnel vision. In fact, the very successes that have gained them recognition can limit their problem-solving abilities should they take on the attitude that experience has provided them the "solutions" before any new analyses are undertaken.

For example, we estimated that of the 25,769 elderly persons in Franklin County 75 years of age and over, 4,167 were handicapped (161.73 per 1,000) and 9,543 were impaired (37%). Expert A might recommend a home care program with a public health nursing emphasis, Expert B might suggest a new program with a strong case management focus, and Expert C might propose a program based in the local senior center that would provide both nutritional and social interaction services. Each of these experts brings the recommendations with him or her, and this is to be expected.

To counter this possibility, such consultations should be initiated only after a basic programmatic strategy has been outlined by the planning staff: community support services, residential care, respite care, nutritional programs, and so on. Consultants, then, are relied on to offer suggestions based on their substantive expertise: estimating numbers at risk, establishing feasible targets, and designing relevant programs or interventions.

USING RESOURCE INVENTORIES
(NORMATIVE NEED)

A resource inventory is basically a mapping strategy in that it at-tempts to amass a considerable amount of information so that the total system can be identified and its boundaries established. The inventory usually begins with an identifiable at-risk population group, such as the aged, single-parent families, the mentally handicapped, or sub-stance abusers. Program planners attempt to identify all agencies, public and private, that offer service to these subpopulations. To carry out an inventory (for planning purposes) requires going beyond a simple list-ing. Optimally, this activity involves the development of discrete and meaningful categories so that services can be grouped by function and purpose, by the eligibility criteria they use (in a standardized format), and by their perception of their overall capacity to meet greater demand.

Table 4.4 presents an example of the type of form that might be used as the first step in conducting a resource inventory attempting to identify and assess the capacity of a community system for the elderly. In this example, all agencies that possibly offer services to the aged in Franklin County are contacted (more often than not by phone) and asked whether they offer any of the preidentified services listed on the form. The interviewer (a) merely checks those services provided by the agency and (b) asks the respondent whether the agency is in a position to meet the needs of all who request that service and meet the agency's eligibility criteria or whether it has waiting lists or refers clients to other resources. The information in Table 4.4 shows that the Franklin County Commu-nity Action Agency offers six of the listed services. Moreover, it has sufficient resources to provide information/referral, employment refer-ral, and housing assistance to all who have requested assistance in those areas, and although it does offer legal services, case management ser-vices, and counseling, it is not able to provide these services to all who request them. Following this, the information is aggregated by service: The planners are in a position to document how many agencies in Franklin County are providing transportation services, counseling, in-formation/referral, and so forth. This is the planner's equivalent of the geologist's surface survey. After program planners have completed this phase, they are in a position to collect more detailed information from each agency providing services to the population.

Table 4.4

Resource Inventory, Franklin County Services for the Elderly,

Franklin County Community Action Agency

Service	Available and Adequate	Available but Inadequate	Not Available
Transportation			X
Homemaker			X
Home health			X
Legal		X	
Respite			X
Meals on Wheels			X
Congregate meals			X
Home repairs/weatherization			X
Information/referral	X		
Case management		X	
Counseling		X	
Employment referral	X		
Housing assistance	X		
Socialization/recreation			X

Strengths and Limitations of Resource Inventories

The critical problems in developing resource inventories are in the areas of standardization and of applying mechanisms to reduce definitional disagreements. What is "case management"? What is "counseling"? Do all service providers define the activity the same way? We have found that it is not uncommon for agencies to use the same terminology but carry out quite different activities under those headings. Many communities have resolved this problem by designing a taxonomy of common terms covering problems, needs, and services. This was partly a response to purchase-of-service contract requirements and partly a realization that without such a system, effectiveness-based program planning on a communitywide basis would be impossible.

Through the resource inventory, the program planner is in a position to evaluate whether the existing system is functioning to capacity, whether specific agencies in the system are capable of serving more people, and whether there is an overlap of services. This assessment may result in the conclusion that there is a need for growth and expansion or, just as likely, that better coordination can meet increased demand. For example, rather than each agency providing case management services or information and referral, agreements for sharing this function might be negotiated, thus reducing the need to develop more of these services.

It is useful to include a survey of service providers under the heading "Resource Inventories." Asking service providers to identify the problems or needs of at-risk groups is quite different from both asking people themselves what their needs are and analyzing utilization data. A survey of providers generates statements of normative need—what the providers consider the problems to be—based on their day-to-day practice.

In that many new initiatives are likely to build on the existing system (i.e., modification and/or expansion), program planners seek more than the opinions of the existing human service leadership. Indirectly, these providers are invited to become members of the planning team, a strategy that could potentially generate a sense of cooperation and reduce the likelihood of domain or turf protection when the implementation stage is reached. A resource inventory may provide formal information on the system, but the provider survey may give insight into the real capacity of the system to change.

Finally, it is important to recognize that service providers are likely to make recommendations based on their knowledge of consumers and not necessarily based on the nonuser population. This perspective emphasizes demand and not need. Despite this limitation, the information received can be extremely useful for needs assessment as long as those analyzing the findings understand the context in which the data were collected.

USING SERVICE STATISTICS
(EXPRESSED NEED)

The collection and analysis of utilization data build on the previous activity, the inventory of resources. Whereas the task in the above section was to identify whether an agency was providing services and, if so, whether that provision was adequate (the agency was expected to respond yes or no in Table 4.4), the program planner now uses that information as the basis for collecting service reports from direct-service agencies. The reports provide a rough measure of agency effort expended and are valuable for the maintenance of support activities and for establishing monitoring procedures. These data, often referred to as *utilization data,* reflect activity under each category/service of the inventory (Table 4.5), such as transportation, homemaker, and home health, and are descriptive of (a) who was receiving (b) what (c) from whom and (d) at what cost.

Following the initial resource inventory, the Franklin County Community Action Agency was asked to generate more detailed information on the six services they offer to elderly persons. These data identify the number of clients served in an average month, the number of units of specific services provided, and the cost per unit of service. As with the initial data (Table 4.4), these data can be aggregated across agencies, giving the planner a fairly comprehensive picture of capacity of the current "human service system."

The "who" data describe the characteristics of the utilizers. Although in theory all agencies in this example would provide services for the elderly, in practice services may be restricted to a subset of the aged, whether defined by age, functional ability, family status, or income. Or within an agency some services are more likely to be targeted to one subgroup, whereas others are targeted to another: For example, respite care may be available only to family members caring for frail elderly parents who are unable to care for their own needs, employment services may be available only to those who are able to work and whose incomes are below a certain level, and information and referral services may be available to all.

The "what" data describe not only the services provided but also the volume of those services. How many units of services are provided to what types of clients with what type of problems over some agreed-on standard period (e.g., monthly, quarterly, semiannually, or annually)? For example, we might find that one agency provided 50 days of respite care to 15 families over a 1-month period. Although the norm was 3 days, one family was provided only 1 day and another 6 days.

The "from whom" data document staffing ratios or caseloads. The average caseload for a caseworker providing counseling services might be 15, whereas that for a case manager might be 25.

The "at what cost" data are gross financial data that can be used to demonstrate the level of commitment for a specific service across agencies and to extrapolate the level of resources that might be necessary if services were to expand. For example, we found that one agency in an average month provided 30 counseling sessions to 20 elderly persons. The agency spent $27,000 annually for this service (this includes both direct and indirect costs), or $2,250 per month. Using this

Table 4.5
Service Utilization Survey, Franklin County Community Action Agency

Service	No. of Clients Served/Month	No. of Units Delivered/Month	Cost per Unit
Transportation			
Homemaker			
Home health			
Legal	25	25	$37.50
Respite			
Meals on Wheels			
Congregate meals			
Home repairs/weatherization			
Information/referral	75	100	$18.75
Case management	50	225	$18.75
Counseling	20	30	$40.00
Employment referral	5	5	$25.00
Housing assistance	15	15	$20.00
Socialization/recreation			

NOTE: One unit is defined as follows: Legal = 30 minutes; information/referral = 15 minutes; case management = 15 minutes; counseling = 1 hour; employment and referral = 30 minutes; housing assistance = 30 minutes.

as a base, we can derive a unit cost of $75 per session ($2,250/30). These concepts are discussed in greater detail in Chapter 9.

In using this approach to a resource inventory, program planners are now in a position to aggregate the above data across agencies and produce a comprehensive picture of services currently being provided by the human service delivery system at the community level.

**Strengths and Limitations
of Service Statistics**

The obvious advantage of this approach is the availability and accessibility of the data, assuming that the issue of confidentiality can be resolved. It is clearly more economical in terms of resources and time to rely on existing data than on newly collected special survey data. Needs assessment using available data can be described as a "low-profile" activity that minimizes the potential problem, already discussed, of increasing expectations among recipients or potential recipients. Furthermore, agencies will have data that cover extended periods of time, thus allowing the planner to analyze trends in service delivery and demand.

The major limitation of service statistics is that they do not provide adequate data about prevalence or unmet need, data that are essential for effectiveness-based program planning. From a planning perspective, the practice of using data that are descriptive of service utilizers and those on the waiting lists to "plan" for the total population is fraught with danger. In fact, it is possible that the characteristics of the groups are markedly different, and often these differences are what determine utilization.

Waiting lists, on the other hand, are affected by actual service provision. For example, in one community, waiting lists for residential care placements had remained fairly constant over a 10-year period. Although there had been significant increases in resources over that period, these facilities were always operating at full capacity. As more places became available, they were filled from the existing waiting lists; as people moved from the waiting lists, their places were filled by others. Although the factors associated with this situation are complex, one reason was that increases in service provision raised expectations, and this, in turn, was translated into demand. If it is known that there are limited resources and that the waiting lists are lengthy, many people will see no value in even applying for help. If, on the other hand, people find that additional services are available, they are more likely to apply.

Service statistics do, however, have value. Utilization data can be used to identify the characteristics of the subpopulations in contact with the human services agencies: who they are, where they live, the types of services they receive, and the extent to which they are helped. These data can be used to assess the capacity of agencies to deliver services and, if the program planners anticipate increased demand, the capacity to expand.

Such information can produce census lists, admission and discharge statistics, and other types of population reports useful for planning and policy formulation. It is then possible to extract information indicating trends in caseloads, patient characteristics, and program needs for forecasting and research activities. Such information can also provide the basis for examining the treatment process. As information on individuals and families is accumulated, it becomes possible to identify service needs for total populations and potential caseloads. It also becomes possible to determine cost patterns incurred in providing services to recipient groups with common problems or needs and, as a result, to offer a more rational basis for adjusting priorities and program plans.

CONDUCTING A SOCIAL SURVEY
(PERCEIVED NEED)

Of all the approaches, the social or community survey is, in many ways, the most powerful method available for assessing need. In that it is concerned with collecting information from people residing in the community, it provides original data tailored to the specific needs of the geographic area in question. Furthermore, it is the one strategy that can produce information on the attitudes of consumers and potential consumers.

The social survey usually has two foci: (a) the identification of the respondent's perception of need and (b) the determination of knowledge about existing services. Both are important for planning. The first provides information useful in the delineation of targets; the second may identify barriers to utilization, whether financial, physical, or attitudinal. Information about these barriers might indicate a need not only for a particular service but also for various supportive services (e.g., outreach, transportation, advocacy, education) that could be instrumental in achieving program success.

The purpose of a survey is to provide a valid description of a situation. It begins by defining the problem in conceptual and operational terms. Program planners can then construct appropriate data collection instruments, draw a sample, conduct interviews, analyze the data, and produce planning recommendations. (It is beyond the purview of this book to discuss the technical aspects of survey research, but interested readers are referred to such texts as Babbie, 1983).

A survey also offers other benefits. If a survey identifies shortages or barriers to utilization, it can serve to legitimate change. In this sense, it becomes a tool for action and a stimulus for marshaling support. As a process tool, it can heighten the awareness of a community and thus serve an educational purpose. To achieve this, the community survey must involve agency representatives, community leaders, and actual and potential consumers in the planning and implementation of the survey itself. Involvement of this kind can produce support for the recommendations that will follow. Finally, although most surveys offer only a static description of a community at one point in time, they establish baseline data and reference points for evaluation at a later time.

Strengths and Limitations of Social or Community Surveys

Time and expense are major considerations in conducting social or community surveys. The amount of time and effort involved in the initial phases of the survey are usually underestimated. To many, a survey is equated with the actual fieldwork, the interviewing of respondents, and a program planner may spend little time on the design of the survey itself. Data items and questions are often included with minimal thought given as to their usefulness for the planning task.

The analysis strategy, however, is not something to put off until after the data are collected. It should begin in the design phase of a survey. Before any data item is included, the program planner should know why the information is being sought (the rationale) and how it will be incorporated in the analysis. This requires careful design preparation and much discussion. Otherwise, it is likely that the analysis will become a fishing expedition, and those responsible for the analysis may become lost in a morass of information.

A number of technical concerns need to be addressed in the creation of survey instruments. Pretests need to be conducted to determine whether the questions are understandable, whether they elicit the types of responses desired, and whether they motivate the respondents to participate. These matters touch on the issues of validity and reliability. A critical concern is the sampling procedure used. All too often, surveys are based on methodologically and statistically inadequate samples. Rather than discussing such a technically complex issue here, we will merely suggest that a sampling expert be brought in to develop an appropriate strategy. Without some confidence in the final sample, it is impossible to generalize to the total target population, a requirement essential for the planning of social services.

Although the social survey is probably the most powerful method of determining need in a community, it does have severe limitations that should be weighed. The more information (variables) you add, the more respondents you will need in the survey. Sample size is a function of the number of variables to be used in the analysis, and in a survey of social service need, the required number of respondents can be relatively large. For example, on the simplest level, two dichotomous variables result in 4 cells, three variables in 8 cells, four in 16 cells, and five in 32 cells,

cells that have to be filled (see Tables 4.6 and 4.7). But in most surveys, few of the variables of concern are dichotomous (e.g., either/or, yes/no); most are continuous (e.g., the actual age of a person, the actual family income, the number of years of school completed). To reduce data to either dichotomous or multiple categories is to lose information and limit the types of statistical analysis that can be used.

Sample size is directly related to costs. Social survey organizations such as the National Opinion Research Center put the cost of one interview at $100 or more. These costs include the actual interview as well as the training and supervision of the interviewers, expenses, and prorated costs for coding and analysis. A sample of 1,000, then, will cost over $100,000. A final concern is the time involved in designing and implementing a survey. A conservative estimate would be 6 to 9 months from design through analysis.

Given these limitations, program planners should exhaust available data sources before finally deciding on the survey. Is it really necessary? Planners should consider the time and financial costs as well as the potential danger of raising expectations that might not be met. If these are not outweighed by the benefits to be derived, then an original survey should not be conducted.

HOLDING A PUBLIC FORUM
(PERCEIVED NEED)

The public hearing approach to needs assessment usually takes the form of an open meeting to which the general public is invited and at which they are welcomed to offer testimony. Quite apart from political or community relations aspects, such meetings may be required by law. Since the 1960s, such hearings have been conducted through neighborhood meetings first encouraged by Office of Economic Opportunity (OEO)-organized community action agencies, later stimulated by programs such as Model Cities and revenue sharing (especially community development programs) and, since the mid-1970s, the Title XX amendments to the Social Security Act.

Ideally, those attending the meetings are able to articulate their own needs, to represent the concerns of their neighbors, and, in some instances, to speak for organized constituencies. Needs and priorities are then determined by a consensus of those involved in the process

Table 4.6
Dummy Table: Age by Gender

Gender	Under 65	65 and Over
Female	1	2
Male	3	4
Total		

Table 4.7
Dummy Table: Age by Gender by Living Status

	Under 65		65 and Over	
Gender	Living Alone	Living with Family	Living Alone	Living with Family
Female	1	2	3	4
Male	5	6	7	8
Total				

or through tabulation of articulated concerns to be prioritized at a later time.

Strengths and Limitations of Public Hearings

Public meetings have the advantage of compatibility with democratic decision making. They are less costly than surveys in terms of both money and time, and they tend to encourage clarification of issues and cross- fertilization of ideas through open discussion. The major problem in this approach is the issue of representation. Do the elderly who attend a meeting represent their individual needs or those of the broader group? Do all interested (or potentially affected) groups attend the meetings, or are some self-excluded because of perceived stigma attached to their needs (such as welfare recipients)? Is it possible that those with the greatest need feel uncomfortable or embarrassed in attempting to articulate their concerns in the presence of more educated professionals? Experience to date suggests that attendees usually are not representative, that some groups are more aggressive than others and more familiar with lobbying strategies, and that different communication patterns are often a barrier.

Program planners need to anticipate these possible problems before deciding to hold these meetings. First, planners should recognize that an announcement of a meeting in the press or on radio and television will not produce a cross section of the community. Use of the media in traditional ways will not prove successful if our concern is to attract consumers or potential consumers of human services. Resources should therefore be allocated to help reach important target groups, resources that include outreach and community organization activities in places such as neighborhood shopping centers, churches, social service agencies, and the schools, to name only a few. Second, planners must assume that attendance per se will not necessarily result in equal and effective participation by all present. Process techniques that attempt to structure participation should be introduced. Delbecq, Vandeven, and Gustafson (1975) described in considerable detail a number of group techniques for needs assessment and problem analysis. Two of these approaches are the nominal group technique (NGT) and the Delphi technique; these are useful for involving various participants early in the analysis phase and helping them to identify problems, clarify issues, and express values and preferences.

SELECTING THE BEST METHOD

None of these methods should be seen as "better" than the others. The methods are not mutually exclusive, and by choosing one, program planners do not automatically reject others. Each contributes distinct information. What is important is that in each planning effort, those responsible for planning determine available resources and constraints and then decide what is feasible.

APPROACHES USEFUL FOR LOCATING
CONCENTRATIONS OF HIGH-RISK GROUPS

The preceding section was concerned with approaches for estimating the needs of high-risk target populations. The primary focus was on the determination of the characteristics and numbers of specific population groups, such as the elderly, the handicapped, or abused spouses. For human service planning, the emphasis was on the aggregation of people with similar needs. Another task for the program planner is to locate concentrations of these high-risk groups by carrying out a spatial or geographic analysis.

An Overview of the Issues

Program planners are expected to formulate plans, develop policies for plan implementation, formulate criteria for priority setting and resource allocation, and establish a monitoring system. Needs assessment, though related to all of these activities, has a major input to priority setting and resource allocation considerations. In general, this assumes that when resources are scarce, the decision maker is interested in identifying concentrations of subpopulations in need; furthermore, it assumes a commitment to channeling resources in such a way that areas with greater need will receive larger amounts of resources. This concern falls into the category of relative need, discussed earlier.

An Example of the Need for Spatial Analysis

County-based indicators, to take one example, though useful for state planning, have proven to be inadequate for local planning. A county might be ranked relatively low (in terms of risk) compared with other counties but still have geographic pockets of high need. County indicators are usually made up of averages, and statistical averages often mask subcounty conditions. For example, in a study of five southern counties, various health and social indicators suggested that their status was similar to the overall state average (Moroney, 1973). After subareas (or neighborhoods) were delineated, however, it was found that, in some subareas, mortality rates were almost twice as high as those found in others, the crude death rates were almost three times as high, the out-of-wedlock pregnancy rates were 10 times higher, residential fire rates were three times higher, and arrest rates were six times higher. Social problems and social needs are not uniformly distributed in geographic space, and part of the planning task is to find these variations.

Spatial Analysis Defined

Spatial analysis is the use of social indicators to classify geographical areas into typologies. The construction of these social indicators of need involves combining more than one variable to form an indicator. The process can be viewed as a device helping planners to assess the status of a community, to establish general priorities, to measure program impact, and to document change over time.

The underlying assumption of indicator construction is that no one variable by itself is capable of tapping into complex social phenomena. Rather, what is needed is a construct that can summarize large amounts of data that are a part of these phenomena. In this sense, a health status indicator might include a combination of such factors as mortality rates, morbidity rates, and accessibility of medical care. An indicator of social equality might include measures of access to educational resources, employment, housing availability, and participation in community decision making.

Program planners are faced with multiple databases and literally hundreds of variables that may or may not be important in determining need levels and in developing programs to meet these needs. It is inefficient, if not impossible, for the planner to obtain a coherent and easily understandable picture of the character of a geographic area by dealing separately with these variables and their permutations. Quite apart from the issue of efficiency is the concern for clarity and comprehension. Decision makers not involved in planning and faced with a deluge of information have considerable difficulty in perceiving its relevance. It would be naive for those who participated in the planning to expect them to wade through the data morass that these planning efforts tend to produce. Carefully selected information and succinct display are more likely to have an impact on decision making.

Factor analysis is a statistical technique that can be used to take a large number of variables and reduce them to a smaller number of constructs or indicators. Underlying factor analysis is the notion that if a large number of variables are intercorrelated, these interrelationships may be due to the presence of one or more underlying factors. Those variables that are most highly correlated with the underlying factor should be highly related to each other. However, it must be emphasized that if the factors cannot be interpreted—if the related variables do not make conceptual sense—factor analysis is of little value to program planners.

Factor Analysis: An Example

The data shown in Table 4.8 are taken from Bell's (1955) study of census tracts in San Francisco. Bell chose these seven variables as important measures of different urban characteristics. The results of the

Table 4.8

Correlation Matrix

	(1)	*(2)*	*(3)*	*(4)*	*(5)*	*(6)*	*(7)*
(1)	1.0	.780	.775	.678	.482	.190	.135
(2)		1.0	.796	.490	.126	.255	.488
(3)			1.0	.555	.260	.051	.360
(4)				1.0	.759	.476	.205
(5)					1.0	.753	.066
(6)						1.0	.248
(7)							1.0

NOTE: Key to variables (+, positive correlation; −, negative correlation): (1) Occupation (+), (2) Education (+), (3) Rent (−), (4) Fertility Rate (+), (5) Women in the Labor Force (−), (6) Single-Family Dwelling Units (+), (7) % in Ethnic Groups (+).

Table 4.9

Factor Analysis

		Factors	
Variable	*I*	*II*	*III*
(1) Occupation	.635	.070	.178
(2) Education	.467	−.105	.209
(3) Income	.602	−.071	−.028
(4) Fertility Rate	.097	.630	.215
(5) Women in the Labor Force	.031	.711	−.029
(6) Single-Family Dwelling Units	−.031	.573	−.183
(7) % in Ethnic Groups	−.098	.106	.496

correlation analysis show that all of the variables are interrelated, some more strongly than others. To determine whether these seven could be reduced to a smaller number of factors, Bell subjected the data to a factor analysis and found three distinct clusters (see Table 4.9). Bell then argued that Variables 1 through 3 were components of "socio-economic status," Variables 4 through 6 measured "family status," and Variable 7 measured "ethnic status."

Since that time, and building on Bell's work, a sizable body of literature has emerged, initially in developing approaches to classifying cities and gaining knowledge of political behavior (Berry, 1972) and later as a support methodology for the planning of human services

Table 4.10

Rank Ordering of Census Tracts, by Level of Risk

Census Tract	Income	Occupation	Education	Family	Overcrowding	Sum/5
001						
002						
003						
...						
...						
095						

NOTE: Key to variables: Income, median family income; Occupation, % semiskilled and unskilled workers; Education, % adults with high school completion; Family, % two-parent families; Overcrowding, more than 1.01 persons per room.

Table 4.11

Indicators, by Socioeconomic Status (SES) Areas

Variable	SES 1	SES 2	SES 3	SES 4
Infant mortality per 1,000 population	35	25	19	14
Crude death rate per 1,000 population	11	7	5	4
Out-of-wedlock pregnancies (%)	34	16	9	3
Residential fires per month	18	7	5	4
Arrests/1,000 population per month	12	7	4	2

(Moroney, 1976; Redich & Goldsmith, 1971; U.S. Bureau of the Census, 1971; Wallace, Gold, & Dooley, 1967). The basic units of analyses are the census tracts, which tend to be relatively small geographic areas (averaging 4,000 to 5,000 population) and are left unchanged from census to census. In some cases, the analysis is complemented by the examination of smaller spatial units such as blocks or block groupings.

Human Service Applications

It was only in the 1960s that the factor-analytic approach was used for human service planning. Wallace et al. (1967) reported on a study in San Francisco that used a combination of factor analysis of census data, expert judgment, and existing health and social data to identify the city's high-risk areas. Five human service professionals independently reviewed the indicators to achieve "consensus indicators." The data were then subjected to a factor analysis. One factor (a general measure of socioeconomic status) accounted for 43% of the total variance and was found to be highly correlated with 29 health and social indicators.

In 1967, a dress rehearsal of the 1970 census was carried out in New Haven, Connecticut (U.S. Bureau of the Census, 1971). Census data were combined with other information to develop a health information system, which, in turn, was to be used to construct social indicators describing health and social conditions at the census tract and block group levels. Using factor analysis, the researchers were able to identify one strong factor, "socioeconomic status," that was highly correlated with the prevalence of a large number of human service problems. Five variables made up the indicator (income, occupation, education, family organization, and overcrowding). The census tracts were ranked on each of the five variables separately, and then the ranks were added and averaged to generate a composite score (see Table 4.10). After the ranking, the tracts were divided into quartiles designated as SES 1, SES 2, SES 3, and SES 4. Data from human service agencies were than transposed against these quartiles; the results are illustrated in Table 4.11.

The strengths of the above approach are as follows: It is efficient in terms of time and money; it will produce rankings of relative social need and risk; it can be used to predict need clustering as well as to provide insight into issues of service design; and it provides baseline data for evaluation. A particular disadvantage of using census data is the data's relatively infrequent updating, although the decennial census is now being updated through special studies between the scheduled periods of data collection. Moreover, the Census Bureau is in the process of arranging for the data to be eventually available through the Internet.

It should be emphasized that the techniques described in this section can be of real significance when properly integrated into local decision making and political processes. Correct and timely identification of high-risk populations by geographic areas, when coupled with the proper use of other techniques described in this chapter, promotes more effective administrative control of limited resources.

CONCLUDING COMMENTS
ON NEEDS ASSESSMENT

The position outlined in this chapter is, in essence, that needs assessment has both qualitative and quantitative dimensions. It involves more than measurement of need, and attention has to be given to what is to be counted. Needs assessment, in this context, begins with problem analysis; only after this is completed can the quantitative aspect be addressed.

In this chapter, a number of methodologies were explored that are useful for determining levels of need. These methods are interdependent insofar as none by itself provides a total assessment and each can be classified under one of the four definitions of need. Strengths and limitations for each approach were identified, and it was argued that the critical factors in determining which of these will be used are time and resource constraints.

We argued that even though needs assessments techniques can produce estimates of need rather than exact numbers, these estimates can be used both to educate the general public and to marshal support from decision makers and elected officials. Furthermore, targets can be translated into resources and budget estimates. The formulation of goals and objectives is directly influenced by the needs assessment task. Insofar as objectives have to be stated in measurable, time-bound terms, the needs assessment provides target data. Finally, estimates of need become the basis for the evaluation of program adequacy.

The next chapter builds on the preceding three and takes us, step by step, through the process of developing a program hypothesis—the linchpin of effectiveness-based program planning.

Part III

PLANNING, DESIGNING, AND TRACKING THE INTERVENTION

Chapter 5

SELECTING THE APPROPRIATE INTERVENTION STRATEGY

Over the last three chapters, we have defined and made distinctions among conditions, social problems, and social need. Furthermore, we have demonstrated the importance of not deciding on a solution prematurely but instead beginning with a condition, transforming that condition into a social problem, and then translating a problem into a social need that will be targeted for action. Finally, we have discussed ways to generate estimates of the numbers with particular social needs, to describe the characteristics of those with these needs, and to locate geographic areas with high numbers of those with needs.

The next task is to take all of the above and devise an intervention strategy. In this chapter, we introduce the *program hypothesis* and its central function in shaping the goals, objectives, and design of the program and, eventually, the monitoring and evaluation of the program.

THE PROGRAM HYPOTHESIS

Most human service professionals would probably argue that because they are action oriented and not researchers, their primary concern is to solve problems and not to test hypotheses. The fact of the matter is, however, that when they design programs they are also proposing hypotheses. Granted, most administrators and program planners do not explicitly offer and document tentative assumptions that are then translated into testable logical or empirical consequences. Still, most design their programs with hypotheses in mind, albeit simplistic ones at times. The most rudimentary form of a hypothesis would be the administrator's "hunch," based on practical experience, that a particular problem or situation will respond to a particular form of intervention—for example, that parenting classes will prevent child abuse.

We can think of hypotheses as nothing more than a series of "if-then" statements. Effective program design should be viewed as a hypothesis-generating activity (e.g., "If we provide parenting classes, then we will prevent child abuse"). The "if-then" statement then provides the mechanism for program evaluation, which is a hypothesis-testing activity (e.g., was child abuse prevented after parenting classes were provided?). In generating a hypothesis, the program planner is able both to identify meaningful objectives and to structure these objectives in a hierarchical series of statements—objectives that are, in fact, a series of means-ends (or if-then) statements.

We find the basis for these "informed hunches" in the research literature—the literature that identifies the etiology of the problem. It is at this point that theory is joined to practice.

A MATERNAL AND CHILD HEALTH EXAMPLE

The following example of a program hypothesis might be helpful. In the mid-1960s, the U.S. Department of Health, Education and Welfare (now the U.S. Department of Health and Human Services), concerned with the problems of infant mortality and mental retardation, provided funds for the development of a number of maternal and infant care projects. Although this new program seemed, on the surface, to resemble a number of previous programs, at least in terms of services, the underlying or implicit assumptions and hypotheses were quite different. In summary form, the assumptions were as follows:

- Infant mortality and mental retardation are related to the incidence of low birth weight (prematurity).
- Low birth weight is related to untreated illness, trauma, and nutritional deficiency experienced by the mother during the pregnancy.
- These conditions are more likely to be found among certain population groups, such as teenagers, women over 35 years of age, women with

histories of multiple births, women who have had previous premature births, and women with low family incomes.

On the basis of these interrelated assumptions, the following program hypothesis was formulated:

• If we are able to locate high-risk mothers, and • *if* we are able to recruit them to our program, and • *if* we are able to offer services that will effectively deal with those factors associated with prematurity, • *then* we should see a reduction in the incidence of prematurity, and • *then* we should see a reduction in the incidence of infant mortality and mental retardation.

One can easily take the above and translate the terms into a more traditional research framework (this is basically what one does when concerned with program evaluation—the hypothesis-testing function).

We introduce the issue of program evaluation at this point in the process rather than at the end of the process (where it usually is discussed) because it is here that the foundation is laid for the monitoring and evaluation of the program. All too often, planning, design, and evaluation are viewed as loosely connected but separate processes. This failure to connect different parts of the program planning process can produce disastrous evaluations by producing findings that simply do not reflect what a program has produced. Findings from an evaluation that has not been through a disciplined planning process tend to be unrealistically positive, inaccurately negative, or inconclusive. The situation becomes disastrous when these flawed findings are treated as accurate reflections of program performance and are used to extend or discontinue funding, and therefore the life of the program. We do, of course, devote a number of chapters to the issues of monitoring and evaluation later in this volume, but at this point we want to argue the importance of laying the necessary foundation for those functions.

Evaluation begins with our stating a proposed relationship between a program or service (the independent variable) and some desired outcome (the dependent variable). In the example cited above, comprehensive prenatal care (including aggressive case finding and outreach) was the independent variable, and infant mortality and mental retardation were the dependent variables.

Variables may also be intervening variables (in a later chapter, we refer to these as *intermediate outcomes*) insofar as some variables appear in a causal chain between the independent variable and a depen-

dent variable and influence the causal pattern. The concept of intervening variables recognizes the existence of multicausal models in understanding the complex problems that human service professionals
encounter. Often, there is a long and complicated chain of events
between treatment and outcomes. To test the program hypothesis, this
chain must be explicated.

In the maternal and infant care example, the relationship between the
services and the lower incidence of infant mortality is complex. The
program affects these outcomes by improving the nutritional and health
status of high-risk mothers. These, then, are the intervening variables:
a series of steps or events, each of which is the result of a preceding
event and a precondition of the next event. These relationships are
illustrated in Figure 5.1.

TYPES OF PROGRAM HYPOTHESES

Where to Intervene

Throughout these chapters, the notion of causation has been discussed. We are using the term *cause* in the sense of factors associated
with the existence of a condition and not in the more classic sense of
"cause and effect." Smoking, for example, is a factor associated with
cancer, heart disease, and emphysema, but it is not a "cause" in that
nonsmokers also experience these problems and some smokers do not.
Furthermore, linear cause-and-effect relationships are rare when one is
dealing with social problems. Multiple causation or multiple factors
associated with social problems tend to be the rule.

If one hopes to deal successfully with a problem, one should modify
or remove those *factors associated with the condition.* One of the
purposes of the analysis, then, is to identify those factors or preconditions—the etiology of the problem. There are, however, special considerations about certain of these factors. Some do not lend themselves to
intervention at the community level. For example,

- Certain preconditions can be dealt with only at the regional or national
  level (see Example 1 that follows).
- Some preconditions do not lend themselves to intervention because we
  lack the knowledge and/or technology to change them (see Example 2 that
  follows).

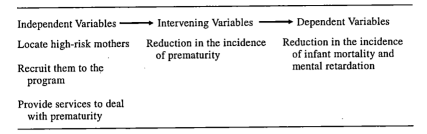

Figure 5.1. The Relationships Between Variables

- Other preconditions may not be addressed because they cannot be controlled, in that controls would be either socially or culturally unacceptable (see Example 3 below).

These distinctions are critical; the following examples are offered only to illustrate the different paths and perspectives generated by different formulations of the problem.

Example 1: Political Economy as a Factor Contributing to Unemployment

It has been argued that many of the problems facing a particular society are "caused" by the specific form of that society's political economy (e.g., capitalism). If one were to begin at this level, proposed solutions would be likely to involve a radical transformation of the existing system or at least its modification. Although the analysis can be theoretically and technically correct, it is unlikely that a planner or administrator at the local level will be in a position to change that system, whether it is a form of capitalism or socialism.

Periodic unemployment for some and more permanent unemployment for others is a fact of life in our society. Our economy is such that (a) cycles of growth are always followed by cycles of decline, (b) inflation historically increases as unemployment declines, and (c) structural and frictional factors in our economy will produce a number of patterns, among which are higher unemployment rates in certain labor markets, regional disparities, the channeling of women and minorities into secondary labor markets with low-paying, dead-end jobs, and the exclusion of others from any labor markets, thus creating a permanent underclass.

Although these problems are "caused" by imperfections in our capitalistic system of relatively free enterprise, our "solutions" are not likely to address the capitalistic system as such but are likely to fall into one or more of the following categories: (a) training those who are unemployed, (b) providing incentives (usually tax) to employers to hire the unemployed and the underemployed, and (c) creating new jobs by attracting new industries to the community. The analysis has shifted from the "causes of unemployment" to the "factors" associated with why some people in a community are unemployed at a specific point in time.

If we were to focus on the economic system as the cause, the original hypothesis might follow this line of reasoning:

> • *If* we were to modify our current economic system in such a way that cycles of growth and decline could be managed and inflation controlled,
> • *then* we would be able to reduce or prevent structural and frictional factors that produce regional disparities, exclusionary employment practices, and the channeling of women and minorities into secondary labor markets, and • *then* we could reduce the numbers of people in the permanent underclass.

Clearly, the actions implied by the above hypothesis are not within the control of a local social service agency. Recognizing, therefore, that the root problem of "imperfections in our economic system" cannot be addressed, we construct a more realistic new hypothesis:

> • *If* we can identify the factors associated with an individual's unemployability, and • *if* we can provide the necessary incentives to make currently unemployable people employable, • *then* the unemployment rate in our community will go down.

The value of this shift in focus from large-scale national issues to local concerns is that it consciously recognizes root causes and determines them to be beyond the purview of local agency limitations, yet translates the social problem of unemployment into a framework that makes it manageable at the local level.

Example 2: The Presence of a Handicapped Child as a Factor Contributing to Child Abuse

This example, one that is on a more micro level than the above, helps clarify further the issues surrounding the program hypothesis. We know from a number of studies that families caring for a severely retarded child are at greater statistical risk of abusing their children than families with nondisabled children. A model that seeks to determine the "cause" of the problem—in this case, child abuse—would identify the cause of the problem as the presence of the handicapping condition.

However, no program is likely to propose a "solution" to this problem—that is, the removal of the condition, severe mental retardation. We do not have the knowledge or the technology to reverse the pathology—to increase an IQ from 50 to 100 or to reverse the physiological aspects of Down's syndrome. Therefore, we would probably conclude that, for intervention purposes, the "cause" of the problem is not simply the presence of a severely retarded child but the stress caused by that presence. Given this, the "solution" to the problem would be the reduction of the stress. The wording of the hypothesis would then shift from "if we can remove the handicap" to "if we can reduce the stress associated with the care of the child who is handicapped."

Example 3: Sexuality and Teenage Pregnancy

Teenage pregnancy will serve as an example of a situation in which a precondition is not addressed because it is not subject to community control or because to try to make it subject to community control would be socially or culturally unacceptable. A major problem facing families, educators, and human service professionals today is the startling increase in the incidence of pregnancy among teens. This problem has a number of subproblems. Each year, 1 in 10 of all teens become pregnant; more than a million adolescent pregnancies occur each year. Over half of these pregnancies are brought to term, and almost 40% end in abortions. One could argue that just as capitalism is the "real" cause of unemployment in the first example and the presence of the severely handicapped child is the "real" cause in the second example, the "real" cause in this example is the act of sex. The solution, then, would involve the reduction or elimination of sexual activity among adolescents. However, given the inability of society to control adolescent sexual activity, most teen pregnancy programs begin at another level, the prevention of conception. The target now is not sexual activity but conception, and interventions focus on reducing the incidence of conception by introducing effective birth control measures. The program hypothesis changes from "if we could prevent sexual activity" to "if we could prevent conception."

In all three of the examples provided, we are likely to move from higher levels of factors to an identification of a factor that we have some chance of changing. Advanced capitalism, the presence of a handi-capped child, or adolescent sexual activity might be the "real" causes, but they are not causes we can deal with on a practical level. Therefore, we call them *preconditions* to the presence of the problem. They help explain—they provide insight—but they are not the targets of the intervention.

THE PROCESS OF DEVELOPING
A PROGRAM HYPOTHESIS

Let us return to Example 1 above. In our discussion of employment, we covered such issues as unemployment and underemployment, struc-tural and frictional factors, and primary and secondary labor markets. We concluded that proposed interventions were likely to emphasize training and job creation and not the more basic causes of these prob-lems.

The following section offers an example of how the problem of unemployment at the local level might be approached and takes the reader through the total process introduced and discussed up to this point.

Statement of a Condition

A recent survey carried out by the County Department of Human Re-sources estimates that of the 10,000 families living in the Morningside neighborhood, 2,000 families had income of less than $10,000.

This statement is a statement of fact and only a statement of fact. There is no interpretation of the fact at this time, nor has a value been placed on the fact. (See Chapter 2 for a full discussion of this process of moving from condition to intervention.)

The concept of "social problem" has been discussed earlier as rela-tive, in that individuals or groups bring a frame of reference, shaped by a value system, to a condition that allows (or forces) them to interpret it. In some cases, this interpretation results in a condition's being labeled a social problem. Furthermore, this interpretation and labeling of the condition becomes the stimulus and justification for action.

Statement of a Social Problem

There are 2,000 families in this neighborhood living in unsafe and sub-standard conditions below minimally acceptable levels for this community. Furthermore, this rate of 20% is almost twice as high as that for any other neighborhood or area in the county. Therefore, resources should be targeted to Morningside to raise the level of family income.

There are three parts to this statement. The first suggests that a family income of $10,000 not only is inadequate but is so low that it places a family at great risk. This is a *qualitative* statement. The second argues that the situation is problematic in its scale or size relative to other parts of the county. This is a *quantitative* statement. These two statements become the basis for the third statement: that something should be done about the situation. This is the *justification for action* statement.

Based on this labeling of the condition as a social problem, which provides a rationale for intervening in the situation, the next task is to determine who these 2,000 families are and why their family income is below $10,000. A survey is commissioned, and a series of community meetings are held over the next few months that produce the following.

Needs Assessment

Of the 2,000 families with income below $10,000,

- 1,000 (50%) are headed by single mothers who are working in marginal jobs with little chance for advancement
- 200 (10%) are headed by fathers who, because of alcohol and other substance problems, are only sporadically employed
- 500 (25%) are headed by mothers who are receiving Aid to Families with Dependent Children (AFDC)
- 200 (10%) are headed by fathers who are employed full time but earn slightly more than the minimum wage and mothers who cannot work because they are needed to care for their preschool-age children
- 100 (5%) are made up of elderly persons

The needs assessment has helped us to understand why these families have incomes of less than $10,000. We now know there are at least five distinct groups of families in this neighborhood, with as many different reasons for their low income level. This type of analysis is critical as we move on in the planning process. It has provided us with the basis for the program hypothesis, or, in this instance, the five program hypotheses.

It also has provided us with *estimates of the numbers* of families in each category, information that becomes crucial when specific interventions are to be designed. The following section takes the first category (mothers in marginal jobs) and walks the reader through the assumptions that eventually become a program hypothesis. Our purpose here is only to demonstrate a line of thinking, an approach that eventually results in services. Different program hypotheses would, of course, be developed for the other four categories because each represents a different subpopulation and because the factors associated with each group's having low income are different. The first program hypothesis would not be an appropriate hypothesis for the others, nor would the services that evolve from this hypothesis be effective for the other families.

Mothers Working in Marginal Jobs

For the 1,000 families headed by single parents (mothers) earning marginal salaries, we would probably consider an intervention that included, at a minimum, the following components:

- Child support enforcement
- Job training/placement
- Child care

It is likely that for at least a percentage of these families, the father is not paying child support. This support is often ordered by a court, yet some fathers refuse to keep up with monthly child support payments. In other instances, the mother, for any number of reasons, never went to court to attempt to collect child support. It is also likely that many of these mothers are restricted to jobs in the secondary labor market because they lack marketable skills. Finally, it is likely that many of these women are restricted to less than full-time employment because of a lack of affordable, accessible child care.

Program Hypothesis: • *If* these women can acquire marketable job skills, and • *if* they are assisted in finding employment in the primary labor market, and • *if* they are relieved of their child care responsibilities by the provision of quality child care, • *then* they are likely to complete their training, secure and retain employment, and raise their standard of living to reasonable levels; and, in some instances, • *if* child support is provided to the mother, • *then* that mother will have more options open to her: Not only will she be in a position to increase her family income, but she will be able to choose between part- and full-time work outside the home and even to return to school as a first step in establishing a career.

PROGRAM HYPOTHESES AND
THE IDEA OF CONSEQUENCES

Thus far, we have discussed the concepts of primary or ultimate causes and the factors associated with primary or ultimate causes. Wherever possible, a program hypothesis should focus as clearly and consistently as possible on causes or on the factors associated with causes. There are, however, many instances in which social problems have gone far beyond primary effects and have reached a stage of secondary and tertiary consequences. One might think of this phenomenon as a series of concentric circles involving a ripple effect. In these cases, it is often necessary for program planners to shift their focus from causes to consequences and target the factors associated with consequences.

Let us continue with our example of adolescent pregnancy and shift our focus from prevention of conception to the problem of adolescents who become pregnant and decide to keep their babies. Some 500,000 infants are born to teenage mothers each year, and the majority are kept by their mothers. The sad fact is that both these mothers and their children are at great risk physically, socially, financially, and emotionally. The following is a brief description of the consequences likely to be experienced by the adolescent who becomes pregnant and decides to keep her child.

The teen is likely to drop out of school. Recent statistics show that only one in three is likely to complete high school within 12 years of the birth of the first child. Given this poor educational background, the teenage mother will have difficulty finding employment, and when she does, it is likely to be work in the secondary labor market. If she finds a job, it will be one with little chance for advancement and minimal health and welfare benefits. She will experience cyclic layoffs from that job. This teen is also likely to be unmarried and to spend some time on welfare (AFDC).

We know that many pregnant teenagers either receive no prenatal care or begin that care late in the pregnancy. This results in medical and health complications for the young mother and the infant. Infant mortality rates are 2.4 times higher for infants born to teenagers than for infants born to mothers from any other age group. The mothers themselves experience a mortality rate 60% higher than that of older mothers. A significant percentage of births to teenage mothers are premature (i.e., low birth weight), a condition associated with the presence of mental retardation and other handicapping conditions.

We also know that teenage mothers are at greater risk of abusing and/or neglecting their children—they are children responsible for raising children. Adolescence is an extremely difficult age for anyone; it is even more difficult for an adolescent who is also a mother. Finally, the unmarried adolescent mother is likely to experience repeat pregnancies.

The foregoing discussion has identified the following possible consequences of adolescent pregnancy and childbirth:

- Dropping out of school
- Difficulty finding employment
- Poor-quality employment
- Dependence on AFDC
- Little or no prenatal care
- Medical and health complications
- Infant mortality
- Risk of death in childbirth
- Premature birth
- Risk of mental retardation for the child
- Risk of child abuse or neglect
- Risk of repeat pregnancies

Our next step is to link factors to consequences. For the sake of illustration, Table 5.1 shows four possible consequences of adolescents' keeping their babies—possible child abuse, infant medical or mental problems, unemployment, and dropping out of school—and identifies factors associated with these consequences.

In the same way that we developed program hypotheses around causes and factors, we can develop them around consequences and factors:

Table 5.1
Consequences of Adolescent Pregnancy

Consequence	Factor
Abuse	Lack of parenting skills
	Lack of bonding
Infant medical or mental problems	Trauma
	Infectious disease
	Poor nutrition
Unemployment	Lack of marketable skills
	Lack of high school diploma
	Lack of good work habits
	Lack of child care
	Lack of transportation
School dropout	Lack of child care
	Lack of family support
	Lack of transportation

• *If* child care is provided for the teenage single mother, and • *if* her family will support her remaining in school, and • *if* she is provided transportation, • *then* she is likely to remain in school and receive her high school diploma.

The discussion in this chapter on causes and consequences, and factors associated with each, can be depicted as shown in Table 5.2, using adolescent pregnancy as an example. The factors associated with either causes or consequences are appropriate candidates for the focus of intervention. Program planners often must choose between causes and consequences, and also among factors, on the basis of resources available. The more comprehensive the coverage, the greater the likelihood of addressing the problem in its entirety.

FROM PROGRAM HYPOTHESIS TO SERVICE

The strength of the above transformation of conditions into problems—and eventually problems into needs—rests on our willingness and ability to propose a set of relational statements (if-then, means-

Table 5.2

Causes and Consequences of Adolescent Pregnancy

Primary Cause	*Secondary Cause*	*Factor*	*Consequence of Adolescent Parenting*	*Factor*
Sexual activity	Conception	Lack of knowledge about conception	Child abuse and neglect	Poor parenting skills
				Lack of bonding
		Lack of availability of contraceptives	Infant medical or mental problems	Infectious disease; poor nutrition
				Unemployment Lack of marketable skills
		Peer pressure	School dropout	Lack of child care; lack of
		Emotional problems		family support

ends) that explain not only what we will do but also why we are doing it. It is our rationale not only for taking action but also for the action we take. If program planners were to stop here, we would be left with a series of statements that might be logically consistent and theoretically correct, but the exercise would have produced nothing of value for clients.

The value of effectiveness-based program planning rests in the ability to create, design, and implement a relevant service that is likely to reduce or eliminate the problem. If the problem analysis and the resulting program hypothesis produce nothing of value for clients and community, then the exercise has been a waste of time.

**Incorporating Problem Analysis
Into Program Design**

There are, unfortunately, numerous examples of elaborate analyses that have been carried out, often at great expense in time and resources,

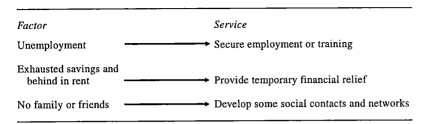

Factor		Service
Unemployment	⟶	Secure employment or training
Exhausted savings and behind in rent	⟶	Provide temporary financial relief
No family or friends	⟶	Develop some social contacts and networks

Figure 5.2. Relationship Between Risk Factors and Possible Services

and have then been ignored when the program's services are developed. This is not unlike a physician ordering an elaborate series of laboratory tests and then ignoring their findings and prescribing something inconsistent with the diagnosis simply because his or her prescribed treatment is easier, more convenient, or cheaper than the "correct" prescription. Let us turn to an example of direct client service to illustrate.

A social caseworker, working in a program attempting to reduce stress among families where there is a high risk of child abuse, finds, during the assessment process, that a particular family is at risk because (a) the father is unemployed, (b) the family has exhausted their savings, (c) they are 3 months behind in their rent and have been told to leave their apartment, and (d) they moved to the city only 6 months before and had not established any friends and have no relatives living within 1,000 miles. These factors, then, should produce the prescription illustrated in Figure 5.2.

What if the case plan identified only family counseling and parent training classes? Given the assessment, we would have to question the selection of these two services. There are no relationships among problem, cause, and solution. It should be obvious that unless emergency assistance is provided, the family will join the ranks of the homeless, and that unless the father is helped in preparing for, finding, and holding a job, and unless the family is linked to an informal or formal support group, the children are likely to be abused.

Program planners make the same mistakes when they fail to make connections among causes, consequences, factors, and service. The introduction of an innovative planning process cannot end with "business as usual": that is, the decision to continue offering the services that have been and are being offered with the rationale that we have to offer them because we are organized to offer them. When program planners ignore the inconsistencies between cause/consequences/factors, on the one hand, and services, on the other, they are dooming a program to waste resources, to provide ineffective services, and ultimately to fail. New discoveries call for new, innovative, or redesigned services.

We address the task of designing or redesigning services in Chapter 7. But first, in the next chapter, we focus on moving from the program hypothesis to the setting of goals and objectives—statements that become, in effect, the beacons toward which we move as we develop new, innovative, or redesigned services. Goals and objectives succinctly summarize the problem analysis, needs assessment, and program hypothesis components of the plan and guide the design of the service.

Chapter 6

SETTING GOALS AND OBJECTIVES

Setting goals and objectives is the fourth major component of the effectiveness-based program planning process, the first three being problem analysis, needs assessment, and establishing the program hypothesis. Up to this point, much of the activity has focused on gathering data and information about the problem and thinking creatively about cause-and-effect relationships.

The development of goals and objectives provides a framework for action by establishing the expectation that program planners describe in clear terms what they are attempting to achieve and how it is to be achieved. Furthermore, it is an extremely important phase of the planning process inasmuch as it provides the framework for the monitoring and evaluation sections of the program plan.

FROM PROGRAM HYPOTHESIS
TO GOALS AND OBJECTIVES

In Chapter 5, we introduced the idea that the design of a relevant and effective program or service is dependent on the development of a clear and logical hypothesis based on knowledge about the problem and the population. The program hypothesis is made up of two sets of subhypotheses: a hypothesis of etiology and a working intervention hypothesis. When all the information accumulated about the problem and the population has been distilled into an understanding of cause-and-effect relationships, a working intervention hypothesis is drafted, designed to address root causes as identified in the hypothesis of etiology.

Earlier we introduced an example of efforts to deal with teen pregnancy. The following statements could act as a hypothesis of etiology, which would then lead to a working intervention hypothesis:

Because of the following factors:
- Increased exposure to a culture of early sexual activity
- Reduced or nonexistent sanctions from family and community
- Peer pressure to become sexually active
- Failure to make use of available methods of contraception
- Lack of interest in education
- Lack of career goals

The result is:
- Pregnant, unmarried women in their teens
- Inadequate income to support themselves and their children
- Inadequate parenting skills
- Poor-quality education
- Limited employment/career opportunities

A working intervention hypothesis based on the above might read as follows:

If the following actions are taken with a population at risk of teen pregnancy:
- Promoting a change in priorities and values
- Enlisting the support of parents and families in reinforcing these changed values
- Promoting practices to avoid pregnancy
- Providing academic support services
- Providing mentors to generate interest in education and career planning

Then the following results can be expected:
- A reduction in feelings of peer pressure to become sexually active among program participants
- Reduced incidence of unprotected sex
- Higher levels of academic performance and high school graduation

- Pursuit of post-high school careers, technical training, or higher education
- A reduction in the incidence of pregnancy among program participants

Earlier, we suggested that this phase of the planning process is concerned with linking the problem analysis to an action plan. In the program hypothesis example, the hypothesis of etiology explains our current understanding of cause-and-effect relationships. The working intervention hypothesis then focuses its activities (interventions) on the "causes," with an expectation that, if successful, it will have a positive impact on the "effects." The next task is to translate these statements into a goals-objectives framework.

Benefits of the Program Hypothesis

The above approach—beginning with problem analysis, moving to needs assessment, developing a program hypothesis, and developing a hierarchical set of goals and objectives—will produce a number of benefits that cannot be produced from any other process. These benefits are listed below, and each is discussed in turn.

The Program Hypothesis Helps Focus Programs on Problems Rather Than on Activities

In the above example, our problem analysis, program hypothesis, and eventually our goals and objectives are all focused on ways (the "how") to lower or prevent the incidence of teen pregnancy and to provide the kind of support needed by the target population for long-term self-sufficiency. Because the program hypothesis is problem directed, it forces us constantly to think about the purpose of our program and not about the details of the actual services.

A traditional approach would tend to focus on the organization's units and the specialized services they provide—services that eventually take on purposes and lives of their own. In this example, in the absence of problem-oriented goals and objectives based on a program hypothesis, a plan might be developed focused on the provision of casework services, leaving the decision about what the participants need to the judgment of many different caseworkers. This approach could very well result in trial and error and ignore all the research and evaluation findings that point to specific factors that, in combination, increase the risk of teen pregnancy.

The Program Hypothesis Can Link
Program Activities to Outcomes

This linkage between means and ends specified in the working intervention hypothesis is critical in that it allows the administrator to determine whether a program is working. This sentence is deceptive in its apparent simplicity. There are, however, two distinct questions involved, both of which are the essence of program evaluation:

1. Did we actually implement the program we designed?
2. To what extent did we achieve the proposed results?

If a working intervention hypothesis is a series of statements that includes, at a minimal level, a relationship between identified programs and anticipated results, we need to determine two things: (a) whether the intervention was implemented as designed and (b) the extent to which the expected results were achieved. This, then, forms the basis for ever-increasing precision in matching programs to problem and need and ultimately for supporting, rejecting, or modifying the program hypothesis.

The Program Hypothesis Can Provide
a Basis for Long-Range Planning

The system we are outlining requires that the planner think beyond the present, or, in other words, beyond a single year. By planning programs around problems and by linking activities to identified results or outcomes, we are encouraged to focus efforts on long-term effects. Most of the problems we are concerned with are complex. Many cannot be successfully dealt with in a single year's time frame. Many are of such a scale that only a portion of the people in need can be served in a single year. We need, then, to identify multiple-year objectives and to generate multiple-year estimates of resources needed to achieve these objectives.

For example, our needs assessment might provide an estimate of 250 young women in a particular school at any given time who meet our definition of being at high risk of pregnancy. In our program planning, we might decide that during the first year we can effectively serve only

75 to 100 women. We would still want to develop, during the second
and subsequent years, the capacity to serve a greater number and the
resources needed to accomplish this.

The Program Hypothesis Can Provide a
Framework for Continuous Monitoring and
Evaluation of the Service Provision Process

The system we are describing is one that will have different levels of
outcomes. One set can be described as the ultimate results expected
from the program. Another can be described as intermediate results. In
our example, the ultimate result is the reduction of teen pregnancy.
Realistically, we should not expect to observe meaningful changes in
the number of teen pregnancies in the first year in which the program
was initiated, especially in view of the program's attempt to somehow
change values within the teen culture. However, this does not mean that
we should ignore evaluation until the end of the second year. We should
take intermediate measures so that we can be in a position to take
corrective action when it can make a difference (i.e., early in the
program's life).

Again, our program hypothesis and accompanying goals and objectives allow us to begin our evaluation at an early date. We have posited
a relationship between values, peer pressure, use of contraception,
education career goals, and teen pregnancy. Are we finding that the
program is having success in its attempt to change values? Are there
measurable improvements in use of various methods of contraception?
Are attitudes toward education and career changing, and if so, are these
changed attitudes resulting in improved academic performance? If the
program hypothesis is correct, and if the interventions are effective,
these are some of the factors that can be measured early in the life of
the program, and we can plan to measure changes in the teen pregnancy
rate at a later time. The relationships between program hypothesis,
intermediate outcomes, and final outcomes are illustrated in Table 6.1.

The Program Hypothesis Can Provide a Database
for Cost-Benefit and Cost-Effectiveness Studies

The final contribution of this system is that it gives us the ability to
tie cost data to program data. The program hypothesis provides a
framework for goals and objectives relating resources to outcomes. Cost
data allow us to take the next step, which is the assessment of how much

Table 6.1

The Relationship Between Program Hypothesis,
Intermediate Outcomes, and Final Outcomes

Program Hypothesis	Intermediate Outcomes	Final Outcomes
If teens who are at high risk of pregnancy can change their priorities and values, make responsible decisions about sexual activity, become focused on career planning, and improve academic performance, then the incidence of teen pregnancy will be reduced.	Changed priorities Use of contraceptives or abstinence Have a career plan Passing grades	Reduce the incidence of unprotected sex Reduce the incidence of teen pregnancy Increase graduation rates

these outcomes have cost. This allows the administrator to address the
following questions:

1. Is the program cost-effective?
2. Could we achieve the same results at a lower cost?

This issue is the focus of later chapters dealing with budgeting.

THE FUNCTION OF A MISSION STATEMENT

Having addressed the benefits to be derived from this system and the
rationale behind the system, let us now turn to its specific components.
The first is the mission statement of the agency that will implement the
program. Program goals and objectives are influenced by the host
agency's mission statement, or statement of overall purpose. This statement is usually given formal approval and sanction by legislators in
public agencies and by boards in private agencies. It provides a "continuing philosophical perspective and makes explicit the reason for the
existence of the organization" (Kettner, Daley, & Nichols, 1985,
p. 118).

Another way of describing the purpose of a mission statement is that
it establishes broad and relatively permanent parameters within which

goals are developed and specific programs designed. A mission state-ment includes, at minimum, a target population and a statement of the agency's vision for what ideally might be achieved in collaboration between the agency and the target population. Some agencies develop elaborate explanations of their mission statements; others limit them to one sentence or one paragraph.

A family service agency might have as its mission "to promote family strength and stability in a manner that allows each individual to achieve his/her potential while, at the same time, supporting strong and produc-tive interrelationships among family members." An agency providing services to alcohol and drug addicts might have as its mission "to promote and support the achievement of a positive and productive lifestyle for those formerly addicted to chemical substances." The key is that a mission statement should focus on what lies ahead for its clients/consumers if the agency is successful in addressing their prob-lems and meeting their needs.

Mission statements are intended to be visionary and should be reevaluated when societal conditions are altered or when the problems that the agency was established to resolve are no longer present (e.g., a health clinic may decide to focus exclusively on the treatment of pa-tients with AIDS). When an agency continually changes or modifies its mission statement, that agency is usually found to be experiencing profound and pervasive internal problems. Implicit in the relative per-manence of mission is an understanding that the problems or conditions of concern to the agency are broad enough in scope and scale that they are unlikely to be achieved in the near future. Just as the mission statements "to promote family stability" and "to promote and protect a chemical dependency-free lifestyle" are legitimate statements in the year 2000, so they are likely to be relevant in 2025. Even though the concept of family stability might be operationalized differently in the future, the concept will continue to have validity.

THE FORMULATION OF GOALS

Program goals are intended to be compatible with the agency's mission. Goals are statements of expected outcomes dealing with the problem that the program is attempting to prevent, eradicate, or ameliorate. Goals need not be measurable or achievable. They simply provide programmatic direction.

In our example dealing with pregnant teens, we hope to reduce teen pregnancy and promote self-sufficiency among the at-risk population. A goal statement might read as follows: "to improve the chances that at-risk young women in the Jefferson School District will graduate from high school." Another might read: "to increase the commitment to career goals among at risk young women in the Jefferson School District." To be appropriate goal statements, both of the above should clearly fall under the mission statement of the agency—in this case, "to promote family strength and stability in a manner that allows each individual to achieve his/her potential while, at the same time, supporting strong and productive interrelationships among family members."

In working toward these goals, we move a few small steps in the direction of furthering the mission of the total organization, understanding that the mission is something that is never fully achieved. Still, goals should be statements of expected long-range accomplishments. They should be ambitious and idealistic as long as they meet the criteria discussed above, are consistent with the agency's mission statement, and state expected outcomes. They do not propose any time limits (i.e., stating that the goal will be achieved in 1, 5, or 10 years), nor are they capable of being measured as written. Time frames and measurement criteria are formulated only when we turn our attention to objectives.

Given this purposeful ambiguity, why develop goals for programs? Basically, they serve the same function for programs that mission statements serve for organizations. They provide a beacon that serves as a constant focal point and lends a sense of direction to the program. They are the reasons for which the program is funded and implemented. They are statements of preferences or values.

Goals statements are also political statements and are written in such a way that they tend to build consensus. Who can be opposed to "reducing the incidence of drug use among 8- to 12-year-olds in Canyon City" or "increasing the employment rate of welfare recipients in Springfield"? Goal statements become rallying causes around which we attempt to gather support for a program. Disagreement will inevitably arise when we attempt to set out the best means to work toward that goal, but we do not want disagreement at this level. Rather, we want cooperation through co-optation.

THE FORMULATION OF OBJECTIVES

In effectiveness-based program planning, one should be able to make explicit two things about a program: (a) the results that are to be achieved and (b) the manner in which these results will be achieved.

The specification of results is a statement of the "ends" or expectations of the program, and in the program planning literature these ends are referred to as *outcome objectives*. The specification of service provision is an articulation of the "means" that will be used to achieve the ends, and these are referred to as *process objectives*. Finally, under process objectives, we find listings of specific activities that represent a further breakdown or refinement of the details of program implementation.

Throughout the literature, a variety of terms are used by planners to distinguish these three different levels, including *strategies, milestones, operational objectives,* and *program objectives*. In the following discussion, we will use the program planning terms *outcome objectives, process objectives,* and *activities*. The hierarchy is similar to that depicted in Figure 6.1.

REQUIREMENTS FOR ALL OBJECTIVES

Whether the objectives deal with outcomes, processes, or activities, all have a number of elements in common. A good objective is *clear, specific, measurable, time limited,* and *realistic* and represents a *commitment*. These elements can be addressed through the following questions:

- Is the objective clear? Does it mean the same thing to anyone who reads the statement?
- Does the objective specify results to be achieved, including numbers and changes in conditions?
- Is the objective written in such a way that it can be measured? Are measurement criteria incorporated into the objective?
- Does the statement indicate a time limit within which or a target date by which the objective will be achieved?
- Is the objective realistic given our technology and knowledge as well as available resources?

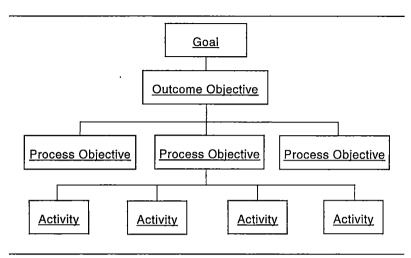

Figure 6.1. Hierarchy of Goals, Objectives, and Activities

- Does the objective identify who has responsibility for achieving the process objectives and their subsets of activities?

If we reduced the above principles of a good objective down into specific criteria by which a good objective can be judged, we would state first that all wording throughout must be clear. Beyond clarity, we would look for five specific elements:

1. Time frame
2. Target of the change
3. Products (process) or results (outcomes) to be achieved
4. Criteria by which the products or results will be documented, monitored, or measured
5. Responsibility for implementing and measuring achievement of the objective

Clarity

The critical test is that anyone who reads an objective will understand it: There is a minimum of ambiguity, and everyone will interpret the objective in approximately the same way. For example, a statement such as "to improve the quality of interaction between spouses" could have many interpretations. It is vague and uncertain without further modifiers and descriptors. A better, more measurable statement would be "to reduce the number of conflicts between spouses by at least 50%."

Precision becomes extremely important as the program goes through its implementation stage. By the time of implementation, the initial authors of the goals and objectives may not be available for interpretation, nor should they have to be if the goals have been crafted correctly.

One way to ensure clarity (and, later, measurability) is to develop objectives that have behavioral aspects. Examples of these would include statements that begin with verbs such as *write, list, increase, reduce, terminate,* or *demonstrate.* Examples that use vague and nonbehavioral (i.e., not observable) referents might include statements that begin with verbs such as *understand, know, realize, feel, believe,* or *enable.*

Time Frames

Wherever possible, time frames should be stated as specific dates, including month, day, and year. These, then, become the dates on which readings are taken to evaluate whether the program is meeting its objectives. Multiple-year planning is usually necessary, given the complexity of most social service program expectations. When multiple-year outcome objectives are developed, they may be stated as follows:

- By June 30, 20XX
- By the end of the sixth month
- By the end of the third year

There may be times when a date cannot be specified for an objective. This may happen, for example, when a program plan is being developed, but the dates for implementation are unknown. In instances such as these, it may be necessary to specify a time frame rather than a specific date: for example, "By the end of the sixth month, at least 30 clients will have been placed in jobs where they are able to use the computer skills learned in training."

Specific dates are preferable because they are so much more useful for monitoring purposes, but when a program is faced with an uncertain start date, objectives may have to use flexible time frames that can later be translated into specific dates.

Target of Change

Objectives also specify the population or the elements that are expected to be changed if the objective is achieved. *Outcome objectives* focus on populations; *process objectives* sometimes focus on inanimate objects, such as the completion of a report or the design of an element of the program. The following are client populations that might be specified in an outcome objective:

- 100 pregnant teens
- 75 low-income families
- 90 abusing and neglecting families

The following are milestones achieved or products produced that might be specified in a process objective:

- Case managers will be hired.
- An interim report will be produced.
- A screening system will be designed.

Products and Results

The purpose of a program planning effort is the accomplishment of client changes that are achievable within stated time frames. To get to the point of successfully achieving client changes, certain processes must first be implemented and followed through to completion. So that processes not be allowed to continue on indefinitely without concrete, measurable achievement, milestones should be identified that can be used to mark the completion of the process.

Client outcomes, on the other hand, identify what positive changes should have been achieved by clients by the time they have completed the program. For example:

- Process: 100 clients will have been recruited.
- Outcome: 50 families will report improved communication.

Deciding how much to promise in terms of client outcomes is a critical decision in program planning. Occasionally, program planners think that the more they promise, the more likely it is that they will obtain funding for their programs. In most instances, this strategy backfires. Either the funding source recognizes that the projected results are unrealistic or, if the program is funded, program planners often find that they have put themselves and the implementers of the program in the untenable position of attempting to achieve unachievable outcomes and, eventually, of attempting to explain why they did not.

This type of behavior begins to affect an agency's credibility. A program's goals and objectives should be seen as a contract. If requested resources are made available, then stated outcomes will be achieved. An objective that is well written technically (one that meets the above criteria) but that cannot possibly be accomplished can be a serious waste of time, energy, and resources. It is better in the long run not to get such a program funded than to waste valuable resources that might have been used more effectively in another program with realistic objectives.

Criteria for Measurement

If the objective cannot be measured, the program cannot be evaluated—or at least we will never be able to know whether the objective has been achieved. The corollary of this is that we need to state in the planning phase not only what we hope to achieve (such as a reduction in child abuse or an increase in job placements) but also the criteria of acceptable performance: for example,

- To reduce child abuse by 15% as measured by referrals recorded in the Child Abuse Central Registry (outcome objective)
- To recruit 100 parents with a history of abuse as documented by child protective services case records (process objective)

To ensure that measurement criteria have been included, one should always look for the phrase *as measured (or documented) by* in a complete objective. Outcome objectives will use the term *measured,* whereas process objectives will often use the term *documented.*

Responsibility

The final issue is that of accountability for implementation of the objective. Up to this point our concern has been that objectives be clear, specific, measurable, time based, and realistic. The last factor in the equation is the ability to fix responsibility for carrying out and reporting on the objective's attainment. The statement (at the process and activity level) should include an identification of a title (e.g., supervisor, program administrator) or a person. For example, in the following process objective, the supervisor is designated as the responsible person: "By June 1, 20XX, to complete the first phase of the outreach, screening, and assessment of 50 women who have been identified as being high risk as documented in a report written by the social work supervisor."

Not all writers of objectives include the name or title of the person responsible in the objective itself. Nevertheless, the principle of identifying person(s) responsible is an important one. In the same manner that we identify a specific date of completion for the objective so that we will know *when* the objective is to be completed, we identify a person or title so that we will know *who* is to be held accountable for ensuring that the plan for achieving the objective is monitored and that all responsible parties are keeping their commitments.

OUTCOME OBJECTIVES

Outcome objectives are extremely important parts of a program plan in that they explain the reason for the existence of the program as well as projecting measurable results. Outcome objectives flow directly from the problem analysis phase in a number of ways. First and foremost, an outcome objective is a statement that is intended to reflect a reduction in the incidence or prevalence of the problem. Outcome objectives should state clearly what effect the intervention is expected to have on the target population—for example,

- To increase the graduation rate among high-risk adolescents
- To prevent the reoccurrence of child abuse or neglect in 25 families
- To return 100 children in foster care to their natural parents

The problem analysis section will provide the numbers necessary to meet the criteria of measurability and specificity discussed above. By identifying the numbers of individuals or families with a particular problem, we have established the outside limits for the program. Given agency, personnel, and resource constraints, we identify the number of clients that we realistically expect to be able to serve during a given period of time. Now the task is to *predict* our success rate. The following are examples of outcome objectives:

- By June 30, 20XX, to increase the graduation rate among high risk adolescents by 40%, as documented in school records

- By December 31, 20XX, to prevent the reoccurrence of child abuse and neglect in 75% of the families participating in this program, as documented by referrals to the Child Abuse Central Registry
- By August 1, 20XX, to improve the relationship between 50 adolescents and their natural parents as measured by the Parent/Adolescent Communication Scale

To restate, outcome objectives flow from the problem analysis phase and focus on a reduction of the problem or an improvement in the quality of life of the program's target population. They are statements that translate a program goal into precise and measurable language. Once the outcome objectives are clearly conceptualized and stated, their companion process objectives should begin to become clear. These are addressed in the next section.

Given the complexity of the problems that we are attempting to resolve, it is often necessary to think of outcome objectives in hierarchical terms. Invariably, we will have levels of outcomes, all dealing with a positive change in the quality of life of the clients, with lower-level outcomes to be achieved before the next level.

The highest level of outcome reflects the reason for existence of the program—for example,

- To reduce the rate of teen pregnancy
- To increase the number of homeless with marketable skills
- To reduce the number of adolescents who participate in street gangs

Most programs designed to achieve these outcomes would require a mix of interventions. With teen pregnancy, as we have discussed earlier, it could be a combination of attempting to change values, increasing use of contraception, improving academic performance, and strengthening commitment to career goals. With the homeless, it could be a combination of learning basic job-finding skills (such as resume preparation and interviewing) and learning a skill (such as short-order cooking). With street gangs, it could be a combination of developing a relationship with a mentor, participating in after-school activities, and improving academic performance.

In each instance, it is expected that if clients improve in the areas specified in the previous paragraph, they will achieve the stated outcome or result. We know (or believe) this because our research done during the problem analysis phase supports this hypothesis.

What must be recognized, however, is that each of the interventions designed to achieve the outcome objective also has expected outcomes. If one phase of the intervention is designed to change values and priorities, then there must be a measurable outcome for that phase. Likewise, there must be measurable outcomes for increasing use of methods of contraception, improving academic performance, and strengthening commitment to career goals. It is these outcomes *in combination* that we believe will enable an adolescent at risk to avoid pregnancy. So to understand all the necessary components of the program, we must understand whether each individual client (as well as all clients aggregated) achieved expected outcomes. Once we know that these lower-level outcomes have been achieved, we can begin to support or reject the intervention hypothesis that states that achievement of these lower-level outcomes will lead to a reduction in the teen pregnancy rate.

In that they represent a hierarchical system, these objectives need to be written as a system and not as discrete objectives. Each has to be logically consistent with the next. If, for example, in the problem analysis we learned that teens were becoming pregnant at an increasingly higher rate because of peer pressure and because of a culture that increasingly accepts unmarried teen mothers, it would not be logical to state that successful completion of a course on sex education would reduce the rate of teen pregnancy.

If there are, as in this example, two levels of outcomes, we might want to distinguish them as *final* (i.e., reduction in teen pregnancy rate) and *intermediate* (i.e., improved academic performance and others). Some programs may have as many as three levels of outcomes, but most are likely to have at least two. We can describe these as final and intermediate. A child abuse program, for example, might be designed as follows:

- *Final outcome*: to prevent the incidence of child abuse in 100 high-risk families
- *Intermediate outcomes*: (a) to increase parenting skills, (b) to increase the utilization of respite care, and (c) to increase the amount of discretionary income available to at least 200 target families

Diagrammatically, the teen pregnancy example might be presented as in Figure 6.2.

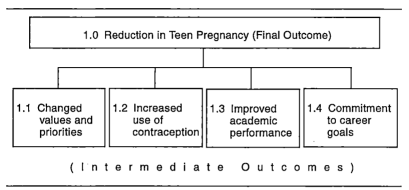

Figure 6.2. Relationship Between Intermediate and Final Outcomes

PROCESS OBJECTIVES AND ACTIVITIES

Once the ends (outcome objectives) have been developed, we are in a position to specify the means (process objectives) by which we hope to achieve the stated results. Again, we return to the program hypothesis, which incorporates in skeleton form the assumed relationships between means (if the following actions are taken . . .) and ends (then the following results can be expected). The "if" statements in the hypothesis dealing with the means become the basis for the process objectives, just as the "then" statements dealing with the ends become the basis for the outcome objectives.

In the teen pregnancy example above, we identified four intermediate outcome objectives. Process objectives become the vehicles by which we describe how these outcomes will be achieved. Process objectives are always related to the lowest level of outcome objectives. We assume that highest-level outcome objectives will be achieved through the attainment of the lower-level outcome objectives (i.e., the incidence of teen pregnancy will be reduced through changed values and priorities, and so on).

Process objectives, then, are intended to spell out the milestones necessary to achieve the intermediate outcome objectives. Like all objectives, well-written process objectives require the five basic parts: (a) time frame, (b) target (population or product), (c) result (the tangible expectation of this process), (d) criterion (how the result will be measured or documented), and (e) responsibility (who is responsible for ensuring the completion of this process objective). Just as with outcome objectives, we find that process objectives have their own set of verbs and descriptors—for example,

- To increase the level of services or number of cases
- To provide case management
- To serve hot meals
- To recruit program participants
- To train volunteers
- To make home visits

Let us use one of our earlier examples to illustrate the relationship between outcome and process.

Outcome Objective (Final)

1.0. By June 30, 20XX, to reduce the number of adolescents in the Roosevelt School District who belong to identified violent street gangs, as documented by city police records

Outcome Objectives (Intermediate)

1.1. By May 15, 20XX, to reduce the number of nights that 100 at-risk adolescents participate in activities of violent street gangs and to increase the number of times these same adolescents participate in formally organized evening activities together with parent or parents, as documented by attendance records

1.2. By September 15, 20XX, to increase the self-esteem of at least 100 at-risk adolescents as measured by the Murphy Self-Esteem Scale

1.3. By December 31, 20XX, to improve the attendance and academic performance of at least 100 at-risk adolescents, as documented by school records

Examples of process objectives for Intermediate Outcome Objective 1.1 might include the following:

Process Objectives

1.1.1. To recruit at least 100 at-risk adolescents and their parents into the gang prevention program

1.1.2. To provide social and recreational activities for at least 100 families two evenings per week for at least 50 weeks per year

1.1.3. To provide parent/child communication training at least 25 evenings during the year

1.1.4. To provide a mentor for each family

A second example illustrates objectives related to the incidence of child abuse:

Outcome Objective (Final)

1.0. By December 31, 20XX, to reduce the incidence of child abuse in 75% of the high-risk families who participate in the program, as measured by reports from the child abuse registry

Outcome Objective (Intermediate)

1.1. By June 30, 20XX, to demonstrate reduction in stress in at least 90% of client families on those stress factors that cause a family to be at risk; success to be measured by a family's moving at least two points in a positive direction on the Sullivan Stress Scale

Process Objectives

1.1.1. By September 1, 20XX, to develop a screening process for all families referred to the program, as documented by the completion and approval of a screening instrument and a flowchart of the process

1.1.2. By December 1, 20XX, to develop a stress profile on at least 30 families using the Sullivan Stress Scale, as documented in case records and monthly project report

1.1.3. By March 1, 20XX, to provide case management services to at least 100 families, as documented in the case records

In establishing dates for outcome and process objectives, remember that the processes must be completed *before* you can expect to measure the achievement of the expected outcome.

ACTIVITIES

Our next and final task in structuring the plan is to take each process objective and break it down into specific tasks that must be completed to achieve the process objectives. These we refer to as *activities* in the classification system suggested earlier in this chapter. In the above example, we might find the screening process objective (Process Objective 1.1.1) to include the following activities:

1.1.1.1. Convene a task force to develop a screening instrument. Due date: July 1.

1.1.1.2. Review instruments used in other programs. Due date: July 15.

1.1.1.3. Draft a screening instrument and a flowchart. Due date: July 22.

1.1.1.4. Circulate draft instrument and flowchart for review and comment. Due date: July 29.

1.1.1.5. Incorporate feedback. Due date: August 5.

1.1.1.6. Finalize instrument and flowchart. Due date: August 15.

Diagrammatically, the completed system would appear as shown in Figure 6.3. The numbering system proposed here is merely a suggestion. There are no hard-and-fast rules that make one numbering or lettering system superior to another. The intent is simply that they be coded in some way that makes for easy identification and that provides an easily understandable scheme to illustrate interrelationships among goals, objectives, and activities. With the numbering scheme used above, those working with Activity 1.1.1.6, for example, will always know that this activity relates to Final Outcome Objective 1.0, to Intermediate Outcome Objective 1.1, and to Process Objective 1.1.1.

Is It Worth the Effort?

When all of the above elements have been fully developed, the complete document represents a plan ready for implementation. A major criticism of this management-by-objectives technology is that it is extremely time consuming, taking staff time away from an already full schedule. This is a valid criticism. In actual practice, however, it comes down to a simple question of business as usual versus a redesign of the system to allow for program planning and evaluation. This system offers the conceptual tools to set up services as ongoing *in vivo* experiments designed to inform practitioners and administrators about whether a program is working. Further, it spells out staff activities in precise language, thereby permitting a proactive approach to ensuring program success.

When programs continue business as usual, they can only hope they are successful, and interpretation of success is made by direct service workers based on impressions of client improvement. When principles of effectiveness-based program planning are used, program success can

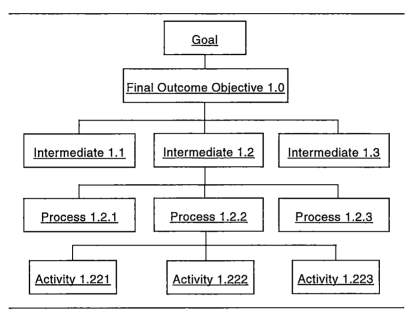

Figure 6.3. A Suggested Numbering Scheme for Goals, Objectives, and Activities

be measured and documented. All indications are that this type of documentation will be increasingly required for future funding. We will say more about this in the chapter on evaluation.

Chapter 7

DESIGNING EFFECTIVE PROGRAMS

THE SIGNIFICANCE OF PROGRAM DESIGN

Like the earlier phases of effectiveness-based program planning discussed in the previous chapters, program design is an activity that requires careful analysis and attention to detail. Historically in social services program planning, program design has not always received this attention to detail. For many years, program design was all but overlooked in planning programs. For the vast majority of social service programs, program design involved simply hiring caseworkers, assigning clients, and instructing the workers to provide casework. Although this approach is simple in its design and allows maximum flexibility for practitioners, it fails to deal with critical questions of relevance of services provided, accountability, and measurement of effectiveness.

Let us explore these issues by contrasting two programs for elderly, isolated seniors. Program A has five caseworkers, each of whom carries 30 cases. Caseworkers decide how often to meet with clients. When they meet, they attempt to determine needs and to find resources in the community to meet those needs. After each session, caseworkers write narrative recordings of case activity in the case record.

Program B is structured differently. Program B has an intake and screening worker, two case managers, a meal coordinator, a transportation coordinator, and a socialization and recreation specialist. Program B staff identify at-risk seniors in the community, transport them to the senior center, screen and assess to determine unmet needs, and build a case plan designed to meet unmet needs to the greatest extent possible, including a daily noon meal and transportation to and from the center.

When a client completes Program A, a caseworker writes a narrative explanation of why the client is no longer in the program and describes the client's progress and status as of the point of termination. On completion of Program B, a case manager administers a posttest on nutrition, social isolation, and general mobility and secures agreement from the client to participate in a 6-month follow-up evaluation. In Program B's case records, case managers record test scores, itemize barriers, and code the special units from which each client receives services. The case manager enters the data or turns them over to a data entry person to be entered into the computer.

Which is the better program? The answer to that question depends on your perspective on the purpose of social service programs. Program A clearly provides for a stronger and more comprehensive relationship between caseworker and client. Program B, however, is clearly superior when effectiveness and accountability are the issues. Program B's design is based on a hypothesis that the major barriers to full participation for isolated elderly include transportation and socialization and recreation opportunities, including congregate meals. Regular analysis of their data will enable Program B's staff to discover whether this hypothesis is correct and to make adjustments as needed to make the program more effective.

The major differences between these programs are differences of precision, specificity, and detail. Program A caseworkers may also discover that socialization, recreation, and congregate meals are important factors in success for isolated elderly. Each caseworker, however, would have to make this discovery independently and decide to act on it. For Program B, the *problem analysis* produced the findings, and the *goals and objectives* established the direction. Let us examine how planners, using effectiveness-based program planning principles, move from goals and objectives to program design.

DESIGNING THE ELEMENTS OF A SYSTEM

As with all sciences, bringing precision and understanding to a phenomenon involves breaking it down into some basic elements. One analytic framework that has proved very useful to business and industry as well as to the social sciences is the systems framework. A greater understanding of programs can be achieved by breaking them down into elements associated with system inputs, throughputs, outputs, and outcomes (Martin & Kettner, 1996). *Inputs* are defined as resources and raw materials, *throughputs* as the conversion process, *outputs* as service products or service completions, and *outcomes* as measurable changes in the client's life situation or circumstances.

Use of these four simple concepts has enabled such diverse organizations as General Motors, IBM, and Microsoft to pinpoint areas of inefficiency or ineffectiveness, to remedy them, and to calculate cost and price in a way that consistently helps them to retain a competitive edge. Rosenberg and Brody (1974) also used this framework to analyze effectiveness in four state public social service agencies.

DEFINING THE ELEMENTS OF A PROGRAM

Applying these concepts to a social service program, we break the system down into its input, throughput, output, and outcome elements.

Inputs

Inputs in a program include five elements representing an agency's resources and raw materials: clients, staff, material resources, facilities, and equipment. Clients represent the raw materials in a human service system; the other elements represent the resources that will be used to "convert" the clients from persons with problems and needs to persons who have been able to resolve problems and meet needs.

Each element needs to be further defined, and we provide examples of how they might be defined in Table 7.1. As each element is defined, it is important to remember that at some point we will have to put in place a data collection system for use in monitoring and evaluation. For this reason, it is useful to define each of the above elements in terms that will be useful for monitoring, evaluation, and reporting purposes. For example, what breakdown of such factors as age, ethnicity, or income will be useful later on when it is necessary to analyze the population served? With these future data and information needs in mind, then, we begin the task of defining the data elements associated with program inputs (see Table 7.1).

Table 7.1

Variables Related to Program Inputs

Variable	Example	Purpose
Client-Related Variables		
Eligibility	Age, residence, income	To ensure that those served are eligible for the program
Demographic or descriptive variables	Race, gender, income, education, employment, census tract	To record elements that may later prove helpful in describing population served, to ensure that the targeted population is being served, and to identify those client characteristics that seem to be associated with success or failure in the program
Social history factors	History of substance abuse, mental health history, violence, etc.—whatever is considered to be relevant	To identify factors that may later be useful in evaluating the types of clients for whom the program is effective or not effective
Client problem and strength profile	Alcohol abuse, drug abuse, parenting skills, money management skills	To identify areas of concern that will become the focus of intervention. Problems are scaled so that assessment will reveal those areas where problems are significant, but also those areas where there are strengths.
Staff-Related Variables		
Demographic or descriptive variables	Gender, ethnicity, education, experience	To identify staff variables that might later be useful in determining what types of workers seem to be most effective with what types of clients or problems
Accreditation or licensing	Licenses, certificates, degrees	To collect data that will be readily available when called for by accrediting or licensing bodies

Table 7.1

Continued

Variable	Example	Purpose
Physical Resources		
Material resources	Food, clothing, toys, or cash provided directly to clients	To collect data that will be helpful in defining what resources seem to affect client change or improvement
Facilities	Residences used to house clients; office facilities used for client treatment	To collect data that may help to understand whether a facility, such as a particular type of residential treatment setting, affects client improvement when compared to other treatment settings
Equipment	Vehicles, computers, medical or other equipment used in direct client service	To collect data about equipment used by or in direct service to clients that may affect the helping process. Data would not be collected on equipment used by staff, only on equipment used directly with and by clients.

Throughputs

Throughput refers to the intervention or program. It is during the service provision process that resources, including staff, material resources, facilities, and equipment, are used to help clients so that they may complete the service process (output) and, it is hoped, resolve their problems (outcome).

Throughputs in social service programs are typically such activities as counseling; job training; provision of day care, residential treatment, and shelter; dispensing of food baskets; and provision of information and referral. To bring some degree of uniformity to the process, it becomes necessary, once again, to identify and define each data element that is part of throughput. These elements include service definition, service tasks, and method of intervention.

Service Definition

The *service definition* is usually a simple one- or two-sentence definition of services to be provided. Its function is to narrow down the service activity from something that might cover a whole range of client problems and needs to something that is focused on a specific aspect of client problems and needs. For example, the broad category "drug treatment" can include the following: detoxification; inpatient or out-patient medical treatment; individual, group, or family counseling; methadone maintenance; job training and placement; and follow-up supportive services.

Simply describing a program as a drug treatment program does not sufficiently narrow its scope in a way that informs relevant parties what the program is intended to accomplish. A definition such as "This program or service is intended to provide outpatient detoxification to cocaine addicts ages 18 and older" helps those who need to know whom and what the program is for.

A comprehensive listing of service definitions has been developed by the United Way of America (1976) in a volume titled *UWASIS II: A Taxonomy of Social Goals and Human Service Programs,* in which more than 230 services are labeled and defined. An example from the UWASIS directory is the definition of prejob guidance: "Pre-job guid-ance is a program designed to help individuals who need to learn the basic tools of obtaining employment to suit their particular skills and talents" (p. 208). Another listing of service definitions is the *Arizona Dictionary and Taxonomy of Human Services* (Department of Economic Security, 1995). The service of "adoption placement" is defined as follows: "This service provides the selection of a family and placement, and supervision of a child until the adoption is finalized."

The service of "adult day care/adult day health care" is defined as follows:

> This service provides planned care, supervision, activities, personal care, personal living skills training, meals, and health monitoring in a group setting during a portion of a 24-hour day. Adult day health services may also include preventive, therapeutic and restorative health related ser-vices. (Arizona Department of Economic Security, 1995)

Service Tasks

Service tasks help to define the activities that go into the provision of the service. If, for example, a program or service is developed to reduce unemployment among high school dropouts, what activities make up the service? Such activities as screening and assessment, job-hunting skills, résumé preparation, job training, job placement, and follow-up might be considered to be part of a complete package. To ensure some degree of comparability in what clients receive, it is important that some thought be given to identifying and defining service tasks.

Often, service tasks follow a chronological order of services to a client. In such cases, it is helpful in the planning and design phases for program planners to develop a client flowchart that tracks a client from entry to exit. Figure 7.1 illustrates a client flow through a system. In a counseling program, for example, a client typically goes through a process involving the following steps:

1. Intake and screening
2. Problem identification and assessment
3. Case planning
4. Implementation of the case plan
5. Monitoring of service provision processes
6. Evaluation of effects of service on the client
7. Termination of the client from services
8. Follow-up

Specifying tasks in this way and bringing increasing degrees of precision to their definition helps to introduce at least some degree of uniformity to what helping professionals provide and can serve a similar function to that of protocols in medicine. It serves to bring a clearer focus to the question of who does what with clients, for what purpose, and under what conditions. It not only addresses the accountability question but also permits ongoing evaluation of effectiveness. If a particular approach is effective, the treatment can be repeated. If it is not, problem areas can be pinpointed and the treatment modified. A service protocol can be developed by beginning with the flowchart of client services and adding a narrative chart that includes an explanation of what activities are to be carried out at each step in the process and

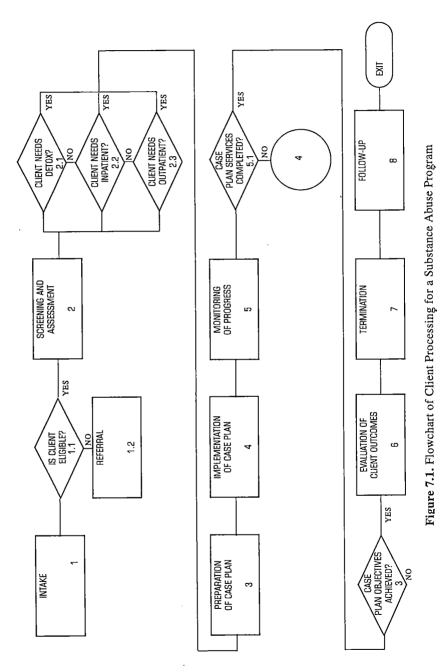

Figure 7.1. Flowchart of Client Processing for a Substance Abuse Program

what documentation is necessary. An illustration of such a service protocol is included as Table 7.2.

Method of Intervention

The third element of throughput is the *method of intervention.* Defining the method of intervention requires that program planners specify in advance the ways the service may be delivered. For example, meals for the elderly can be provided in a congregate setting or can be delivered to the elderly person's home. Job training can be carried out in a classroom setting or on the job. Counseling can be offered to individuals, in groups, or in families. Models of counseling range from psychotherapy to behavior modification. In that the method of treatment is based on an understanding of the problem and on the program hypothesis, it is important to specify a proven method of treatment or service delivery if such a method exists. Table 7.3 illustrates throughput elements.

Outputs

The purpose of measuring output is to determine (a) how much of an available service a client actually received and (b) whether the client completed treatment or received the full complement of services as specified in the program design. The "how much" question is answered by defining *units of service,* and the answer is referred to as an *intermediate output.* The "service completion" question is answered by defining what we mean by completion, and the answer is referred to as a *final output.* A third focus—quality of service provided—also emerges in current discussions of output measures. Quality performance measures are discussed in one of the following sections in this chapter.

Units of Service

Units of service can be measured in three different ways: (a) as episodes or contact units, (b) as material units, or (c) as time units (Martin & Kettner, 1996). An *episode* or *contact* unit is defined as one contact between a worker and a client. It is used when the recording of client contact information is important but when the actual duration (time) of the contact is not considered important.

A *material* unit of service is a tangible resource provided to a client and can include such items as a meal, a food basket, articles of clothing, cash, or a prescription. Material units are generally considered to be the

Table 7.2

Narrative Chart

Process Number	Title	Procedures	Documents
1	Intake	Case manager completes the intake form; determines eligibility; takes a social history.	Intake Form; Eligibility Form; Social History Form
1.1	Is Client Eligible?	Case manager determines if client is eligible on basis of residence and income. If client is eligible, client proceeds to the next step. If not, client is referred to other services.	
2	Screening and Assessment	Case manager and client complete the appropriate client assessment scales. On basis of findings, case manager determines which program the client will enter.	Individual Functioning Scale; Substance Abuse Diagnostic Scale
2.1	Client Needs Detox?	If the Substance Abuse Diagnostic Scale reveals that the client needs detox services before entering a rehabilitation program, the client will enter the detox program.	Detox Program Admissions Form
2.2	Client Needs Inpatient?	If the Substance Abuse Diagnostic Scale reveals that the client needs inpatient services, the client will enter the inpatient program.	Inpatient Program Admissions Form
2.3	Client Needs Outpatient?	If the Substance Abuse Diagnostic Scale reveals that the client can benefit from outpatient services, the client will enter the outpatient program.	Outpatient Program Admissions Form
3	Preparation of Case Plan	On the basis of the findings from the screening and assessment, client and case manager agree on goals, objectives, and activities and a time frame for accomplishment.	Case Planning Form
4	Implementation of Case Plan	Case manager meets with client to clarify expectations and plan for client and case manager activities.	Case Notes and Service Provision Form

Table 7.2

Continued

Process Number	Title	Procedures	Documents
5	Monitoring of Progress	Case manager meets periodically with client to review goals and objectives and to monitor progress.	Case Notes and Service Provision Form
5.1	Case Plan Services Completed?	During the monitoring phase, case manager continually refers to the case plan to determine when tasks and activities have been completed; the case plan remains at the implementation and monitoring stages until services have been completed.	Case Notes and Service Completion Form
5.2	Case Plan Objectives Achieved?	When the case plan services have been completed, the case manager determines whether the case plan objectives have been achieved; if not, case manager and client go back to the case planning process.	Case Notes and Service Completion Form
6	Evaluation of Client Outcomes	If it is determined that the case plan objectives have been achieved, case manager and client readminister the client and family assessment scales to determine changes achieved since the point of initial assessment.	Individual Functioning Scale; Family Functioning Scale
7	Termination	Case manager explores with client how changes achieved can be stabilized and made permanent; final session with client ends the episode of service.	Case Notes and Case Closure Form
8	Follow-Up	Case manager makes at least one follow-up telephone call or in-person visit between 1 and 2 months after termination. If additional services are needed, and if client is willing to pursue further treatment, client returns to Process 3, preparation of a new case plan.	Case Notes and Follow-Up Information Form

Table 7.3

Throughput Elements

Element	Examples	· Purpose
Service definition	This program is intended to provide outpatient detoxification to cocaine addicts ages 18 and older	To provide a formal definition as a basis for common understanding and agreement about the services to be provided
Service tasks	Intake and screening, problem identification, development of a case plan, and so on	To ensure some degree of uniformity in services received by similar clients with similar problems
Method of intervention	Group counseling, groups no larger than 8, meet 2 hours per day for 21 consecutive days from 7 to 9 a.m.	To ensure uniformity in the way services are provided within the same program

least precise of the three types of units of service because of the variation that can exist between individual units. For example, the number of items in two food baskets can vary widely, but each basket is still counted as one unit of service.

A *time* unit can be expressed in minutes, hours, days, weeks, or months, depending on the information needs of individual human service programs. A time unit is generally considered the most precise of the three types of units of service because it is expressed in standardized increments. When time is used as a unit of service, it is important to state whether the time refers only to direct client contact time or whether support activity time (e.g., completing paperwork, attending client staffings, etc.) is also included. Ultimately, units of service are used for a number of purposes, including a determination of cost per unit of service, so decisions about defining units of service should be made with a good deal of care and attention to their purpose.

The ways in which units of service may be used become evident when we calculate how many units a program can provide in 1 year. Let us assume that there are five counselors and that each one can see 20 clients per week at 48 weeks per year (allowing for 2 weeks for vacation and 10 paid holidays for each counselor in a year). Each counselor, then, has a capacity to provide 48×20, or 960, units of counseling per year. The entire program, with five counselors, can provide 4,800 units per year. (In a later chapter we will discuss how a unit cost is calculated.) In the same manner for any given program, examination of resources provides a basis for calculating the number of units to be provided in a given year.

The measurements most commonly used in rank order are the time, episode, and material units. They help provide a degree of comparability from program to program, even though they still are not exact measures. A child care day usually runs from 6:00 a.m. to 6:00 p.m., and even though some children may be in child care for 6 hours, some for 8 hours, and some for 12 hours, for the purpose of measuring volume, all are considered to have received one child-care day of services. It may simply not be worth the time and effort involved to calculate the hours and minutes for the purposes for which the measure is used.

By the same token, one food basket generally represents one unit of service in a food distribution program. One could be more precise by calculating how many pounds of cheese, how many cans of soup, how many quarts of milk, and so on, but, again, for the purposes for which units of service are used, a food basket consisting of a standard mix of groceries is an acceptable and useful definition. Table 7.4 illustrates time, episode, and material units of service.

Service Completion

The second data element involved in defining output is that of service completion and is referred to as a final output. The question that must be answered is, When is a client finished with a service? For some services, output is easily and clearly defined; for others, it is problematic. In most training programs, for example (or even in a university setting, for that matter), a number of training sessions or class sessions are required for successful completion of the course. One intermediate output unit might be attendance at one class, and a final output might be defined as one client's completing all the requirements of an automobile mechanics training course. A prenatal care program might consist of at least six monthly prenatal visits with a physician, and successful completion of a detoxification program might be defined as completion of a 60-day stay in an inpatient detox unit. Table 7.5 provides examples of intermediate and final outputs.

For other services, final outputs are more difficult to define. In ongoing services such as day care or long-term residential care for the elderly, it is not useful to define final outputs in terms of exit or "graduation" from a program because these programs are not designed

Table 7.4

Calculating Units of Service

Type of Unit	*Design Elements Needed to Calculate*	*How to Calculate Units*
Time	Staff time and service type	Calculate how many time units one staff member can provide in 1 week, multiply by 52 weeks, then multiply by number of FTE[a] staff
Episode	Staff/client encounters and service type	Calculate how many episodes one staff member can complete in 1 week, multiply by 52 weeks,[b] then multiply by number of FTE staff
Material	Material resources (food, clothing, cash)	Given raw materials for 1 week (e.g., $1,000 cash), calculate how many material units (e.g., ten $100 stipends) can be created, multiply by 52 weeks

a. Full-time equivalent.
b. Weeks can be adjusted for holidays and vacations.

to move clients in and out at a steady and predictable pace. Clients in these programs may remain for many years, yet it does not make sense to measure program completion only after an extended period of years. Most monitoring and evaluation systems require at least annual reporting.

Because of the potentially great variability (from a few days to several years), the "completion" or "graduation" type of definition for final outputs is not helpful and can be misleading. Instead, the program designers should define the final output in terms of a fixed number of days of care or of the completion of a short-term treatment plan. For example, one might define an output as "completion of an individual care plan" for day care or "completion of the prescribed services for a 3-month period" in the case of long-term residential care for the elderly.

Building milestones into the service design permits measures to be taken at certain selected points to determine whether the treatment plan is having the desired effects. Its purpose is to ensure that the full service mix, as intended by the designers of the program, has been received by a client. Defining output before implementation of a program also enables evaluators to distinguish between someone who completes the program and someone who drops out. These two groups need to be evaluated separately, but if output is defined simply as an exit from the program, it is impossible to distinguish completers from dropouts for evaluation purposes. Table 7.6 illustrates calculation of intermediate and final outputs.

Table 7.5

Output as an Element of Service Design

Element	Example	Purpose
Intermediate output	One unit of family counseling	To measure the volume of service provided to each consumer, using predefined units of service
Final output	Participation in at least ten 1-hour marital counseling sessions	To ensure agreement among program personnel and clients as to what constitutes full participation and to ensure that, in evaluating outcomes, distinctions are made between completers and dropouts

Table 7.6

Calculating Output Units

Type of Unit	Design Elements Needed to Calculate	How to Calculate Units
Intermediate output	Staff time and service type	Calculate the number of units that can be provided by one staff member in 1 week. Multiply by 52 weeks, then multiply by number of full-time equivalent staff
Final output	Definition of service completion; number of units of service needed for one client to meet the requirements specified in the definition	Calculate how long it takes one client to complete the service, given number of staff and resources available; calculate how many of those time slots are available in 1 week; multiply by 52 weeks

Quality

Over the years, as units of service have become more clearly conceptualized and defined, funding sources have tended to base contracts and
reimbursement plans on the number of units of service actually delivered and in some cases on the number of final output or service com-

pletion units. This emphasis has, in turn, led to a concern about what is often referred to as "bean counting," an exclusive focus on quantity to the exclusion of quality.

It is easy to see how this emphasis can come about. If my agency is reimbursed and rewarded for the number of interviews our staff conduct, I as a program manager for the agency may be tempted to cut down on the time of an interview and squeeze in 10 or 12 interviews per worker per day, regardless of the quality of those interviews. On the other hand, if we are held responsible for meeting certain standards of quality in our interviews, and if we are reimbursed on the basis of both efficiency (the number of units) and quality (meeting the standards), then I find I must balance both of these factors. This is the principle behind quality.

However, quality, unlike quantity (units of service) tends to be more elusive and is defined differently depending on one's perspective. In business and industry, customers have tended to be the final arbiters of what constitutes quality (Crosby, 1980, 1985; Deming, 1986; Juran, 1988, 1989). In human services, customer (client) perspectives are important but are not the sole criteria for determination of quality. Other perspectives, including professionals, formally appointed decision makers such as board members, and funding sources, also demand input in determining what constitutes quality.

Because of the many perspectives on quality in human services, it is necessary that quality dimensions be agreed on as a part of the program design, that they be defined, that quality data be collected, and that service quality be monitored and evaluated on a regular basis.

Quality is frequently addressed through the use of standards. A standard is a specification accepted by recognized authorities that is regularly and widely used and has a recognized and permanent status (Kettner & Martin, 1987). For many of the elements of program design, standards will be imposed by outside sources. For example, wherever licensing, certification, or accreditation is a concern, standards must be identified and incorporated as a part of the program. If food is served, standards will be imposed by the health department. If medical services and facilities are a part of the program, the Joint Commission on Accreditation of Healthcare Organizations will impose standards.

In most instances, it is necessary to identify and operationalize standards. In some instances, however, it will be necessary to develop them. It is often a judgment call, for example, what credentials casework or counseling staff should have. Some drug treatment programs operate exclusively with ex-addicts, regardless of educational background.

Some programs insist on a staff member's having at least a master's degree and prefer a Ph.D. Some positions require bilingual staff, and defining a qualification such as bilingual depends on preestablished standards for the ability to speak two languages. In many ways, standards serve as protection for clients or consumers in that they affect the services provided. Martin (1993) made a contribution to the measurement of quality by identifying 14 generally recognized quality dimensions (see Table 7.7).

Working from this table, program planners (in conjunction with clients and other stakeholders) can determine which of these quality dimensions are the most important for a given program. Quality dimensions to be used in the program must then be operationally defined. For example, the quality dimension of "accessibility" could be defined as having services within walking distance for at least 80% of clients, and the quality dimension of "responsiveness" could be defined as ensuring that at least 75% of clients who come to the agency for services are seen within 10 minutes of their scheduled appointment time.

Once the quality dimensions are selected and defined, they must be melded with units of service (intermediate outputs) and tracked. For example, in tracking responsiveness, each time a client comes to the agency for services, it will be necessary to record whether that client was seen within 10 minutes of the scheduled appointment time. Or if the quality dimension of "competency" is used and defined in terms of having an MSW and 3 years of counseling experience, it will be necessary to record the number of client counseling sessions that met this standard and the number that did not.

In measuring quality over the course of a year, two different sets of units will be recorded and tracked: (a) the number of units of a given service provided to clients and (b), of those units provided, the number that met the preestablished standard. Following this format, any quality standard established within a field can be used in conjunction with outputs to determine the extent to which quality dimensions are being achieved within a program.

In instances in which quality dimensions are too difficult, time consuming, or cumbersome to track, the client satisfaction approach may be used. When this option is selected, it is still necessary to select quality dimensions, but they are measured by translating them into questions to be asked of clients: for example, "Did your home-delivered meals arrive on time (within 10 minutes of scheduled delivery time)?" and "Do your home-delivered meals arrive hot?" The findings are then

Table 7.7

Dimensions of Quality

Dimension	Definition
Accessibility	The product or service is easy to access or acquire
Assurance	The staff are friendly, polite, considerate, and knowledgeable
Communication	Customers are kept informed, in language they can understand, about the product or service and any changes thereto
Competence	Staff possess the requisite knowledge and skills to provide the product or service
Conformity	The product or service meets standards
Deficiency	Any quality characteristic not otherwise identified that adversely affects customer satisfaction
Durability	The performance, result, or outcome does not dissipate quickly
Empathy	Staff demonstrate an understanding of and provide individualized attention to customers
Humaneness	The product or service is provided in a manner that protects the dignity and self-worth of the customer
Performance	The product or service does what it is supposed to do
Reliability	The ability to provide the product or service in a dependable and consistent manner with minimal variation over time or between customers
Responsiveness	The timeliness of employees in providing products and services
Security	The product or service is provided in a safe setting and is free from risk or danger
Tangibles	The physical appearance of facilities, equipment, personnel, and published materials

SOURCE: Adapted from Martin (1993).

turned into percentages of clients who answer "yes" to determine whether the quality standard has been achieved.

Outcomes

In the human service literature, a great deal of attention has been devoted over the past decade to outcome evaluation. For many funding sources, it has become the sine qua non for program planning and proposal writing. The question that must be answered is, Do clients improve as a result of services?

An *outcome* is defined as a measurable change in quality of life achieved by a client between entry into and exit from a program.

Outcome measures can be placed into one of four categories: numerical counts, standardized measures, level of functioning scales, or client satisfaction (Kuechler, Velasquez, & White, 1988; Martin, 1988).

Numeric Counts

Numeric counts are nominal measures related to client flow. They require yes or no answers to specific questions, such as the following: Was the client placed in a job on completion of WIN training? Did the child return home following residential treatment? Was another crime committed by the juvenile subsequent to treatment? The answers are then converted into percentages to determine the extent to which the expected outcome was achieved. Numeric counts are relatively easy to define and interpret, and many programs already collect these data. Calculating the number of families in the Child Abuse Prevention Program who are reported for child abuse in each of the next 5 years is an example of how numeric counts might be used. Recidivism is also a commonly used numeric count.

Standardized Measures

Standardized measures are objective instruments that have been validated and are widely used by practitioners. Examples include the Minnesota Multiphasic Personality Inventory (MMPI) and standardized intelligence tests such as the Stanford-Binet. Several volumes have been devoted to standardized measures of quality-of-life factors. For example, Kane and Kane (1981) developed measures for the elderly, and Fischer and Corcoran (1994) developed measures for families and children. Martin and Kettner (1996) identified a variety of different perspectives from which standardized measures have been developed, including population, problem, behavior, attitude, intrapersonal functioning, interpersonal functioning, development personality traits, achievement, knowledge, aptitude, and services (see Table 7.8).

The following is an illustration of a question from a Generalized Contentment Scale developed by Hudson (1982):

I feel that I am appreciated by others:

1 = rarely or none of the time
2 = a little of the time
3 = some of the time
4 = a good part of the time
5 = most or all of the time

Table 7.8

Focus of Standardized Measures

Focus	Example
Population	Young Children's Social Desirability Scale (YCSD) A 26-item scale for measuring young children's need for social approval
Problem	Child Abuse Potential (CAP) Inventory A 160-item scale for measuring potential for child abuse in parents and prospective parents
Behavior	Preschool Behavior Rating Scale A set of 20 scales rating preschool development on several different dimensions
Attitude	Maryland Parent Attitude Survey (MPAS) A 95-item scale for measuring attitudes of parents toward child rearing
Intrapersonal functioning	Generalized Expectancy for Success Scale Measures an individual's belief in ability to attain goals
Interpersonal functioning	Index of Family Relations A 25-item scale for measuring family relationships
Development	Developmental Profile II A 186-item scale for measuring child development up to age 9
Personality traits	Liking People Scale Measures whether an individual approaches or avoids social interaction
Achievement	Career Skills Assessment Program Measures student competency in areas important to career development
Knowledge	Knowledge Scale A 73-item scale for measuring a parent's knowledge of appropriate growth and behavior in children up to age 2
Aptitude	Differential Aptitude Tests An integrated series of measures for assessing verbal reasoning, spelling, need for education, and vocational guidance
Services	Seattle/King County Four C's Evaluation Checklist for In-Home Care, Day Care Homes, and Day Care Centers Measures child health and nutrition and staff-child interactions

SOURCE: Martin and Kettner (1996).

Level-of-Functioning Scales

Level-of-functioning scales are instruments developed by staff and other local experts familiar with a particular population and problem and are specific to a program or service. They require that practitioners rate their clients on several aspects of functioning. For example, the chronically mentally ill may be rated on such factors as self-care, decision-making ability, and interpersonal interaction. The developmentally disabled may be rated on activities of daily living, functional communication, interaction skills, and other factors. For each scale, indicators are specified and clients are rated at intake, at intervals during their participation in the program, and at exit from a program on a multipoint scale ranging from low to high functioning on each item. The following is an illustration of a level-of-functioning measure for social isolation:

1	2	3	4	5
Social isolation is a major problem		A social network is neither a strength nor a problem		Social contacts represent a strength

With this type of scale, Points 2 and 4 would be used if the client seemed to fall somewhere in between these descriptions.

Client Satisfaction

The fourth measure is *client satisfaction.* Several studies have demonstrated a significant correlation between satisfaction and other, more tangible positive outcomes (Martin, 1988; Millar, Hatry, & Koss, 1977). Martin's research with services such as transportation and ambulance services has demonstrated that although it is possible to measure such factors as response time, arrival at destination time, cost per trip, and cost per mile, client satisfaction proves to be a much less costly and equally valid and reliable measure and therefore would be indicated for these services. This does not mean, however, that client satisfaction should be considered the preferred measure across the board.

In response to early demands for program evaluation, many service providers have opted for client satisfaction, apparently because it appears to be the easiest information to collect. However, correlations have not been established in all services between client satisfaction and improved quality of life, and program planners need to be cautious about overuse and unrealistically high expectations for this measure.

Measuring client satisfaction requires the development of questions with responses ranging from "very satisfied" to "very dissatisfied" and options in between. The following is an example of a client satisfaction question:

How satisfied were you in terms of resolving the problem that brought you to this agency in the first place?

1 = very satisfied
2 = somewhat satisfied
3 = neither satisfied nor dissatisfied
4 = somewhat dissatisfied
5 = very dissatisfied

Intermediate Outcomes
and Final Outcomes

As with objectives and outputs, there are two types of outcomes: intermediate outcomes and final outcomes. Intermediate outcomes are those changes in quality of life for the client (such as improved skills or placement in a job) that can be measured at the point of completion of the services provided—that is, at the point of final output. Final outcomes are those changes in quality of life for the client (such as self-sufficiency or stabilization in a job and a career path) that are measured at a designated follow-up point. Table 7.9 illustrates outcomes as an element of service design.

Intermediate and final outcomes may be the same or they may be different. For example, to use the teen pregnancy example from Chapter 6, in measuring intermediate outcomes, we would want to know if there was a change in values, if use of contraception increased, if academic performance improved, and if there was a commitment to career goals. If all of these things happened, then we would expect that the final outcome of reduced incidence of teen pregnancy would be achieved. However, there might also be a program in which the expected intermediate outcome would be that a client would have a job and the expected final outcome would be that the client will still have the same job.

Intermediate outcomes can be documented by using any of the four measures: numerical counts, standardized measures, level-of-functioning scales, or client satisfaction instruments. Numerical counts would include such outcomes as reduction in depression for a counseling program or reduction in recidivism for a program working with first-time juvenile offenders. With standardized measures or level-of-functioning

Table 7.9

Outcomes as Elements of Service Design

Element	Example	Purpose
Intermediate outcome	Ability to prepare a resume, to identify at least three valid job opportunities, and to complete at least three job interviews	To identify and define what a client should be able to do or should have accomplished at the point of termination from the program or episode of service
Final outcome	To hold a job that pays above minimum wage and a career path of at least two levels of promotion for at least 1 year	To identify and define outcome expectations for a client after a specified period of postservice time has elapsed

scales, pre- and post-assessments are required. The difference between the pre- and post-scores represents an indicator of intermediate outcome. These scores indicate such factors as improvement in self-esteem, improvement in intrafamily communication, or an acceptable level of performance in activities of daily living. Client satisfaction scores provide a one-time statement of a client's perception of the usefulness of the services provided and are used as an indicator of an outcome, with high satisfaction indicating a positive outcome and low satisfaction indicating a negative outcome.

Likewise, in determining final outcomes, it is possible to use any of the four measures. Numerical counts or level-of-functioning scales, however, are the more likely candidates for final outcomes. This is because final outcome expectations are likely to be broader and more ambitious than intermediate outcome expectations and therefore need measures that are broader than a single standardized test or a client satisfaction score can provide. Final outcome measures typically encompass such quality-of-life factors as stability of living conditions, family relationships, employment, education, and other major life activities and achievements. Many of these domains have standardized numerical count indicators such as employment status, income, grade in school, and grade point average. These tend to be more useful measures of final outcome expectations. Table 7.10 illustrates how outcomes indicators are used to calculate outcome units.

Table 7.10

Calculating Outcome Units

Type of Unit	Design Elements Needed to Calculate	How to Calculate Units
Intermediate outcome	Definition of intermediate outcome; the number of clients who achieve final outputs; the number of clients who achieve intermediate outcomes	Calculate the number of completions (final outputs) possible; if every client who achieves final outputs is successful as defined by intermediate outcomes, the rate is 100%. Calculate the actual rate by dividing actual successes by actual number of completers.
Final outcome	Definition of final outcome; the number of clients who achieve intermediate outcomes; the number of clients who achieve final outcomes	Calculate the number of clients who achieve intermediate outcomes; if every one of them also achieves final outcomes, the rate is 100%. Calculate the actual rate by dividing actual successes by actual number achieving intermediate outcomes.

THE RELATIONSHIP BETWEEN OBJECTIVES AND SYSTEM COMPONENTS

In Chapter 6, we discussed in some detail the importance of distinguishing between process objectives and outcome objectives. At this point, it should be evident that there are some relationships between objectives and the input, throughput, output, and outcome components of a program or system. Throughputs and outputs are related to process objectives in that they are the activities or means we are introducing to achieve the program's ends. Intermediate and final outcome objectives have a direct relationship to intermediate and final outcomes as elements of design. Table 7.11 depicts the relationship.

In summary, we have focused in this section on the input, throughput, output, and outcome components of a system. This framework is used to identify and define each element of program design. *Inputs* include

Table 7.11

Relationship Between Objectives and System Components

Type of Objective	*Purpose*	*Related System Component*	*Purpose*
Process objective	To define the services to be provided within the program	Throughput	To achieve consensus on a formal service definition, service tasks, and methodology
		Final output	To specify what combination of services must have been received by a client to constitute a completion of services
Intermediate outcome objective	To define results to be expected on completion of service	Intermediate outcomes	To specify what indicators will be used and how they will be measured
Final outcome objective	To define results to be achieved after a specified period of postservice time has elapsed	Final outcomes	To specify what indicators will be used and how they will be measured

client, staff, and physical resource elements; *throughputs* include service delivery elements; *outputs* include service completion elements, with *intermediate outputs* referring to completion of a unit of service and *final outputs* referring to completion of the full complement of services prescribed; and *outcomes* include measures of life changes for clients, with *intermediate outcomes* referring to changes at the point of completion of services and *final outcomes* referring to changes achieved or maintained as of a specified point of follow-up.

Specifying the Program Hypothesis

Program hypothesis, as discussed in Chapter 5, is a term used to sum up the assumptions and expectations of a program. It is probably fair to say that every program has one, whether or not it is made explicit. For example, when a law or policy change mandates that welfare benefits be terminated after a set period of time and recipients be required to go to work, there is an implied hypothesis that terminating welfare benefits will lead to self-sufficiency. When the law requires termination of parental rights under certain conditions of abuse and neglect, there is an implied hypothesis that the children affected will turn out to be physically and emotionally healthier if they are raised in an environment where they are free from abuse and neglect.

In Chapter 5, we introduced the example of a program hypothesis related to the problem of child abuse. The purpose then was to lay the foundation for the development of goals and objectives. As part of that process, we reviewed the various theories of why people abuse their children (etiology) and developed a hypothesis of etiology and a working intervention hypothesis. Continuing this line of reasoning, we argued that if a program is designed to teach parenting skills, it should be made clear that the intent is to deal only with those parents who lack knowledge and skill in parenting. For those who need extensive counseling to deal with their own abused childhoods, for those who need jobs, or for those who need social contacts or help with child care, parent training alone will probably not be effective.

The program hypothesis guides the definition and selection of the elements of program design, including client characteristics, staff characteristics, service definition, tasks, and methodology, as well as output and outcome definitions. It establishes the framework that brings internal consistency and integrity to the program.

In sum, the following questions might be asked as they relate to each system component:

Inputs

- What types of clients (in terms of demographic or descriptive characteristics) do we expect will benefit from this program, given our assumptions and our program hypothesis?

- What types of staff should be employed in this program to provide the expected services and serve the clientele we have defined? Is gender, ethnicity, or age a consideration? What degrees, certification, or experience should staff members have?

- What resources, facilities, or equipment will be needed to carry out the services and meet the needs of clients?

Throughputs

- What kinds of services, service tasks, and methods of intervention are most relevant to address the problems and work with the client population as defined in the program design?

Outputs

- Given program expectations, what mix of services represents a full complement of services, and what is the minimum volume or quantity of these services that could be expected to produce a measurable result?

Outcomes

- Given the program hypothesis, what outcomes can we expect to achieve, and, by implication, what outcomes do we not expect to achieve, given the limitations of the program?

This list is not intended to be exhaustive, but it illustrates the types of questions that, if answered in a manner consistent with the program hypothesis, will help to ensure program consistency and integrity. As program planners think through and define these elements, the fit between client need and service or program design should be greatly enhanced.

Defining the elements of program design is a critical step in effectiveness-based program planning. It is the step that lays the groundwork for practitioners to discover what interventions are most likely to produce positive results, given a target population and a problem, and what interventions are not effective. In the place of a hit-or-miss human service technology, definitions of the elements of program design provide for a more precise assessment of client problems and needs, together with a prescription for the mix of services most likely to alleviate the problems and meet the needs. Using these definitions, data collection systems can increasingly inform program planners, managers, and practitioners of the success or failure of a wide range of intervention technologies.

In summary, we have pointed out in this section that a program hypothesis

1. helps make explicit assumptions about program expectations;

2. establishes a framework that can be used to bring internal consistency to the program; and
3. should be used to examine inputs, throughputs, outputs, and outcomes for their internal consistency.

By attending to the elements of program design as described in this chapter, program planners can ensure that a program has been designed in a manner that is comprehensive, that attends to detail, and that can demonstrate internal consistency and integrity. By establishing the relationships between and among (a) resources and raw materials (inputs), (b) the processing system (throughputs), (c) the completion of an episode of service (output), and (d) a change in the quality of life of the client served (outcome), program planners can feel confident that the program is logical, can be implemented, and can be evaluated.

Chapter 8

BUILDING A MANAGEMENT INFORMATION SYSTEM

DOCUMENTATION PRACTICES IN SOCIAL SERVICES

Beginning as far back as the early days of the Charity Organization Society in the 1870s, social service administrators and practitioners have recognized the need to gather certain basic information about clients and to keep a record of contacts. From a case record that, in the early years of social work, included a simple face sheet on which identifying information was recorded, case records have become massive volumes that document sometimes more than a decade of activities, events, and legal proceedings.

In a great many cases, social service programs deal with populations for whom some social, legal, and/or financial responsibility falls into the public domain. Examples are dependent and neglected children, the mentally ill who cannot afford to pay for their own services, those on public assistance, and those in public hospitals or institutions. For each of these client populations, demands for documentation build over time. A new program is added—a form is designed to document clients' participation. A legislator campaigns on a platform of having those who can afford it pay a part of the cost of their own services—a form is added to ensure that a financial investigation has been conducted. A judge makes a ruling on a child's rights to medical treatment—a new form is created to ensure protection of the rights of all children to medical treatment.

Child welfare staff in some states estimate that the number of forms that might conceivably be included in a child's record in a protective services case runs around 150. As a result, agency files have become, in some ways, a reflection of the agendas of attorneys, physicians, legislators, program directors, advocacy groups, and citizens' advisory groups. Each interest group wants assurances that the case record contains documentation that their concerns have been addressed. And although this may contribute to the protection of a client's legal rights and entitlements, it does little or nothing to provide a database that can contribute to improving the overall operations of the program.

Although the above describes a problem in child welfare, it is not uncommon in many other types of agencies, private as well as public. Data collected to address the concerns of community interest groups or funding sources are rarely used in a manner that produces helpful information about program performance.

The dilemma is an ironic one. Few other professions or disciplines feel more overwhelmed by paperwork than does social work. Yet, for all the paper produced, very little is useful for program monitoring and evaluation purposes. One data set (usually narrative) describes the casework process, the contacts made, and the client's responses. A second data set (usually computerized) feeds into a reporting system, designed to produce reports required by funding sources. Neither focuses on improving the quality and relevance of services provided to clients.

Effectiveness-based program planning requires that data be generated that will support decision making based on what is in the best interests of clients—on information about what services are most effective with what types of clients and what types of problems. The remainder of this chapter focuses on building a management information system to provide data and information on program operations. This will require decisions grounded in a concern for maximizing the volume, achieving the highest possible quality, and ensuring the relevance of services provided.

BUILDING AN EFFECTIVENESS-BASED
MANAGEMENT INFORMATION SYSTEM

There are several ways that program planners can approach the construction of management information systems useful for effectiveness-based program planning. Considerations include the state of existing case records, satisfaction with existing data collection documents, computer capability, data entry capacity, and executive and staff readiness for and commitment to a system change.

We first use an example of a complete original design of a management information system and examine the steps staff might go through to create an ideal system. We then briefly consider the realities of redesigning an existing system.

DESIGNING A NEW MANAGEMENT INFORMATION SYSTEM

In creating a new data collection system, we return once again to the elements of program design—the elements associated with program inputs, throughputs, outputs, and outcomes—to guide us in the construction of the system. Each element has implications for data collection. But before we reexamine the elements, it is important to revisit the problem analysis completed at the beginning of the program planning process and to identify the questions to be answered by our system.

Historically, many creators of data collection and processing systems have ignored this first step of identifying questions to be answered and have instead skipped directly to the creation of data collection forms. Although this approach may be "chronologically" sound, it can produce information that is useful only to some users of the resulting data and information but not to all. We propose an approach that leads to the development of a data collection system that not only has relevance to all of its users but also is efficient.

The steps involved in designing and implementing such a system are these:

1. Identify the questions to be answered.
2. Identify the data elements needed.
3. Develop a strategy for analysis.
4. Design output tables.
5. Design data collection procedures and instruments.
6. Develop data entry procedures.
7. Compile and analyze the data.

The details involved in carrying out each of these steps are covered in the following sections.

Step 1: Identify the Questions
to Be Answered

If the program planning process proposed in this book has been followed from the beginning, an efficient way to generate questions to be answered is to revisit the problem analysis and the working intervention hypothesis. The objective here is to revisit the reasons for developing the program and the problems it is intended to alleviate or resolve.

For the sake of illustration, we turn to an example of a retirement community that has become alarmed about the increasing number of suicides and suicide attempts. The residents are concerned about the unnecessary and tragic loss of members of the community, and the developers are concerned about the impact on future marketing attempts if this information becomes public. Together the developers and a voluntary citizen's council have undertaken a problem analysis that has revealed the following hypothesis of etiology:

Because of the following factors:
- Loss of role and identity after retirement
- Lack of meaningful and personally fulfilling activity
- Feelings of loneliness that come with a move to a new location
- Loss of loved ones, especially loss of a spouse
- Change in socioeconomic status

The result has been:
- Loss of self-esteem
- Social isolation
- Reduced discretionary income
- Depression (especially among White men over age 65)
- An increasing number of suicides and suicide attempts

The working intervention hypothesis is stated as follows:

If we initiate the following intervention:
- Recruit members of the at-risk population through outreach sponsored by local churches and civic groups

- Provide opportunities for participation in therapeutic group discussion
- Increase the participation of the at-risk population in social and recreational activities
- Increase the participation of the at-risk population in part-time employment or voluntary activities

Then we will expect the following results from those who participate in the program:

- An increase in self-esteem
- An increase in the number of social contacts
- An increase in the number of participants who secure part-time employment or do volunteer work
- A decrease in the number of participants diagnosed as depressed
- A decrease in the number of suicides and suicide attempts

What questions do these working hypotheses suggest? Some of the following come to mind:

- Can we recruit members of the at-risk population through outreach sponsored by local churches and civic groups? If our recruitment efforts are unsuccessful, none of the other program components will be of value to the at-risk population.
- Do members of the at-risk population reveal the same characteristics as those identified in the literature: namely, a loss of role and identity, lack of personally fulfilling activity, feelings of isolation, loss of a spouse or other loved one, or change in socioeconomic status? If the population recruited to participate in this program does not match this profile, then the relevance of the intervention as designed is questionable.
- If members of the at-risk population do have some of the same characteristics as those identified in the literature, have these factors resulted in such feelings as low self-esteem, in depression, or in actual suicide attempts? These are the feelings and behaviors we are attempting to change or eliminate. We must be certain that they are, in fact, manifested in the at-risk population to test the intervention hypothesis.
- Are members of the at-risk population participating in the planned socialization and recreation activities? If so, how often? Are they finding part-time employment or voluntary work that is personally fulfilling?
- Do program participants, after spending time in the planned activities, demonstrate improved self-esteem, elimination of or milder forms of depression, and an absence of suicidal thoughts or attempts?

These types of questions will prove to be very useful in identifying data elements to be collected as well as in developing a strategy for analysis.

Step 2: Identify Data Elements

Data elements are the individual information items that, taken together (i.e., aggregated), present a source of information that will answer questions about program process and outcome. Data elements should be organized around program inputs, throughputs, outputs, and outcomes. They can be further organized around the following headings and subheadings:

Program Inputs

- Client demographic and descriptive characteristics
- Client social history data
- Client problem/strength profile
- Staff demographic and descriptive characteristics
- Material resources provided to clients
- Facilities used by clients
- Equipment used by clients

Program Throughputs

- Services provided
- Service tasks
- Method of intervention

Program Outputs

- Intermediate outputs (units of service provided)
- Final outputs (service completions)

Program Outcomes

- Intermediate outcomes (change at the point of service completion)
- Final outcomes (change at the designated point of follow-up)

Program Inputs

Client demographic and descriptive characteristics. As discussed in Chapter 7, one of the first data elements to be considered is that of client demographic and descriptive characteristics. The task at this point is not one of developing data collection forms but one of identifying and justifying what data are to be collected. Only when this task is completed can we turn to the task of instrument development. Demographic and descriptive characteristics typically include such elements as

- Age
- Ethnicity
- Education
- Income
- Marital status

Considering the questions to be answered in the program to prevent elderly suicide, in addition to the above characteristics, we would want to know something about the number of social contacts per week, location of nuclear family members, location of extended family members, employment status, involvement in volunteer activities, and other such characteristics. These factors, to a large extent, will help us to determine whether we are actually working with the intended population.

Client social history data. Social history data may help provide clues to factors in clients' backgrounds that are related to their current situations. It is usually an expectation of caseworkers that they take a social history on their clients at the point of intake so that they can determine patterns of behavior and behavioral changes over time, as well as documenting legal considerations.

To be useful for a management information system, social history data must have a "research" focus. In other words, there must be a reason, based on the problem analysis, to believe that a particular variable may have some relevance to the program, its clients, and the outcomes achieved.

With the suicide prevention program, for example, we know that separation from loved ones can lead to depression. We may, therefore, want to explore (in a quantified way) the nature of an elderly client's relationship to children, siblings, or significant others. This could be explored by asking questions such as "How many of your children did you communicate with at least once a week before moving to this area, and how many do you communicate with at least weekly now?" Additional questions can be used to determine the frequency of contact with other family and friends.

Client problem/strength profile. Clients usually come to social service agencies for help with a problem, so it is important to know how many clients, during the course of a year, identified a particular problem (e.g., marital conflict) as their reason for coming to the agency. This information can be drawn from assessment tools completed at the point of intake by the intake and screening person, by the client, by a third party, or by some combination of these.

By using a simple scaling device on which the scale ranges from "a serious problem" at the low end of the scale to "an area of strength" at the high end, a problem and strength profile can be developed for individual clients as well as for all program participants. These assessment tools, either purchased from the author of a standardized scale or developed by staff, can be designed to determine (a) problems being experienced by clients, (b) level of severity, (c) areas of strength, and (d) degree of strength. A simple 1 to 5 scale could be used, where 1 = *severe problem,* 2 = *problem,* 3 = *neither a problem or a strength,* 4 = *strength,* and 5 = *major strength.* Many types of measurement scales are available, and most will yield useful information about problems and strengths. The following scale might be used with a target group of single males 65 and over who are considered to be at risk of suicide:

1.	Participation in social and/or recreational activities	1	2	3	4	5
2.	Participation in personally fulfilling activities	.1	2	3	4	5
3.	Relationship with friends	1	2	3	4	5
4.	Relationship with nuclear family members	1	2	3	4	5
5.	Relationship with extended family members	1	2	3	4	5
6.	Ability to adjust to loss of a loved one	1	2	3	4	5
7.	Sense of self-confidence/self-esteem	1	2	3	4	5
8.	Current socioeconomic status	1	2	3	4	5

Some of the questions to be answered by these data might include these:

- What problems are most prevalent?
- What strengths are most prevalent?
- Do any problems reveal a high correlation with any demographic or social history factors (e.g., low participation may be correlated with recent loss)?
- Are there any predominant "problem profiles" or problems that tend to cluster together (e.g., low participation in personally fulfilling activities correlated with low sense of self-confidence/self-esteem)?

- Are there any predominant "strength profiles" or correlations with other factors?

Staff descriptive characteristics. Descriptive characteristics about staff are not likely to be entered into a program's management information system, but it may be useful to record them elsewhere (perhaps in a personnel management information system). Typically, in a management information system designed to record program and service data, there will be some mechanism for connecting clients to workers (e.g., through a worker identification number).

If, at some point, program analysts or evaluators want to look at successful cases to determine if any particular staff characteristics were correlated with client success, capturing staff descriptive characteristics will be important to help identify what factors about staff, if any, make a difference in terms of client outcomes. It may also be important to record client demographic information if accrediting organizations need to know about such factors as education and experience. Some of the staff descriptive characteristics that might be useful include the following:

- Education
- License or certification
- Number of years of experience
- Type(s) of professional experience
- Ethnicity
- Sex

Some of the questions to be explored might include these:

- How do education and/or experience correlate with client satisfaction and client outcomes?
- When worker demographics are matched up with client demographics, what are the relationships, if any, to completion of the service plan and to outcomes?

Material resources. When material resources such as cash, food, or clothing are provided for clients, it is important that these items be tracked so that it can be determined whether they are significant to the helping process. If food, clothing, and emergency financial aid were available as support services for the career planning program, some of the data elements to be tracked would include

- Number of food baskets
- Articles of clothing for client
- Articles of clothing for client's child(ren)
- Amount of financial aid

Amount and frequency of receipt of each of these and other such data would be added as the system was developed. Questions of interest in this area might include these:

- Does the need for material resources correlate with any particular pattern of client demographics? Of client problems? Of current living arrangements?
- Are there any patterns of problems that tend to predict requests for food baskets or financial aid?

Facilities. In a way, facilities can also be considered a resource used for the benefit of clients. By tracking facilities, it may be possible to discover that certain locations or settings are more conducive than others to success. Or in the case of residential treatment, it may be valuable to learn whether clients assigned to a private room adjust better and make better progress than those who share a room with others.

Each time a client takes advantage of services provided, it may be useful to record the facility where this takes place. Categories might include the following:

- Office visit, main office
- Office visit, branch office
- Home visit, client's home
- Home visit, relative or friend's home
- School
- Other community facility

Some of the questions to be explored are these:

- Is there a relationship between facility location and keeping appointments?
- Does it appear that certain clients clearly prefer home visits? Do some prefer other locations?

Equipment. The importance of equipment will vary by program. In a transportation program, the vehicle is an important resource. In a word processor training program, computers and software are important pieces of equipment. Tracking who used what software could help in determining what word-processing software seems to work best for beginners and for intermediate and advanced students, for example. In a program for seniors, there may be reasons to use communications equipment such as citizen's band radios or cellular telephones to keep in touch with those who live a great distance from the center or agency, or medical reasons to loan durable medical equipment. There also may be a correlation between a transportation service and social participation. Some of the equipment-related questions to be answered might include these:

- What equipment is most needed by clients?
- What level of use of equipment correlates with successful client outcomes?
- What is the unit cost of equipment currently used by clients? How would this compare with contracting with another provider for use of this equipment?

Program Throughputs

Service tasks. The concept of service tasks, introduced in Chapter 7, is used to define the helping process and to break it down into a series of stages or phases. This breakdown is important because, by tying tasks to units of service, the management information system can help to identify what tasks were provided in what volume over what period of time. In the absence of service tasks, the service process defaults to just one, simple, undifferentiated task called "casework." By defining service tasks, it is possible, for example, to determine how many units of service (either in the aggregate or by a particular worker) are devoted to each task. A program evaluator may learn that the more time spent in intake and screening, the better the eventual outcome of service. Service tasks that might be used in a program to serve the at-risk elderly might include

- Outreach
- Intake
- Screening
- Case planning
- Provision of transportation
- Provision of center activities

- Provision of meals
- One-to-one counseling
- Group counseling
- Outcome evaluation
- Termination
- Follow-up

These data elements could help to answer such questions as the following:

- How much time is being spent on each service task?
- Do patterns vary by worker and type of client?
- What correlations exist between time spent on service tasks and outcomes?

Method of intervention. Defining the method of intervention will help evaluators and program staff to learn whether one particular method is more effective than others with certain types of clients. This, then, can lead to adjustments in types of treatment prescribed, depending on the likelihood of success, based on findings. Data on method of counseling services might be defined in terms of individual, group, or family counseling. Data on socialization and recreation services might be defined in terms of those provided on site by the staff and those provided in the community. Meals can either be provided in a congregate setting or be home delivered. The program evaluator is interested in any possible relationship between method of intervention and rates of success.

Questions that might be answered by collecting data on method of intervention might include these:

- Are there types of clients that respond better to one type of counseling than to another?
- What correlations exist between time spent in counseling and successful outcomes?

Program Outputs

Intermediate outputs. Intermediate outputs are defined as units of service and can be measured in any one of three different ways: (a) an episode or contact unit, (b) a material unit, or (c) a time unit. Each service included as part of service tasks must define an accompanying unit of service. For example, one inquiry about the services provided by a senior center might be defined as an episode or contact unit. The evaluator is interested in the number of contacts per week/month/year, not necessarily in the length of each contact. One meal provided in a congregate setting is an example of a material unit. If the center typically serves a noon meal to 50 seniors per day, that will be defined as 50 units of service per day or 250 units during a normal 5-day week. If, in addition, a caseworker spends 1 hour per week in a counseling session with selected seniors, a unit of counseling can be defined as 1 hour, and the evaluator will be interested in the total number of units of counseling provided by the center each week/month/year.

The total number of units provided is a measure of productivity and can be useful in answering such questions as these:

- What is the average number of units provided by each caseworker each week?
- What is the average number of units of each type provided to each client each week?
- Are there correlations between types of units provided and client outcomes?

Final outputs. Final outputs are defined as service completions and require that each service provided have a definition of what is meant by "completion." For example, in the senior center, completion might be defined as a client's participation in at least 80% of activities prescribed in the treatment plan for a period of 90 days. Detailed enough records must be kept to make a distinction as to whether the client actually received services or ceased contact following the assessment process and whether he or she should be considered a "dropout" from the program. The following items illustrate the type of data that would be collected to measure service completions for each client and, in the aggregate, for an entire program:

- Activities prescribed
- Activities attended
- Number of counseling sessions prescribed
- Number of counseling sessions attended

- Number of weeks of congregate meals prescribed
- Number of weeks of congregate meals attended

This information helps to determine whether clients are actually carrying out the treatment plans prescribed and, if not, to probe for reasons why not. Some of the questions to be answered include these:

- What percentage of clients complete the prescribed treatment plan?
- What factors influence completion and dropout?
- Are there any significant relationships between completing a plan and positive client outcomes?

Program Outcomes

Intermediate client outcomes. Intermediate client outcomes are defined as those client changes achieved at the point of termination from a program. Client outcomes are measured by conducting an assessment at the point of intake and producing a baseline in terms of client behavior or performance. Assessments may be done in terms of numeric counts, standardized measures, level-of-functioning scales or client satisfaction (see Chapter 7).

When standardized measures or level-of-functioning scales are used, outcomes are calculated by administering the same measurement device at the completion of service as was used at intake (a pre-post assessment). The purpose is to determine whether there has been progress in solving the problems presented at intake, whether they have remained the same, or whether they have gotten worse. In this case, we would revisit the eight factors assessed at intake and once again rate each on a scale from 1 to 5, with 1 representing a serious problem and 5 representing a strength, assuming that each point on the scale would be operationally defined for each item.

1.	Participation in social and/or recreational activities	1	2	3	4	5
2.	Participation in personally fulfilling activities	1	2	3	4	5
3.	Relationship with friends	1	2	3	4	5
4.	Relationship with nuclear family members	1	2	3	4	5
5.	Relationship with extended family members	1	2	3	4	5
6.	Ability to adjust to loss of a loved one	1	2	3	4	5
7.	Sense of self-confidence/self-esteem	1	2	3	4	5
8.	Current socioeconomic status	1	2	3	4	5

These types of measurements emphasize the central issues of effectiveness-based program planning. If all has gone according to plan, the initial assessment will reveal problems and strengths. The treatment plan will focus on dealing with the problems. If the treatment plan has been implemented, if the client has completed all the services prescribed, and if the plan has worked, the problem areas should show some improvement. If case managers have collected all needed data during the process, these data can now be aggregated and can begin to inform staff about overall program effectiveness. Questions to be addressed include these:

- What types of problems seem most often resolved?
- Which types seem most resistant to change?
- Are there any patterns in the types of clients who seem to be most successful and least successful with certain problems?

Final outcomes. Final outcomes are identified and defined by returning to the purpose for which the program was created, or what we have in Chapter 6 called "final objectives." In this example, the program was created to reduce the number of suicide attempts and suicides among program participants. Final outcome measurements are always taken in a follow-up contact with clients, using numerical counts, standardized measures, level-of-functioning scales, or client satisfaction measures (see Chapter 7).

The period of time that should elapse between the end of the program and the follow-up is a judgment that must be made by those familiar with the program and depends on the results to be achieved. An outcome such as "no suicide attempts" might require follow-up for several years. If the final outcome required that we measure whether the at-risk population has improved in self-esteem or decreased in severity of depression, we might have to administer a standardized scale once a year for as long as the client remains in the program and in a follow-up between 6 months and 1 year after termination. It should be recognized that in some programs, such as long-term care for the elderly, formal, planned termination may never happen. Clients may remain until death. In cases such as these, periodic measurements may be taken after an episode of service (such as a quarterly or annual treatment plan) has been completed to determine whether the effects of that plan remain over time.

Questions to be addressed in analyzing these data would include these:

- What types of clients seem to be having the most success in this program? What are their characteristics?
- For what types of clients does this program seem to be least effective? What are their characteristics?
- What factors seem to contribute to success and failure?
- What elements of the program should be redesigned?
- What mix of services, given to which types of seniors in what volume, has the highest probability of leading to successful outcomes?

Step 3: Develop a Strategy for Analysis

The third step in designing a management information system involves examining every variable that will be a part of the system and developing a matrix to help in selecting the variables to be used later in data analysis. Each variable should be numbered so that it can be used later to build a codebook and a data entry system.

At this point it becomes important to begin to categorize variables by the ways in which they will ultimately be used. The compound question we are attempting to answer might be phrased as follows:

1. What types of clients?
2. Experiencing what types of problems?
3. Receiving what types and volume of services?
4. Get what results?
5. At what cost?

Each part of this compound question may require development of a subset of data; examples of the types of data needed are shown below for each part of the question:

1. What types of clients?
   - Demographic, descriptive, and social history data
2. Experiencing what types of problems?
   - Problem profile data
3. Receiving what types and volume of services?
   - Service tasks data
   - Intermediate output (service units) data
   - Material resources data

- Method-of-intervention data
- Staff-descriptive data
- Final output (service completion) data

4. Get what results?
   - Intermediate outcome data
   - Final outcome data

5. At what cost?
   - Unit costs data (cost per unit of service; cost per service completion; cost per successful client outcome)

Each of these subsets of data elements makes up a part of a comprehensive list of all variables that will form the basis for the management information system. Although the itemization of relevant variables is a tedious and time-consuming task, it is a necessary step to reach the point where an effectiveness-based data system can be useful to answer critical questions about effectiveness and efficiency of service provision.

Once all variables to be incorporated into the system have been listed, variables to be aggregated should be identified. The aggregation and cross-tabulation of variables begin to reveal patterns in client progress, programmatic interventions, and client responses that will help to answer the questions identified in Step 1 and will shape future program modifications.

One way of ensuring that every possible comparison is considered is, first, to list each variable in the data collection system. Next, questions related to each variable should be identified. All levels of staff, supervisors, administration, and board members should have input into framing these questions. Finally, the variables needed for cross-tabulation (we are not suggesting that testing for relationships will only be done through the use of contingency table analysis; rather, we use the term to include all appropriate statistical methods) should be listed. Some sample variables, questions and cross-tabulations are illustrated in Table 8.1.

Step 4: Design Output Tables

An output table is a data display of columns and rows that is used as a basic document for building management information. (The term *output,* in this context, does not in any way refer to output as a part of the program design discussed in Chapter 7 and in this chapter. Rather, it is used in a data-processing context as the format for data aggrega-

Table 8.1

Selecting Variables for Monitoring
and Evaluation for a Job Placement Program

Variable	Questions to Be Answered	Possible Cross-Tabulations
Age	How many clients are there in each age grouping?	None
	In each age grouping, how many clients are male/female? How many are from each ethnic group? How many are high school graduates? How many are employed?	Gender Ethnicity Education Employment
Education	How many clients have successfully completed each level of education: grade school, junior high school, high school, community college, university?	None
	For each level of educational achievement, how many clients are male/female? How many are in each ethnic group? How many are employed? How many have income over $30,000?	Gender Ethnicity Employment Income
Completion of service	How many clients successfully completed the program as pre-scribed in the planning process?	None
	Of those who successfully completed employment-related services, how many are employed at the point of service completion? How many are employed 6 months after service completion? How many are earning at least 15% above minimum wage?	Employment at completion Employment at follow-up Salary/wages at follow-up

tion.) In building management information, a series of tables is created, each of which is used for a special purpose. For example, a simple output table to guide analysis of our senior center program might be designed as shown in Table 8.2.

Table 8.2

Output Table to Guide Analysis of Senior Center Program

	Age			
Ethnicity	*65-69*	*70-74*	*75-79*	*80+*
African American				
American Indian				
Asian American				
Hispanic/Latino				
White				

Or an output table designed to assess program outcomes might use the following variables:

Participation

1. Number of clients who participated in at least 80% of meals
2. Number of clients who participated in at least 80% of planned activities

Socialization

3. Number demonstrating an improvement in socialization skills
4. Number demonstrating a decline in socialization skills

The person or task force responsible for the development of these tables might begin this task by returning to the problem analysis to review the factors that were found to be related to the problem and population. By drafting a series of questions and asking for review and comment from key agency personnel, board members, or others considered to be experts in the field, one can generate a useful set of questions. Individuals who are familiar with the problem, the population, and the program from different perspectives will invariably identify different sets of questions because their interests and need for information differ.

When a final draft of questions to be answered has been produced and approved, output tables can then be developed. Ideally, output tables can be clustered by the purposes for which they were created—planning, administration, program evaluation, budgeting, clinical supervision, and other such purposes. In instances where these purposes have been

Table 8.3

Profile of At-Risk Seniors (Those for Whom
Characteristics Listed Are a Problem or a Serious Problem)

Characteristics of Seniors	Ages 60 to 69		Ages 70 to 79		Ages 80 and Over	
	No.	%	No.	%	No.	%
1. Participation in social and/or recreational activities						
2. Participation in personally fulfilling activities						
3. Relationship with friends						
4. Relationship with nuclear family members						
5. Relationship with extended family members						
6. Ability to adjust to loss of a loved one						
7. Sense of self-confidence/self-esteem						
8. Current socioeconomic status						

combined into one complex table, the result is often a table that very few understand or find useful. On the other hand, when tables are created that are considered by the users to be relevant to their need for information, they serve as building blocks for a valuable and highly useful management information system.

For example, a table created for the purpose of planning programs and services might look something like Table 8.3. This table clusters three age groupings and proposes to display the number and percentage of clients (at-risk seniors) in each group who have been identified in the initial assessment as having a problem (indicated by a score of 1 or 2) in each of the eight problem areas identified.

A supervisor, on the other hand, might want weekly reports describing the service activities of the program's case managers. In this way, the supervisor will be able to monitor how much time is being spent on each phase of the process and whether patterns differ by worker (see Table 8.4).

Step 5: Design Data Collection
Procedures and Instruments

After examining the list of variables and the matrix created in the previous steps, a picture of data elements to be included in the management information system should begin to emerge. A comprehensive list of data elements should be produced and examined one more time before incorporating these elements into data collection instruments.

Table 8.4

Weekly Report of Service Activity[a]

Case Manager	No. of Cases	Intake	Assessment	Case Planning	Implementation/ Monitoring	Evaluation	Termination	Follow-Up	Total[b]
A. Graham	27	1.0	2.0	2.5	14.3	2.0	1.0	5.5	28.30
T. Jacobs	33	1.75	1.5	2.0	12.5	2.25	1.75	4.9	26.65
F. Parham	24	1.5	2.25	1.25	15.6	2.0	1.25	6.3	30.15
M. Chase	39	1.25	1.0	1.5	19.3	1.5	1.5	4.2	30.25
L. Patrick	35	.50	1.50	2.5	10.2	1.0	1.0	6.5	23.20

a. Number of units of service spent on each activity in the service process this week (1 unit = 1 hour).

b. Totals reflect only time spent and direct client contact.

If a data element is on the list but has no relevance in any output table and is not used for any reporting purpose, consideration should be given to dropping it or setting it aside for collection and use in another way. Adding data elements that do not contribute to useful information often happens when those involved in the creation of the management information system attempt to incorporate elements that fall into the category of "nice to know." For example, it might be nice to know if at-risk seniors had siblings who were diagnosed as depressed, but if there is no plan for using the information, it should be set aside and perhaps collected in another way (e.g., through counseling sessions) rather than incorporated into the regular collection of management information.

Once the list has been pared down to essential and useful data elements, they should be organized by data source. For example, all demographic and descriptive information should be incorporated into a form to be completed by an intake worker, drawing on information provided by client, family, guardian, and/or referral source. Assessment of client's problem/strength profile may be drawn from several sources, including, but not limited to, (a) client self-report, (b) family members, (c) other professionals involved with the client, and (d) client's caseworker, intake worker, and/or therapist.

One concern when creating the data collection system is to keep forms to a minimum. Each form that must be completed represents time that may be taken away from concentrating on the interventions needed by a client. For each form, the data source and frequency of data collection should be established. Frequency will usually be one time only, daily, weekly, or monthly when it has to do with information about clients. A sample intake form is shown in Figure 8.1.

In collecting the type of data we are proposing, it is critical that this activity be completed in a timely manner and not put off until the caseworker "has time." When the data are used as a basis for decision making about the program, accuracy at each stage of data collection, entry, and retrieval is vital. A daily report coding caseworker activity with each client he or she has seen that day can often be completed in 10 minutes or less. Trying to remember back a week or longer, even when notes were taken, can create reliability problems in interpreting the data.

When the necessary data collection documents have been designed, the flowchart of client progress through the program can once again be put to good use. Names of the documents to be completed can be added to the flowchart, along with indications of the points at which they

INTAKE FORM
CENTERVILLE CHILD AND FAMILY TREATMENT CENTER

Name _____

        Last   First   Middle

Date of Birth _____ Soc Sec Number _____

Client Address _____

           Number and Street

_____

City   State   ZIP Code   Home Phone

Sex ____ Education (years) ____ Monthly Income _____

Employed ____ Yes ____ No   If yes, complete the next line.

Employment _____

          Name

_____

        Address

ETHNICITY	MARITAL STATUS	LIVING ARRANGEMENTS
____ Asian	____ Never married	____ Alone
____ Black	____ Married	____ With spouse
____ Caucasian	____ Widowed	____ With children
____ Hispanic	____ Separated	____ With relatives
____ Native American	____ Divorced	____ With nonrelatives
____ Other	____ Unknown	____ Other

Number in household contributing to family income _____

Number in household dependent on family income _____

ADULTS IN HOUSEHOLD

Name	Age	Sex	Ethnicity	Income

CHILDREN IN HOUSEHOLD

Name	Age	Sex	Ethnicity	Grade

Figure 8.1. Sample Intake Form

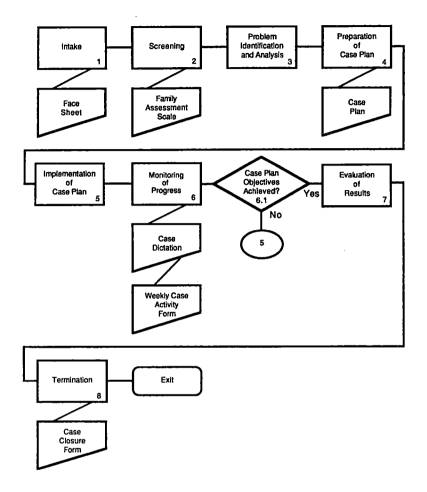

Figure 8.2. Flowchart of Client Processing and Documentation

should be completed. This provides a helpful overview of the process, the data collection points, and even, if necessary, the distribution of copies of the data collection forms. A sample flowchart is illustrated in Figure 8.2.

One final step that may be useful in the developing data collection procedures is the creation of a narrative chart to accompany the flowchart. The narrative chart allows for a more detailed description of procedures and documentation at each stage of the helping process and acts as a sort of protocol designed to ensure some degree of uniformity in the way clients are served and documents are completed. This can be especially important in cases that involve legal matters (see Chapter 7, Table 7.2).

In summary, four questions should be answered during the creation of data collection forms:

1. What is the purpose of the form?
2. What data elements should be included on the form?
3. Who will collect the data?
4. At what intervals (one time only, daily, weekly, monthly, or other) will the data be collected?

Step 6: Develop Data Entry Procedures

During Step 6, the information system moves from collection of raw data on individual clients to aggregation of data on all clients on whom data are reported. Setting up this process requires the creation of a codebook—a document used to translate client data into numbers that can be processed by a computer.

Setting up a codebook requires a return to the comprehensive list of variables identified in Step 5. Each variable must now be assigned (a) a variable name, (b) a variable label, and (c) a value. However, the following is only offered for illustrative purposes. Most statistical packages have their own format requirements.

The variable name is the title assigned to a variable; titles or definitions must also be assigned to subcategories of that variable. For example, here are some possible variable names and their subcategories:

- Case number
- Sex
  1. Female
  2. Male
- Ethnicity
  1. African American
  2. American Indian
  3. Asian American
  4. Hispanic/Latino
  5. White
  6. Other

The variable labels are usually shortened variable names that are used by the computer to identify variables as data are entered, aggregated, retrieved, and printed out in the form of output tables. For the variable names given above, for instance, the variable labels might be

- CASENO
- SEX
- RACE

The value is the number assigned to correspond to a subcategory of a variable. In the interest of saving time and space, and in the interest of translating data into computer language, subcategories of variables are assigned numerical values: For example, the subcategories of "female" and "male" are entered into the computer as 1 and 2. For each variable that includes subcategories, a value is assigned; using the sample variables above, values may be assigned as follows:

Case number	CASENO	001-999
Sex	SEX	
Female		1
Male		2
Ethnicity	ETH	
African American		1
American Indian		2
Asian American		3
Hispanic/Latino		4
White		5

Finally, in that revisions are likely to be needed as the program is implemented, it is always good practice for each version of the codebook to be clearly numbered and dated. Table 8.5 illustrates part of a codebook for the at-risk seniors project we have been using as an example.

The codebook would continue in the format shown in the table until every variable to be included in the system was coded and ready for entry. It should be noted here that the format for data entry varies with the statistical package selected. Each package may have slightly different protocol requirements as to data entry and use of columns. Table 8.5 provides an illustration of only one possible format.

Table 8.5
Sample Codebook for Senior Support Project

Variable	Variable Label
Case Number	CASENO
001-999	
ID No. of Case Manager	IDCM
01 M. Brown	
02 R. Blue	
03 H. Green	
04 S. Black	
.	
.	
.	
10 S. White	
Age of Client	AGE
Actual age in years	
Client's Marital Status	MS
1 Never married	
2 Married	
3 Separated	
4 Divorced	
9 Missing	
Ethnicity	ETH
1 African American	
2 American Indian	
3 Asian American	
4 Caucasian	
5 Hispanic/Latino	
6 Other	

Step 7: Compile and Analyze the Data

Software packages capable of assisting in the process of data analysis are readily available and affordable for even the smallest agency. These packages, whether for statistical analysis, spreadsheet purposes, or report generation, can be used on personal computers. They can produce tables that cover a wide variety of management needs, including descriptive statistics (e.g., frequency distributions) and inferential statistics (e.g., chi-square, correlation, and regression analysis). Appropriate staff may then examine the tables each month for indicators that client or program performance is within an acceptable range for the month. Where it is above or below expectations, further probing is required to reveal why an indicator is not within the expected range.

When analyzing data, staff should always be careful to avoid assumptions, to treat findings conservatively, to probe further, to track a particular phenomenon over time, and to ensure that any action taken is appropriate and warranted. Table 8.6 provides an example. This table illustrates the number and percentage of clients (at-risk seniors) who have been identified in the initial screening as having a problem (defined as at the 1 or 2 level on a 5-point scale) in each of eight potential problem areas. The clients are clustered into three age groups. This data display can potentially be helpful in revealing whether or not those 65 and older tend to develop more serious problems as they age.

If output tables have been designed around the interests and need for information of various stakeholders, tables and reports can be generated at this point directed to these special interests. Clinical supervisors will want to know something about client progress and worker effort for their units. Program managers will want to know about program performance, unit costs, and total program expenditures. The agency director and board will want to know something about overall agency performance, program performance, unit performance, and costs and expenditures to date. All of these perspectives can be addressed and need for information met if the information system has been designed as described in this chapter.

UTILIZING DATA FROM
AN EXISTING SYSTEM

In the vast majority of instances where there is interest in creating an effectiveness-based management information system, years of data collection documents are already in place. Creation of a new system is usually out of the question because of limited time, money, and potential disruption to the existing system. In these instances, a computerized data collection and aggregation system can still be created, but some adjustments will have to be made to the seven-step process discussed above.

Step 1: Identify the Questions to Be Answered

Step 1 should be accomplished in the same manner as in creating a new system. Through a review of the findings from the problem analysis and a series of brainstorming sessions with management and staff, the important questions to be answered for clinical, supervisory, manage-

Table 8.6
Profile of At-Risk Seniors (Those for Whom Characteristics Listed Are a Problem or a Serious Problem)

Characteristics of Seniors	Ages 60 to 69 (N = 75)		Ages 70 to 79 (N = 60)		Ages 80 and Over (N = 45)	
	No.	%	No.	%	No.	%
1. Participation in social and/or recreational activities	22	36.7	35	58.3	27	60
2. Participation in personally fulfilling activities	25	33.3	31	51.7	23	51.1
3. Relationship with friends	15	20	21	35	25	55.6
4. Relationship with nuclear family members	27	36	24	40	32	71.1
5. Relationship with extended family members	31	41.3	29	48.3	37	82.2
6. Ability to adjust to loss of a loved one	22	29.3	27	45	13	28.9
7. Sense of self-confidence/ self-esteem	18	24	22	36.7	19	42.2
8. Current socioeconomic status	16	21.3	23	38.3	34	75.6

ment, administrative, and planning purposes should be identified, organized into a logical scheme, and published for all staff to use as a working document.

Step 2: Identify Data Elements Needed for the System

It is worthwhile to develop a list of data elements independent of the existing system so that a comparison can be made between the list considered to be necessary and the existing data elements included on forms currently in use. Likewise, the exercise of developing a comprehensive matrix to help in the selection of appropriate and useful cross-tabulations can be worthwhile.

Step 3: Develop a Strategy for Analysis

The activities undertaken in working with an existing system are essentially the same as the activities in developing a new system. Dummy tables should be created that display data in a manner that will answer the questions posed in Step 1.

Step 4: Design Output Tables

Step 4 should also be accomplished in the same manner as in creating a new system. Dummy output tables should be created that display data in a manner that will answer the questions identified in Step 1.

Step 5: Design Data Collection
Procedures and Instruments

In Step 5, the assumption is that there are already data collection instruments in place. For this reason, it is important to pull together a sample of all instruments currently in use. In the process of identifying variables to be included on the data collection instruments, it may be worthwhile to develop a worksheet that includes columns to indicate whether each data element is already being collected and, if so, on what form. Only those items needed but not currently being collected will need to be added to the system. Wherever possible, they can be added to existing data collection forms; new forms can then be created to collect data not otherwise covered.

Step 6: Develop Data Entry Procedures

If no codebook has been developed for data entry purposes, one should be created at this point. If one is already in existence, new variables should be added at this point.

Step 7: Compile and Analyze Data

Using the display framework created in Step 3, this final step should be completed in the same way as in creating a new system, developing a plan for production and distribution of data, study and analysis by relevant staff, and feedback and application of findings within the system.

In summary, creation of an outcome-oriented management information system is not a terribly complex process from a conceptual perspective, but it is time consuming and labor intensive. It requires an ability on the part of administrators and staff to identify the key questions to be answered so that the best interests of clients can be served. It requires the ability to create data displays in a manner that will produce the necessary information. It requires the design or redesign of data collection instruments, and it probably increases the demands on the data processing system.

Despite the relatively low cost, movement in many agencies has been very slow in building data and information bases on client outcomes and incorporating them into decision-making processes. Barriers to progress, ironically, seem to come in the form of the many additional requirements and demands placed on administrators and practitioners in the field. A shrinking funding base, increased competition for funds, and increased demand from clients all converge to make today's social service agency an organization seemingly already stretched to its limits and therefore unable to make the breakthroughs needed to convert to an outcome-oriented management information system. For this scenario to change, the effort must be initiated at the local level to reconceptualize the way data are collected, compiled, and used.

Part IV

CALCULATING THE COSTS AND VALUE OF THE INTERVENTION

Chapter 9

LINE-ITEM, FUNCTIONAL, AND PROGRAM BUDGETING SYSTEMS

Although such concepts as program hypotheses, the elements of program design, goals and objectives, outputs, and outcomes are critical components of effectiveness-based program planning, they are simply abstract concepts until backed up by resources. It is in the budgeting process that resources are allocated.

In this chapter, we will identify and define four types of budgeting systems and highlight the value of each as it relates to effectiveness-based program planning.

TYPES OF BUDGETING SYSTEMS

Considerable disagreement exists in the budgeting literature as to the number of separately identifiable budgeting systems and the names that should be ascribed to each. "Line-item," "program," "performance," "program-planning and budgeting" (PPBS), "zero-base" (ZBB), and "outcome" are all budgeting systems identified in the literature (Lynch, 1995; Martin, 1997). Some writers make a distinction between performance and program budgeting; others use the terms interchangeably. The *term functional budgeting* is used to describe many different budgeting systems, and is often used interchangeably with both *performance budgeting* and *program budgeting*.

PPBS and ZBB, when used as originally described by Lee and Johnson (1973) and Phyrr (1973), can be considered as complete budgeting systems to be implemented exactly as prescribed. However, the concepts of PPBS and ZBB can still be incorporated into performance, program, or functional budgeting systems. For example, calculating the cost of achieving program objectives (to be discussed later in this chapter) can draw on the concept of a "decision package" taken from zero-base budgeting.

Given the confusion in the literature, any attempt to classify budgeting systems must be somewhat arbitrary. The approach taken here adopts the taxonomy first proposed by Gundersdorf (1977). He suggested that historically four budgeting systems have tended to predominate in the social services: (a) nonbudgeting systems, (b) line-item budgeting systems, (c) functional budgeting systems, and (d) program budgeting systems. Brief examples of the budget formats used by each of these four budgeting systems are shown in Table 9.1.

As Table 9.1 illustrates, each of these four budgeting systems takes a somewhat different perspective on the operations of a social service agency and its various programs. The differing perspectives can be accounted for by the dual financial/programmatic nature of budgeting. Nonbudgeting and line-item budgeting systems have a financial perspective; they are designed to simply account for revenues and expenditures. Nonbudgeting systems look at revenues and expenses from a "lump-sum" perspective, whereas line-item budgeting systems put revenues and expenses into categories. Functional and program budgeting systems have a programmatic perspective in addition to a financial perspective. Functional budgeting systems provide information about the costs of providing program products and services (intermediate outputs) and service completions (final outputs). Program budgeting systems provide information about the costs associated with achieving program results, accomplishments, or impacts (outcomes).

The different perspectives taken by each of these four budgeting systems determine the elements of the systems framework that each adopts as its focus. The focus, in turn, determines the kind of budgetary data and information that need to be generated by a social services agency and its various programs, how the budgetary data and information are analyzed and presented, and how resources are apportioned between or among agency programs.

Table 9.2 identifies the element(s) of the systems framework that each of the four budgeting systems takes as its focus. Nonbudgeting systems focus primarily on revenues (inputs). For this reason, non-

Table 9.1

Examples of Budget Formats

Nonbudgeting System Format

Revenues	$325,000
Expenses	$325,000

Line-Item Budgeting System Format

Revenues

1.	Government grants and contracts	$150,000
2.	United Way	$100,000
3.	Client fees	$ 50,000
4.	Donations	$ 25,000
	Total	$325,000

Expenses

1.	Salaries and wages	$200,000
2.	Employee-related expenses (ERE) @ .25%	$ 50,000
3.	Rent	$ 20,000
4.	Utilities	$ 12,000
5.	Travel	$ 10,000
6.	Supplies	$ 7,000
7.	Equipment	$ 15,000
8.	Other	$ 11,000
	Total	$325,000

Functional Budgeting System Format

1.	Adult day care services (provide 8,000 days of service at a unit cost of $26.88 per day of service)	$215,000
2.	Adult protective services (conduct 75 home studies at a unit cost of $1,466 per study)	$110,000
	Total	$325,000

Program Budgeting System Format

1.	Adult day care services (prevent the premature institutionalization of 100 elderly persons at a unit cost of $2,150 per person)	$215,000
2.	Adult protective services (place 25 adults in safe homes at a unit cost of $4,400 per placement)	$110,000
	Total	$325,000

---

budgeting systems can also be thought of as "input budgeting." Other characteristics of nonbudgeting systems include the absence of standardized budgetary processes and the lack of standardized budget formats and common budget definitions. Nonbudgeting systems do not

Table 9.2
The Relationship Between Budgeting Systems and the
Elements of the Systems Framework

Type of Budgeting System	Systems Element(s) Focus
Nonbudgeting	Inputs
Line-item budgeting	Inputs and throughputs
Functional budgeting	Inputs and outputs
Program budgeting	Inputs and outcomes

categorize revenues and expenses. Consequently, nonbudgeting systems are concerned only with revenues and expenses in the aggregate, in much the same way as an individual might manage his or her own personal checking account. Given the effectiveness-based program planning approach we have discussed throughout this book—its intent, promise, and requirements—we reject nonbudgeting systems out of hand. We have included them here only because they are mentioned in the literature.

Line-item, functional, and program budgeting systems are all characterized by structured budgetary processes and the use of standardized budget formats and common budget definitions. Line-item budgeting systems focus on expenses (throughputs) and relate expenses to revenues (inputs). For this reason, line-item budgeting systems can also be thought of as "throughput budgeting" or "expense budgeting."

Functional budgeting systems focus on outputs, including program products and services (intermediate outputs), quality products and services (quality outputs), and service completions (final outputs), and on the revenues (inputs) consumed in their production. The ratio of program outputs to program inputs is the classical definition of efficiency or productivity. Consequently, functional budgeting systems can be thought of as "output budgeting," "efficiency budgeting," or "productivity budgeting." Program budgeting systems focus primarily on program results, accomplishments, or impacts (outcomes) and on the revenues (inputs) consumed in their production. Program budgeting systems can be thought of as "outcome budgeting" or "effectiveness budgeting."

As a social service agency moves from a nonbudgeting system to a line-item budgeting system to a functional budgeting system and finally to a program budgeting system, the complexity of the budgetary process increases, as does the budgetary expertise required of agency staff.

To summarize thus far:

- There are four major budgeting systems used in the social services: nonbudgeting systems, line-item budgeting systems, functional budgeting systems, and program budgeting systems.
- Nonbudgeting systems focus primarily on revenues (inputs) and are inadequate to meet the budgeting needs of social service agencies today.
- Line-item budgeting systems focus on expenses (throughputs) and relate revenues (inputs) to expenses.
- Functional budgeting systems focus on program products and services (intermediate outputs), quality products and services (quality outputs), and service completions (final outputs) and on the revenues (inputs) consumed in their production.
- Program budgeting systems focus on program results, accomplishments, and impacts (outcomes) and on the revenues (inputs) consumed in their production.

LINE-ITEM BUDGETING SYSTEMS

Line-item budgeting systems are characterized by the use of a structured budgetary process, standardized budget formats, and common budget definitions. Line-item budgeting systems seek to bring consistency to the budgetary process and to provide a financial overview of a social service agency and its various programs.

Line-item budgeting systems usually cover one fiscal year. A fiscal year is composed of 12 calendar months and tends to follow one of three time frames: (a) from January 1 to December 31 (used by most nonprofit social service agencies), (b) from July 1 to June 30 (used by most state and local government social service agencies), and (c) from October 1 to September 30 (used by the U.S. Department of Health and Human Services and other federal departments and agencies). Regardless of the fiscal year used, all agency budgeting systems are tied to that time frame.

The implementation of a line-item budgeting system in a social service agency involves the following steps:

1. Designing a standardized line-item budget format
2. Developing common budget definitions and terms
3. Identifying all revenues and expenses
4. Balancing the budget

Designing a Standardized
Line-Item Budget Format

The categories of revenues and expenses in a line-item budgeting system are designed to be mutually exclusive and exhaustive. All revenue and expense items should fit into one, and only one, category. The various categories should be sufficient to cover all revenue and expense items. Table 9.3 presents an example of what a standardized line-item budget format might look like.

Developing Common Budget
Definitions and Terms

In an actual social service agency line-item budgeting system, each of the revenue and expense categories shown in Table 9.3 would be operationally defined to provide guidance and ensure uniformity in the treatment of budget items. For example, the term *employee-related expenses* (ERE) would be operationally defined as those additional costs associated with each staff person, including Social Security payments, federal and state withholding taxes, health and dental insurance costs, and retirement costs. The inclusion of a miscellaneous category for both revenues and expenses ensures that the budget format will accommodate all budget items.

Identifying All Revenues and Expenses

Not all social service agency line-item budgeting systems include a complete presentation of both revenues and expenses. Many line-item budgeting systems detail only expenses. The inclusion of all revenues and expenses is the preferred approach because the budget of a social service agency should be balanced. Revenues should be equal to or greater than expenses.

Balancing the Budget

The use of a line-item budgeting system with a standardized budget format that includes all revenues and expenses clearly indicates whether a social service agency's budget is balanced or unbalanced. During the budgetary process, the standardized line-item budget format facilitates the identification and discussion of where proposed expenses might be reduced or where additional revenues might be sought to bring the finalized budget into balance.

Table 9.3
Example of a Line-Item Budgeting System Format

	Revenues		
1.	Contributions (general)		$ _____
2.	Special events		$ _____
3.	United Way allocation		$ _____
4.	Government contracts and grants		$ _____
5.	Membership dues		$ _____
6.	Third-party payments		$ _____
7.	Program income		$ _____
8.	Investment income		$ _____
9.	Miscellaneous		$ _____
		Total Revenues	$ _____
	Expenses		
1.	Salaries and wages		$ _____
2.	Employee-related expenses		$ _____
3.	Rent		$ _____
4.	Utilities		$ _____
5.	Supplies		$ _____
6.	Telephone		$ _____
7.	Equipment		$ _____
8.	Postage and shipping		$ _____
9.	Printing and publications		$ _____
10.	Travel		$ _____
11.	Conferences		$ _____
12.	Miscellaneous		$ _____
		Total Expenses	$ _____

Because balancing the budget can sometimes be a painful organizational experience, a temptation may exist for a social service agency to force a budget into balance. A forced balance is created when agency management consciously overstates revenues or consciously understates expenses. There is an old story about the director of a religiously affiliated social service agency who forced his agency budget into balance each fiscal year by routinely including a revenue category called "unanticipated income." When asked about this unorthodox approach, the director replied that he preferred to trust in divine intervention rather than go through the pain of balancing the budget.

Unless one has connections in high places, forcing the budget of a social service agency into balance is risky business. Balancing the budget at the beginning of the fiscal year may sometimes be a difficult task, but the task becomes increasingly more difficult with each passing month. An unbalanced budget must eventually be balanced. The actual organizational impact of a budget reduction on the operations of a social service agency is equal to the amount of the reduction multiplied by the number of months elapsed in the fiscal year. For example, a $2,000 budget reduction in the sixth month of a fiscal year actually has an organizational impact equal to $12,000 ($2,000 × 6 months).

To summarize:

- Line-item budgeting systems require the design of a standardized budget format that identifies all revenues and expenses.
- All budget categories in a line-item budget should be operationally defined.
- Line-item budgets should be balanced: Revenues should be equal to or greater than expenses.
- It is better to balance a line-item budget at the beginning of the fiscal year rather than later.
- All budgeting systems are usually designed to cover one fiscal year, with varying starting and ending dates depending on the type of social service agency and the source of funding.

THE LINK BETWEEN LINE-ITEM BUDGETING AND FUNCTIONAL OR PROGRAM BUDGETING

The development of either a functional or a program budgeting system for a social service agency actually begins with the agency's line-item budget. The use of a structured budgetary process, standardized budgetary categories, and common budget definitions is also characteristic of functional and program budgeting systems shared with line-item budgeting systems.

The central idea behind both functional and program budgeting systems is to take a social service agency's line-item budget and assign or allocate all expenses to the agency's various programs to determine the total cost of each program. At this point, functional and program budgeting systems diverge. Functional budgeting systems are concerned with the efficiency, or productivity, of a social service agency's various programs and answer the following questions: How much service will a program provide as measured in terms of products and services (intermediate outputs), quality products and services (quality outputs), and service completions (final outputs)? What is the cost per intermediate output (unit of service), per quality output, and per service completion? And what is the total cost of the program? Program budgeting systems are concerned with the effectiveness of a social service agency's various programs and answer the questions, What program results, accomplishments, or impacts (outcomes) are anticipated? And what is the cost per outcome?

Because both functional and program budgeting systems are concerned with determining the total cost of the various programs operated by a social service agency, they have certain implementation steps in common, including the following:

1. Developing the line-item budget identifying all revenues and expenses, *but with emphasis on expenses.*
2. Determining the agency's program structure.
3. Creating the cost allocation plan format.
4. Identifying direct and indirect costs.
5. Assigning direct costs to programs.
6. Allocating indirect costs to programs and determining total program costs.

Developing the Line-Item Budget

The initial step in implementing either a functional or a program budgeting system in a social service agency is the development of a line-item budget that identifies all revenues and expenses. However, it is the expenses that are important in the development of functional and program budgeting systems.

Table 9.4 is an example of a line-item budget format for a hypothetical senior center. This hypothetical senior center and its line-item budget will be used to illustrate how functional and program budgeting systems and formats are derived. The senior center's total budget is $686,000, with three major expense categories: $341,000 in salaries and wages, $85,250 in ERE, and $259,000 in other operating costs.

Determining the Agency's
Program Structure

Determining the social service agency's program structure is the next major step in implementing either a functional or a program budgeting system. *Program structure* refers to the number of distinct programs

Table 9.4
Senior Center Line-Item Budget (Expenses Only)

Salaries and Wages	
Executive director	$ 75,000
Business manager	$ 50,000
Program coordinator (CM)	$ 40,000
Program coordinator (SR)	$ 35,000
Program coordinator (T)	$ 30,000
Social worker	$ 27,000
Recreation aide (SR)	$ 15,000
Cook (CM)	$ 24,000
Janitor	$ 15,000
Van drivers (T)	$ 30,000
Total Salaries and Wages	$341,000
Employee-Related Expenses (@ 25%)	$ 85,250
Other Operating	
1. Rent	$ 22,000
2. Utilities	$ 12,000
3. Telephone	$ 8,000
4. Supplies	$ 10,000
5. Supplies (CM)	$ 20,000
6. Supplies (SR)	$ 15,000
7. Van rentals (T)	$ 28,000
8. Equipment	$ 7,750
9. Printing and duplicating	$ 12,000
10. Travel	$ 10,000
11. Postage and shipping	$ 5,000
12. Food (CM)	$100,000
13. Miscellaneous	$ 10,000
Total Other Operating	$259,750
Total Budget	$686,000

operated by a social service agency. For some social service agencies, this task may be quite simple; for others, determining the number of distinct programs the agency operates may require some reflection and analysis.

A program can be thought of as a set of relatively permanent agency activities or services designed to accomplish a specific set of quantifiable goals and objectives. A program can be composed of a single service or activity or multiple services and activities. For example, a single service such as information and referral or case management that has its own set of quantifiable goals and objectives can constitute a program. Likewise, a complex service such as adult day care that is composed of a mix of services (e.g., congregate meals, recreation and socialization, transportation, health monitoring) can also be treated as a program provided it has its own set of quantifiable goals and objectives.

In the senior center example from Table 9.4, the agency has determined that it has three programs: (a) a congregate meals program, (b) a socialization and recreation program, and (c) a transportation program.

Creating the Cost Allocation Plan Format

The cost allocation plan format is the primary document, or tool, used to derive a functional or program budget from a line-item budget. In the rows of a cost allocation plan (see Table 9.5), the same line items appear that are used in an agency's line-item budget. Each agency program appears in a column heading, and one column is labeled the *indirect cost pool*. With the aid of the cost allocation plan format, the total cost of each program that a social service agency operates can be determined.

Identifying Direct and Indirect Costs

Every item of expense (as identified in a social service's agency's line-item budget) can be classified as either a direct cost or an indirect cost.

Direct costs are those items of expense that are to be incurred by a social service agency for the benefit of only one program. Examples of cost items that are generally treated as direct include:

- The salaries and wages of staff who work for only one program.
- Materials and supplies used for the benefit of only one program.
- Travel costs associated with only one program.
- Equipment used exclusively in one program.
- Any other costs that benefit only one program.

Indirect costs are those items of expense that are to be incurred for the benefit of two or more programs. Indirect costs are sometimes referred to as "overhead costs" or "organizational and maintenance (OM) costs." Indirect costs typically involve the salaries, wages, and

Table 9.5
Senior Center Cost Allocation Plan Format

Budget Line Items	Congregate Meals (CM)	Socialization and Recreation (SR)	Transportation (T)	Indirect Cost Pool
Salaries and Wages				
Executive director				
Business manager				
Program coordinator (CM)				
Program coordinator (SR)				
Program coordinator (T)				
Social worker				
Recreation aide (SR)				
Cook (CM)				
Janitor				
Van drivers (T)				
Total Salaries and Wages				
Employee-Related Expenses (@ 25%)				
Other Operating				
Rent				
Utilities				
Telephone				
Supplies				
Supplies (CM)				
Supplies (SR)				
Van rentals (T)				
Equipment				
Printing and duplicating				
Travel				
Postage and shipping				
Food (CM)				
Miscellaneous				
Column Totals				
Allocate Indirect Costs				
Total Program Costs				

ERE of the executive director and other agency staff whose work benefits two or more programs, as well as other operating expenses that benefit two or more agency programs. Other operating costs that are generally treated as indirect include

- Building rents
- Utilities
- Janitorial services
- Telephones
- Auditing

Assigning Direct Costs to Programs

For a social service agency to determine the total cost of its various programs, each program's direct costs must be determined, as well as each program's relative share of indirect costs. *The total cost of a program is the sum of its direct and indirect costs.* Identifying a program's direct costs is a fairly straightforward activity. If a cost item benefits one—and only one—agency program, the cost is a direct cost to that program. In the senior center line-item budget (Table 9.4), the direct costs are identified as belonging to one of the following: the congregate meals (CM) program, the socialization and recreation (SR) program, or the transportation (T) program. In Table 9.6, these direct costs are assigned to their respective programs using the cost allocation plan format. In addition to the identification of some agency staff (e. g., the program coordinators) as direct costs, certain other operating costs (e. g., supplies for the congregate meals program and van rental expenses for the transportation program) are also identified as direct costs because they benefit only one program.

Allocating Indirect Costs to Programs
and Determining Total Program Costs

Determining each program's relative share of indirect costs is a somewhat more complex undertaking. When a cost item is identified as an indirect cost, the item is first placed in the *indirect cost pool.* The indirect cost pool is a sort of temporary holding category. In the senior center line-item budget (Table 9.4), the executive director and the business manager are both indirect costs because they work in support

Table 9.6
Completed Senior Center Cost Allocation
Plan Using Total Direct Costs

Budget Line Items	Congregate Meals (CM)	Socialization and Recreation (SR)	Transportation (T)	Indirect Cost Pool
Salaries and Wages				
Executive director				$ 75,000
Business manager				$ 50,000
Program coordinator (CM)	$ 40,000			
Program coordinator (SR)		$ 35,000		
Program coordinator (T)			$ 30,000	
Social worker				$ 27,000
Recreation aide (SR)		$ 15,000		
Cook (CM)	$ 24,000			
Janitor				$ 15,000
Van drivers (T)			$ 30,000	
Total Salaries and Wages	$ 64,000	$ 50,000	$ 60,000	$167,000
Employee-Related Expenses				
(@ 25%)	$ 16,000	$ 12,500	$ 15,000	$ 41,750
Other Operating				
Rent				$ 22,000
Utilities				$ 12,000
Telephone				$ 8,000
Supplies				$ 10,000
Supplies (CM)	$ 20,000			
Supplies (SR)		$ 15,000		
Van rentals (T)			$ 28,000	
Equipment				$ 7,750
Printing and duplicating				$ 12,000
Travel				$ 10,000
Postage and shipping				$ 5,000
Food (CM)	$100,000			
Miscellaneous				$ 10,000
Column Totals	$200,000	$ 77,500	$103,000	$305,500
Allocate Indirect Costs	$160,578	$ 62,224	$ 82,698	
Total Program Costs	$360,578	$139,724	$185,698	

of all the agency's programs. In addition, certain other operating costs (rent, utilities, telephone, supplies, equipment, printing and duplicating, travel, postage and shipping, and miscellaneous) are also treated as indirect costs because they benefit two or more of the agency's programs. Consequently, the salary and wages of both the executive director and the business manager, together with their associated ERE and all other operating costs identified as indirect costs, are temporarily placed in the indirect cost pool.

When all indirect costs have been identified and placed in the indirect cost pool, they are totaled and apportioned among the agency's various programs. The process by which indirect costs are apportioned, or allocated, among programs is called *cost allocation.* The actual practice of cost allocation is a technical matter best left to accountants. However, the logic behind cost allocation is not difficult and is essential to a complete understanding of how functional and program budgets are derived from line-item budgets.

Cost allocation involves the selection and application of a methodology, or base, to be used to apportion indirect costs among programs. The cost allocation methodologies, or bases, most frequently used by social service agencies are (a) total direct costs, (b) direct labor costs, (c) direct labor hours, and (d) direct costing (Hay & Wilson, 1995; Horngren, Foster, & Datar, 1997).

Total Direct Cost Methodology

Cost allocation using total direct costs as the methodology or base involves four steps:

1. Determining each program's share of direct costs
2. Totaling all direct costs
3. Determining each program's relative percentage share of indirect costs
4. Allocating the indirect cost pool to each program, using the derived indirect cost rate

Continuing with the ongoing senior center example, Table 9.6 shows the total direct costs (column totals) for each of the three programs: $200,000 for the congregate meals (CM) program, $77,500 for the socialization and recreation (SR) program, and $103,000 for the transportation (T) program, as well as the total indirect costs in the indirect

Table 9.7

Allocating Indirect Costs Using Total Direct Costs

Congregate Meals		Socialization and Recreation		Transportation		Total Direct Costs
$200,000	+	$77,500	+	$103,000	=	$380,500

Indirect Cost Pool = $305,500 $305,500/$380,500 = 80.29% = Indirect Cost Rate

$200,000 × .8029 = $160,578   = Indirect costs to be allocated to the congregate
                                                meals program
$ 77,500 × .8029 = $ 62,224   = Indirect costs to be allocated to the socialization
                                                and recreation program
$103,000 × .8029 = $ 82,698   = Indirect costs to be allocated to the transportation
                                                program

                        $305,500 = Total Indirect Costs

costs pool ($305,500). Cost allocation using total direct costs as the base involves apportioning, or allocating, the indirect cost pool ($305,500) between the three programs according to each program's relative percentage share of total direct costs. Table 9.7 demonstrates the process involved.

The direct costs of all three senior center programs total $380,500. To apportion, or allocate, the indirect cost pool ($305,500) to the three programs, an *indirect cost rate* must be computed. An indirect cost rate is a ratio that expresses the relationship between a program's direct costs and indirect costs. Determining the indirect cost rate using the total direct costs methodology or base involves dividing the indirect cost pool ($305,000) by the total direct costs ($380,500) of all three programs. The resulting percentage (80.29%) is the indirect cost rate. The indirect cost rate is then applied to the total direct costs of each program. For example, the total direct costs of the congregate meals program ($200,000) is multiplied by the indirect cost rate (.8029). The product ($160,578) is the congregate meals program's relative percentage share of indirect costs. Each program's assigned direct costs and allocated indirect costs are then totaled (refer to Table 9.6). The result is the total cost of each program. For example, the total cost of the congregate

Table 9.8

Allocating Indirect Costs Using Direct Labor Costs

	Congregate Meals	Socialization and Recreation	Transportation	Total Direct Labor Costs
Salaries and wages	$64,000	$50,000	$60,000	
Employee-related expenses	16,000	$12,500	$15,000	
Total program direct labor costs	$80,000 +	$62,500 +	$75,000 =	$217,500

Indirect Cost Pool = $305,500 $305,500/$217,500 = 140.461% = Indirect Cost Rate

$80,000 × 1.4046 = $112,368   = Indirect costs to be allocated to the congregate
                                 meals program

$62,500 × 1.4046 = $ 87,787   = Indirect costs to be allocated to the socialization
                                 and recreation program

$75,000 × 1.4046 = $105,345   = Indirect costs to be allocated to the transportation
                                 program

              $305,500   = Total Indirect Costs

meals program is $360,578: $200,000 in assigned direct costs and $160,578 in allocated indirect costs.

Direct Labor Costs Methodology

The second approach to cost allocation is called *direct labor costs*. The process is essentially the same as the total direct costs methodology, except that instead of finding each program's relative percentage share of total direct costs, one determines each program's relative percentage share of direct labor costs and uses it as the base. Direct labor costs are those staffing costs, including ERE, that are considered direct costs. Table 9.8 demonstrates the process involved in allocating indirect costs on the basis of direct labor costs.

As Table 9.8 shows, each program's direct labor costs (salaries, wages, and ERE) are identified: $80,000 for the congregate meals program, $62,500 for the socialization and recreation program, and

$75,000 for the transportation program. The direct labor costs of all three programs combined total $217,500. The *indirect cost rate* is determined using total direct labor costs as the methodology or base. The indirect cost pool ($305,500) is divided by the total direct labor costs ($217,500). The resulting percentage (140.461%) is the indirect cost rate. The indirect cost rate is then applied to each program's direct labor costs. For example, the direct labor costs of the congregate meals program ($80,000) is multiplied by the indirect cost rate (1.4046); the product ($112,368) is the congregate meals program's relative percentage share of the indirect costs. Each program's direct costs and indirect costs are then totaled (see Table 9.9) to determine each program's total cost.

It is interesting to note how much the total cost of each program changes when the cost allocation methodology or base changes. For example, the total cost of the congregate meals program decreases from $360,578 when total direct costs is used as the cost allocation methodology to $312,368 when direct labor costs is used. Much of the difference is attributable to the cost item "food." When total direct costs is used as the cost allocation methodology, the congregate meals program is allocated a larger share of indirect costs because the $100,000 item for "food" is included in the computation, bringing the program's total direct costs to $200,000. When direct labor costs are used, some indirect costs are reallocated away from the congregate meals program because all three programs are relatively equal in terms of these costs.

Direct Labor Hours Methodology

The third approach to cost allocation is called *direct labor hours.* Again, the process is essentially the same as for the total direct costs and the total direct labor costs methodologies, except that now each program's relative percentage share of total direct labor hours is determined and used as the base. *Direct labor hours* means the total annual hours worked by all agency staff that are considered direct costs.

The average work year, taking into consideration weekends and holidays, is generally computed at 2,080 hours. If a particular program in a social service agency has four staff and they are all full-time equivalent (FTE) employees (meaning they all work full time, or 2,080 hours per fiscal year), then the total direct labor hours for the program is 8,320 (2,080 × 4). Returning to the ongoing example of the senior center, Table 9.9 demonstrates that each of the three programs has two

Table 9.9
Completed Senior Center Cost Allocation
Plan Using Direct Labor Costs

Budget Line Items	Congregate Meals (CM)	Socialization and Recreation (SR)	Transportation (T)	Indirect Cost Pool
Salaries and Wages				
Executive director				$ 75,000
Business manager				$ 50,000
Program coordinator (CM)	$ 40,000			
Program coordinator (SR)		$ 35,000		
Program coordinator (T)			$ 30,000	
Social worker				$ 27,000
Recreation aide (SR)		$ 15,000		
Cook (CM)	$ 24,000			
Janitor				$ 15,000
Van drivers (T)			$ 30,000	
Total Salaries and Wages	$ 64,000	$ 50,000	$ 60,000	$167,000
Employee-Related Expenses (@ 25%)	$ 16,000	$ 12,500	$ 15,000	$ 41,750
Other Operating				
Rent				$ 22,000
Utilities				$ 12,000
Telephone				$ 8,000
Supplies				$ 10,000
Supplies (CM)	$ 20,000			
Supplies (SR)		$ 15,000		
Van rentals (T)			$ 28,000	
Equipment				$ 7,750
Printing and duplicating				$ 12,000
Travel				$ 10,000
Postage and shipping				$ 5,000
Food (CM)	$100,000			
Miscellaneous				$ 10,000
Column Totals	$200,000	$ 77,500	$103,000	$305,500
Allocate Indirect Costs	$112,368	$ 87,787	$105,345	
Total Program Costs	$312,368	$165,287	$208,345	

staff persons who are considered direct costs. Table 9.10 details the process involved in using direct labor hours as the cost allocation methodology or base in allocating the indirect cost pool.

Because all three senior center programs have two staff working full time, the number of direct labor hours for each program is 4,160 (2,080 × 2). The total direct labor hours for all three programs is 12,480. The *indirect cost rate* is determined by dividing the indirect cost pool ($305,500) by the total direct labor hours (12,480). The result is an indirect cost rate that, unlike the others, is not a percentage but is, rather, a dollar amount ($24.479) per direct labor hour. The indirect cost rate is then applied to each program's direct labor hours. For example, the direct labor hours for the congregate meals program (4,160) is multiplied by the indirect cost rate ($24,479). The resulting product ($101,833) is the congregate meals program's relative share of the indirect costs. Once again, each program's direct costs and indirect costs are then added together (see Table 9.11) to determine each program's total cost.

The total cost of each of the three senior center programs in Table 9.11, when direct labor hours is used as the cost allocation methodology or base, is slightly different from the total program cost in Table 9.9, where total direct labor costs is used. The primary reason for the difference is that cost allocation using direct labor hours is not affected by differences in salaries, wages, and ERE. For example, the program coordinator for the congregate meals program earns $40,000 a year, whereas the program coordinator for the transportation program earns only $30,000, but they both work the same number of hours (2,080) during the fiscal year. When direct labor costs are used as the base, more indirect costs are allocated to the congregate meals program than to the transportation program because of the differences in salaries, wages, and ERE. When direct labor hours is used as the base, the same amount of indirect costs is allocated to the congregate meals program and the transportation program because their direct cost staff work the same number of hours.

Direct Costing Methodology

The fourth and final approach to cost allocation to be reviewed is called *direct costing*. This methodology involves converting indirect costs to direct costs. The direct costing method requires that a unique

Table 9.10
Allocating Indirect Costs Using Direct Labor Hours

	Congregate Meals		Socialization and Recreation		Transportation		Total Direct Labor Hours
Direct labor hours	4,160	+	4,160	+	4,160	=	12,480

Indirect Cost Pool = $305,500 $305,500/12,480 = $24,479 = Indirect Hourly Rate

4,160 × $24.479 = $101,833	=	Indirect costs to be allocated to the congregate meals program
4,160 × $24.479 = $101,833	=	Indirect costs to be allocated to the socialization and recreation program
4,160 × $24.479 = $101,834	=	Indirect costs to be allocated to the transportation program
$305,500	=	Total Indirect Costs

measure or base be found and used to track and allocate each item of indirect cost. With this approach, each item of indirect cost has its own rationale or base for allocation to programs. The indirect cost item "telephone" from Table 9.11 can be used to illustrate how an item of indirect cost can be converted to a direct cost. The cost item "telephone" (defined for purposes of this example as basic monthly service charges) is generally treated as an indirect cost because the telephone system of a social service agency benefits all programs. One way of converting this item of indirect cost to a direct cost would be to determine the total number of telephones in the senior center and the number used by each of the agency's three programs. Each program's relative percentage share of the total telephones in the agency would then become the base for allocating telephone charges to the agency's programs.

Any item of indirect cost can be converted into a direct cost by finding a measure (e.g., hours, square feet) to serve as the allocation base. The allocation bases shown in Table 9.12 are generally acknowledged as acceptable for purposes of converting indirect costs into direct costs.

Table 9.11

Completed Senior Center Cost Allocation
Plan Using Direct Labor Hours

Budget Line Items	Congregate Meals (CM)	Socialization and Recreation (SR)	Transportation (T)	Indirect Cost Pool
Salaries and Wages				
Executive director				$ 75,000
Business manager				$ 50,000
Program coordinator (CM)	$ 40,000			
Program coordinator (SR)		$ 35,000		
Program coordinator (T)			$ 30,000	
Social worker				$ 27,000
Recreation aide (SR)		$ 15,000		
Cook (CM)	$ 24,000			
Janitor				$ 15,000
Van drivers (T)			$ 30,000	
Total Salaries and Wages	$ 64,000	$ 50,000	$ 60,000	$167,000
Employee-Related Expenses				
(@ 25%)	$ 16,000	$ 12,500	$ 15,000	$ 41,750
Other Operating				
Rent				$ 22,000
Utilities				$ 12,000
Telephone				$ 8,000
Supplies				$ 10,000
Supplies (CM)	$ 20,000			
Supplies (SR)		$ 15,000		
Van rentals (T)			$ 28,000	
Equipment				$ 7,750
Printing and duplicating				$ 12,000
Travel				$ 10,000
Postage and shipping				$ 5,000
Food (CM)	$100,000			
Miscellaneous				$ 10,000
Column Totals	$200,000	$ 77,500	$103,000	$305,500
Allocate Indirect Costs	$101,833	$101,833	$101,834	
Total Program Costs	$301,833	$179,333	$204,834	

Table 9.12

Suggested Bases for the Direct Charging of Indirect Costs

Indirect Cost Item	*Allocation Base*
Accounting	Number of transactions processed for each program
Auditing	Hours worked on each program
Budgeting	Hours worked on each program
Data processing	Hours of computer system use by each program
Employees[a]	Hours worked on each program
Insurance	Square feet of office space occupied by each program
Janitorial	Square feet of office space occupied by each program
Legal	Hours worked for each program
Telephone	Number of telephones
Mail	Number of documents processes
Printing and reproduction	Number of jobs/number of pages
Utilities	Square feet of office space occupied by each program

a. Employees who work for more than one program—such as an agency executive director.

Which Cost Allocation Methodology Is Best?

There is no one best cost allocation methodology for a social service agency to use in allocating indirect costs. Each of the four methodologies presented is more appropriate in some situations and less appropriate in others.

For some social service agencies, a combination of direct costing and one of the other cost allocation methodologies may be more appropriate. With this "combination of methods," those items of indirect cost that *can* be logically and easily converted to a direct cost and directly assigned to the agency's various programs are so assigned. Those items of indirect cost that *cannot* be readily converted to direct costs are allocated to programs by one of the cost allocation methodologies. Another consideration in selecting a cost allocation method is the types of programs operated by the agency. Many social service programs are labor intensive: That is, salaries, wages, and ERE represent 60% or more of agency's expenses for a fiscal year. In such instances, cost allocation using direct labor costs or direct labor hours may be a more equitable approach, provided that all agency programs are similarly labor intensive. Yet another consideration is the preferences of funding sources. Some funding sources may prefer, or even require, the use of a particular cost allocation methodology.

The choice of the most appropriate cost allocation methodology for a social service agency to use is best left to the agency's accountants and auditors after consultation with major funding sources. Nevertheless, the guiding principle in selecting a cost allocation methodology should be to ensure that each program is allocated its fair share of agency indirect costs and that the total program cost figure represents as accurately as possible the real costs of providing agency programs.

Is Cost Allocation Worth the Effort?

Considering the complexity of cost allocation, the question is invariably raised: Is cost allocation really worth the effort? The answer is *yes!* Without resorting to cost allocation, a social service agency does not know the full costs of providing its various programs. In turn, an agency cannot develop accurate costs per unit of service (intermediate output), per quality output, or per service completion (final output). If a social service agency does not know the true unit costs of its various programs, it has no way of determining the service delivery implications of revenue increases or decreases. The knowledge of a program's true unit costs is also basic to the calculation of a break-even point. Likewise, the knowledge of a program's true unit costs is necessary for the setting of fees.

Frequently, government funding sources link contracts or grants to the provision of a specified number of units of service (intermediate outputs) or quality outputs. If a social service agency does not include indirect costs in the computation of its unit costs, then the agency is actually underpricing its services. A social service agency that consistently underprices its services may find itself committed to a contract or grant that actually causes it to lose money.

In summary:

- Functional and program budgeting systems both begin with a social service agency's line-item budget, but with a focus on expenses.
- Direct and indirect costs are then assigned and allocated respectively to programs.
- Direct costs are those items of cost that benefit only one program.
- Indirect costs are those items of cost that benefit two or more programs.
- Four cost allocation methodologies or bases are generally used by social service agencies: total direct costs, direct labor costs, direct labor hours, and direct costing (converting indirect costs to direct costs).

- Cost allocation is essential to the successful financial management of social service agencies and programs today.

FUNCTIONAL BUDGETING SYSTEMS

Determining a program's total costs, including both direct and indirect costs, completes the first six steps required to move from a line-item budgeting system to a functional and program budgeting system. Three additional steps are required to create a functional budgeting system: (a) selecting the program's output measures, (b) establishing the program's output objectives, and (c) computing the program's output costs.

Selecting the Program's Output Measures

A program has three potential output measures: a unit-of-service measure (intermediate output), a quality output measure, and a service completion measure (final output).

Selecting the Unit-of-Service
(Intermediate Output) Measure

The unit of service (intermediate output) serves as a measure of program volume. The concept of a unit of service was discussed in Chapter 7. A unit of service can be defined in terms of time, episode, or material. In defining a unit of service for a program, a social service agency needs to be conscious of the dual financial/programmatic nature of budgeting.

The selection of a unit of service for a program usually involves a trade-off between financial information and programmatic information. As an example, take the situation of a specialized transportation program. Several different units of service could be used, including vehicle miles, trips, and one-way trips. The selection of any one of these units of service constitutes a trade-off between financial considerations and programmatic considerations. Selecting vehicle miles as the unit of service might well be optimum from a financial perspective; this is a standard unit of measure in the transportation industry. Using vehicle miles as the unit of service would provide agency management with detailed cost information about the operation of the agency's vehicles. From a programmatic perspective, however, vehicle miles as a unit of service says absolutely nothing about how much specialized transportation service is being provided. It is often the rule that the more useful a unit of service is as a financial measure, the less useful it is as a programmatic measure, and vice versa.

In selecting a unit of service for a program, a social service agency should keep two points in mind. First, the unit of service serves as the measure by which the productivity (ratio of outputs to inputs) of a program is determined. Thus, the unit of service must say something about how much product or service the program provided (e.g., 100 placements; 1,000 one-way trips). Second, the principal use of functional budgeting systems is in the *management* of programs. Consequently, the unit of service selected should be the one that provides the most useful management information.

Returning to our ongoing senior center example, let us assume that agency management has established the following unit-of-service (intermediate output) measures for each of its three programs: for congregate meals, one meal; for socialization and recreation, 1 hour; and for transportation, one trip.

Selecting the Quality Output Measure

Selecting a quality output measure entails adding a quality dimension to the selected unit of service (intermediate output). Let us assume that agency management has established the following quality output measures for its three programs: for congregate meals, one meal that meets one third of the recommended daily allowance (RDA) of vitamins and minerals; for socialization and recreation, 1 hour when no scheduled activities were canceled; for transportation, one trip when the rider was picked up within 10 minutes of the scheduled pickup time.

Selecting the Service Completion (Final Output) Measure

A service completion (final output) is achieved when a client has completed treatment or received a full complement of services. The three programs provided by our senior center example are such that clients may enter the programs and continue in them for extended periods of time. In other words, there is no readily identifiable point at which one can say that a client has completed treatment or received a full complement of services. Consequently, let us assume that the senior center staff conduct a case plan review of all clients every 3 months to determine if clients still need to continue receiving services. Agency management and staff have determined the average amount of service that clients would receive each 3 months from each of the three programs and have decided to use these data to establish service completions. For the congregate meals program, a service completion is defined as receipt of at least 50 of the 60 meals provided each quarter. For the socialization and recreation program, a service completion is defined as participation in at least 250 hours of activities out of a possible 300 hours provided each quarter. And for the transportation program, a service completion is defined as receipt of a minimum of 100 one-way trips, which would ensure clients' participation in at least 50 meals and 250 hours of activities.

Selecting the Program's Output Objectives

A program has three potential output measures and consequently three potential output objectives. Let us assume that agency management has established the following output objectives for each of its programs for the fiscal year:

	Congregate Meals	*Socialization and Recreation*	*Transportation*
Unit-of-service (intermediate output) objectives	56,000 meals	2,200 hours of service	24,500 one-way trips
Quality objectives (error rate = 5%)	53,200 meals	2,090 hours of service	23,725 one-way trips
Service completions (125 clients each quarter)	500	500	500

Computing the Program's Unit Costs

Once a social service agency has determined output measures and output objectives for each of its programs, the final step in implementing a functional budgeting system is to compute each program's unit costs. Unit costs are computed by dividing the total cost of each program by the total number of outputs (intermediate, quality, and service completions) to be provided during the fiscal year. For example, if a specialized transportation program has a total proposed budget of $150,000 for the fiscal year, and agency management intends to provide 20,000 one-way trips, the unit cost will be $7.50. Some trips will be longer than others and will cost more; some trips will be shorter and cost less. The principle, however, is that the average figure of $7.50 is the single best cost statistic to use; the variations that will naturally occur on either the high or low side will cancel each other out. Once a social service agency has determined a unit cost for each of its programs, a functional budgeting system can be said to be in place: That is, all the information needed to determine the costs of various programmatic functions is now available.

To return to our ongoing senior center example, agency management, using each program's output measures, output objectives, and total cost, can compute (a) a cost per intermediate output, (b) a cost per quality output, and (c) a cost per service completion (see Table 9.13).

As Table 9.13 shows, the functional budget format identifies all three programs operated by the senior center and their unit costs per intermediate output, quality output, and service completion, together with their total program costs (from Table 9.11) and the total agency budget.

To summarize:

- Functional budgeting systems require the designation of output measures, the establishment of output objectives, and the computation of output costs.
- Unit costs are determined by dividing total program cost by total units (intermediate outputs, quality outputs, and service completions) to be provided.
- The output objectives and output costs determine the types of information that will be available to the management of a social service agency for purposes of monitoring and assessing program operations.

PROGRAM BUDGETING SYSTEMS

Once total program costs have been calculated, the final steps in implementing a program budgeting system are (a) selecting an outcome measure and (b) calculating the cost per outcome.

Selecting an Outcome Measure

By definition, each program operated by a social service agency should have a quantifiable outcome measure. For example, the outcome measure for an adoption program might be "one adoption." The adoption program might also have an outcome objective of achieving 25 adoptions during the fiscal year. It is important to differentiate here,

Table 9.13

Senior Center Functional Budgeting System Format

Intermediate Outputs (Units of Service)	
Congregate Meals Program	
Provide 56,000 meals @ a unit cost of $5.39	$301,833
Socialization and Recreation Program	
Provide 2,200 hours of service @ a unit cost of $81.51	$179,333
Transportation Program	
Provide 24,500 one-way trips @ a unit cost of $8.36	$204,834
Total Senior Center Budget	$686,000
Quality Outputs	
Congregate Meals Program	
Provide 53,200 quality meals @ a unit cost of $5.67	$301,833
Socialization and Recreation Program	
Provide 2,090 quality hours of service @ a unit cost of $85.80	$179,333
Transportation Program	
Provide 23,725 quality one-way trips @ a unit cost of $8.63	$204,834
Total Senior Center Budget	$686,000
Final Outputs (Service Completions)	
Congregate Meals Program	
Achieve 500 service completions @ a unit cost of $603.66	$301,833
Socialization and Recreation Program	
Achieve 500 service completions @ a unit cost of $358.66	$179,333
Transportation Program	
Achieve 500 service completions @ a unit cost of $409.66	$204,834
Total Senior Center Budget	$686,000

once again, between a program's results, accomplishments or impacts (outcomes) and its products and services (outputs). The unit of service (intermediate output) for an adoption program might be "one home study" (an episode unit). The unit of service (intermediate output) objective simply identifies the volume or amount of service the program plans to provide. It says nothing about what the accomplishments, results, or impact (outcomes) of service provision will be.

Returning once more to our ongoing senior center example, let us assume that the three programs have identified the following anticipated outcomes: (a) congregate meals, to maintain or improve the nutritional health of senior clients; (b) socialization and recreation, to maintain or improve the socialization of senior clients; and (c) transportation, to enable senior clients to access needed nutrition, socialization, recreation, health, and other social services.

Determining the Cost per Outcome

Let us assume that the management of the senior center has established the following outcome objectives for its three programs: (a) the congregate meals program, to maintain or improve the nutrition of 200 senior clients during the fiscal year; (b) the socialization and recreation program, to maintain or improve the social functioning of 200 senior clients during the fiscal year; and (c) the transportation program, to enable 200 senior clients to access needed nutrition, socialization, recreation, health, and other social services during the fiscal year. With this information and using the total program costs from Table 9.11, a program budget format can be developed for each of the three senior center programs.

A cost per outcome is determined by dividing total program cost by the total outcomes to be achieved. For example, the total cost of the congregate meals program from Table 9.11 is $301,833, and the total outcomes to be achieved are 200. Thus, the cost per outcome is approximately $1,509 ($301,833/200). As Table 9.14 demonstrates, a program budget format identifies all agency programs, the outcomes to be achieved by each program, the cost per outcome for each program, and the total agency budget.

The type of programmatic and financial data and information provided by program budgeting systems is extremely useful for planning purposes. By relating costs to planned results, accomplishment, or impacts (outcomes), a social service agency can determine how effective its various programs are. Hard data and information on program outcomes will also help to increase the credibility of a social service agency with its funding sources, advocacy groups, and clients.

In summary:

- Program budgeting systems require the determination of program outcome objectives and the computation of cost per outcome.

Table 9.14

Senior Center Program Budgeting System Format

Congregate Meals Program	
To maintain or improve the nutrition of 200 senior clients @ a cost per outcome of $1,509.00 and a total program cost of	$301,833
Socialization and Recreation Program	
To maintain or improve the social functioning of 200 senior clients @ a cost per outcome of $897.00 and a total program cost of	$179,333
Transportation Program	
To enable 200 senior clients to access needed nutrition, socialization, recreation, health, and other social services @ a cost per outcome of $1,024 and a total program cost of	$204,834
Total Senior Center Budget	$686,000

- When programs share an outcome objective, cost per outcome is computed by dividing the total program cost of all programs that contribute to the outcome by the number of planned outcomes.
- When programs have their own individual outcome objectives, cost per outcome is computed by dividing each program's total cost by the number of outcomes to be achieved.
- Program budgeting systems provides powerful data and information on the effectiveness of programs.

Readers who would like to practice the budgeting concepts covered in this chapter, including developing program budgets for programs with individual outcome objectives, may want to use the case example found in the appendix to this volume.

Chapter 10

BUDGETING FOR CONTROL, MANAGEMENT, AND PLANNING

The terms *accounting* and *budgeting* are unfortunately often used interchangeably, but budgeting and accounting are not the same thing. Accounting is a financial activity, whereas budgeting is both a programmatic and a financial activity. Accounting and accounting systems are retrospective: They are concerned with the past and present condition of a social service agency and its various programs. Budgeting systems and budget formats are prospective: They are concerned with the present and future condition of a social service agency and its various programs.

THE PRINCIPAL PURPOSES OF BUDGETING

The principal purposes of budgeting have long been acknowledged to be threefold: *control, management,* and *planning* (Schick, 1966). Seldom, however, does the budgeting system (or systems) of most social service agencies fulfill all three purposes. Even in those rare instances when all three purposes are included, the control purposes tend to overshadow the planning and management purposes. The tensions among the three principal purposes of budgeting are attributable to the dual financial/programmatic nature of budgeting. Only when a social service agency is consciously aware of this dual nature of budgeting are the planning, management, and control purposes all given relatively equal consideration in the design of a budgeting system.

For a social service agency to derive the maximum benefit from its budgeting system, the control, management, and planning purposes of budgeting should all be included and assigned relatively equal importance.

The Control Purposes

The control purposes of budgeting deal with ensuring that agency and program expenses do not exceed agency and program revenues and that both are properly accounted for and documented. The control purposes of budgeting come into play in the processes that management uses to bind an agency's organizational elements and staff to its goals and objectives. In an era of diminishing public and private support for social services, the maintenance of control over an agency's resources is essential. It is through the budgeting system and the budget that the resources of a social service agency are controlled. Resources are committed and spent only when they conform to the approved agency budget and when their expenditure works toward the accomplishment of the agency's plans, goals, and objectives.

The Management Purposes

The management purposes of budgeting deal with the procedures used to ensure that agency and program revenues are obtained and spent in an efficient manner to provide as much service as possible. The resources of a social service agency need to be managed to support its programs, services, and other activities. Consequently, the budget needs to be managed. All too often in a social service agency, once the budget is adopted it becomes "set in concrete." Changes become difficult, if not impossible, to make. Flexibility, rather than rigidity, should characterize a social service agency's budgeting system. Just as a social service agency may need to alter its plans from time to time due to some unforeseen event, the budget may also require alteration. Some programs may need to be expanded, others cut back. The ability of a social service agency to operate programs efficiently in a dynamic and constantly changing environment is highly dependent on how well the budget is managed.

Budgeting systems are an important source of management information that can provide feedback about how well the agency and its programs are operating. This information, in turn, can be used to ensure the optimum mix and use of staff, facilities, equipment, and other resources to maximize overall program efficiency or productivity.

The Planning Purposes

The planning purposes of budgeting deal with the determination of what revenues will be used to achieve what goals and objectives and the establishment of policies governing the acquisition and use of those revenues. In this context, a budgeting system is seen not as a stand-alone activity but rather as an integral component of a social service agency's planning system. For example, issues such as where additional revenues should be allocated or where funding reductions should be made are first and foremost planning issues. Consequently, the direction—or redirection—of resources should be decided on in accordance with a social service agency's priorities as articulated in its plans, goals, and objectives. To allocate resources otherwise can lead to situations where the agency's budgeting system actually hinders, rather than facilitates, the achievement of the agency's goals and objectives.

BUDGETING AND THE SYSTEMS FRAMEWORK

To better understand the importance of the control, management, and planning purposes of budgeting in a social service agency, reference is again made to the systems framework (see Figure 10.1). In the systems framework,

1. The *control* purposes of budgeting deal with the relationship between program revenues (inputs) from receipt until expenditure (throughputs) and answer the question, What is the financial condition of the agency and its programs?
2. The *management* purposes of budgeting deal with the relationship between program revenues (inputs) and program outputs, including products and services, as measured by units of service (intermediate outputs), quality outputs, and service completions, and answer the question, How efficient, or productive, is the agency and its programs?
3. The *planning* purposes of budgeting deal with the relationships between revenues (inputs) and the accomplishment of program outcomes and answer the question, How effective is the agency and its programs?

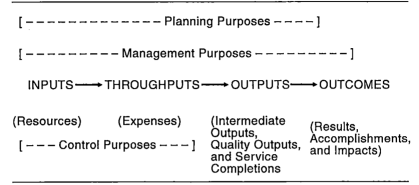

Figure 10.1. The Principal Purposes of Budgeting and the Systems Framework

Collectively, the three principal purposes of budgeting combine to provide a comprehensive picture of the functioning of a social service agency that none is capable of providing separately.

In summary:

- Budgeting and accounting are not the same thing.
- Budgeting has three principal purposes: control, management, and planning.
- The control functions of budgeting deal with keeping agency and program expenses (throughputs) in balance with agency and program revenues (inputs).
- The management purposes of budgeting deal with the utilization of revenues (inputs) to maximize agency and program efficiency or productivity (outputs).
- The planning purposes of budgeting deal with the utilization of revenues (inputs) to accomplish program outcomes.

MODELS OF THE BUDGETARY PROCESS

How do social service agencies and other types of organizations actually make budgeting decisions? Several models have been created in an attempt to describe what actually takes place during the budgetary process. The three major models of the budgetary process are the political model, the incremental model, and the rational planning model.

The *political model* views the budgetary process as primarily one of negotiation. According to the political model, budgeting decisions are seen as the end product of conflict and compromise between competing interests. In this model, a social service agency's program administrators and other employees, together with advocacy groups and clients, are seen as attempting to mobilize political pressure (both within and without the agency) to support their program and to ensure that it receives an equitable allocation of agency resources. Increases in resources are seen as going primarily to those agency programs with the most political support. Conversely, those agency programs with the least amount of political support are deemed more likely to experience resource decreases.

The *incremental model* views the budgetary process as being highly influenced by past budgeting decisions. In this model, a social service agency's programs are seen as being allocated a share of the agency resources based primarily on what each received in previous years with some sort of incremental or marginal increase or decrease. In this model, an agency's programs are all considered to have some merit or they would not have been previously funded.

The *rational planning model* views the budgetary process as a set of rational, logical steps leading to agency budgeting decisions based on needs, priorities, plans, goals, and objectives. Following this model, a social service agency goes through a planning process (such as the effectiveness-based program planning model) that includes a needs analysis, the establishment of agency goals and objectives, and the linking of agency resources to the agency's goals and objectives.

Social service agencies that pursue the political or incremental models of budgeting tend to use budgeting systems that focus on revenues (inputs) and expenditures (throughputs), such as line-item budgeting systems. These agencies seldom gather, analyze, and present budgetary data and information dealing with agency products or services (outputs) or the accomplishment of agency goals and objectives. A budgeting system concerned only with revenues and expenditures seldom challenges the organizational decision-making status quo. Questions about the efficiency or productivity (outputs) and effectiveness (outcomes) of programs—questions that might upset the decision-making status quo—are usually not raised, or if raised, are not answered, because the budgetary information needed to answer the questions is simply not available.

From a social service perspective, the major criticism of both the political and incremental models of the budgetary process is that the various needs of an agency's clients are not considered during the budgetary process. The only factors that really matter are the amount of political pressure that can be mobilized (the political model) or what happened last year or the year before (the incremental model). From a social service perspective, there is frequently an inverse relationship between need and political power and between need and previous funding levels. Client groups with the least political power, such as the homeless, children, and the chronically mentally ill, are frequently the ones most in need. In the same vein, if a social problem, such as the social service needs of HIV/AIDS clients, has only recently been recognized, it has little or no funding history, an essential requirement of the incremental model.

The rational planning model is not without its drawbacks. Critics of the rational planning model point out that implementing this model is time consuming and spends resources that otherwise could be directed toward client services. These critics also argue that in the end, budgeting decisions still wind up being heavily influenced by political and incremental considerations. Information and analysis, these critics argue, is seldom used by decision makers except when it happens to coincide with their own preconceived ideas.

A social service agency concerned about the needs of clients would probably not want to make budgeting decisions based primarily on politics or incrementalism but would instead want to be guided by rational planning. In pursuing the rational planning model, however, there is no guarantee that politics and incrementalism will still not play a major role in shaping a social service agency's budgeting decisions. Nevertheless, when the rational planning model is pursued, the level of budgetary debate is raised. If the level of debate is not raised, and if an alternative decision-making framework is not provided, then the political and incremental approaches to the budgetary process win by default.

A social service agency desiring to pursue the rational planning model of the budgetary process cannot rely solely on a budgeting system that generates, analyzes, and presents budgetary information only on revenues (inputs) and expenditures (throughputs). The level of debate must be raised to at least the level of agency products and services (outputs) and preferably to the level of the accomplishment of agency goals and objectives (outcomes). An additional consideration today is that performance accountability systems such as the Government Performance and Results Act and the Service Efforts and Accomplishments (SEA) reporting initiative of the Governmental Accounting Standards Board necessitate a focus on outputs and outcomes in addition to quality.

BUDGET REDUCTIONS AND INCREASES

Funding reductions are an everyday fact of life for many social service agencies today. Revenue shortfalls force social service agencies to reduce expenses. When it comes to dealing with budget reductions, line-item budgets systems by themselves are inadequate to the task.

A social service agency that uses only a line-item budgeting system cannot inform decision makers, board members, elected officials, advocacy groups, clients, and other stakeholders about the actual effects of funding decreases—or increases, for that matter. The only information that a line-item budgeting system provides is the effects of budget decreases, or increases, on the numbers of program and agency staff; their salaries, wages, and employee-related expenses; travel; equipment; supplies; and so forth. Line-item budgeting systems provide no information at all about the effects of budget decreases, or increases, on the outputs (intermediate, quality, and service completions) that an agency and its programs will be able to provide, or, even more important, the effects on an agency's ability to accomplish its outcomes. To know the effects of budget decreases, or increases, on the outputs of an agency and its programs, one must have a functional budgeting system in place. To know the effects of budget decreases, or increases, on the ability of an agency and its programs to achieve their outcomes, one must have a program budgeting system in place.

Suppose that a social service agency operating a child day care services program is faced with the task of decreasing its budget by $50,000. Table 10.1 illustrates the program effects of this reduction based on the information available from different budgeting systems.

As Table 10.1 points out, if the social service agency uses only a line-item budget system, the effects of a budget reduction can be assessed only in terms of decreases in staffing, staff costs, and other budget line-items. In the case of the child day care program, the infor-

Table 10.1

Budgeting Systems and Budget Reductions

Issue: the implications of a $50,000 budget reduction on a child day care program.

Line-item budgeting system	Reduce the number of child day care staff by 3.
Functional budgeting system	Reduce the number of child care days of service by 4,000.
Program budgeting system	Reduce the number of children provided with a safe and educational day care experience by 50.

---

mation that a line-item budgeting system can provide is that the $50,000 budget reduction will result in three child day care workers being laid off. However, if a functional budgeting system is in place, the child day care staff will be able to point out that a $50,000 budget cutback translates into a reduction of some 4,000 fewer child care days of service. Better still, if a program budgeting system is in place, agency staff can point out that a $50,000 budget cutback means that 50 fewer children will be provided a safe and educational day care experience.

From both an administration perspective and an advocacy perspective, the type of information provided by functional and program budgeting systems is clearly superior to that provided by line-item budgeting systems. Knowledge of the real implications for service delivery and for clients of budget reductions enables staff of social service agencies to begin planning for an orderly reduction in services and clients. For example, intake might be closed so that no new children are accepted. In terms of advocacy, information about the service delivery and client effects of budget reductions can be used by the staff of social service agencies to inform and educate advocacy groups, clients, and, in particular, decision makers. All too frequently, decision makers really do not know the actual implications of their budgeting decision.

To summarize:

- There are three models of the budgetary process: the political model, the incremental model, and the rational planning model.
- The political model of budgeting is influenced by power and strength, the incremental model by history, and the rational planning model by data and information.

- Line-item budgeting systems are inadequate to deal with budget decreases, or increases, because they do not provide information about the effects on agency and program service delivery and clients.
- Functional budgeting systems are needed to provide data and information about the effects of budget increases or decreases on service delivery and program budgeting systems and on program outcomes.

BUDGETING IN SOCIAL
SERVICE AGENCIES TODAY

Most social service agencies today use, at a minimum, a line-item budgeting system. Many have gone beyond line-item budgeting systems and also use functional budgeting systems, program budgeting systems, or both. Because these different budgeting systems provide different perspectives on the operations of a social service agency, it is not unusual to find one or more operating simultaneously in a social service agency. Recent research (Martin, 1997) suggests that social service agencies are moving away from exclusive reliance on line-item budgeting systems and are increasingly making use of functional and program budgeting systems.

Major sources of revenue for social service agencies today include government contracts and grants, the United Way, and private foundations. To make rational budgeting decisions concerning the awarding of contracts and grants to competing social service agencies and programs, government, the United Way, and private foundations frequently make comparisons between agency and program requests. For valid comparisons to be made, a complete financial picture of each competing agency and program must be presented, using a standardized budget format and common budget categories and definitions. At a minimum today, most funding sources generally require the submission of a line-item budget to support a request for funding. Frequently, funding sources have their own standardized line-item budget formats that applicants are required to use.

Because of the performance measurement movement, many government funding sources today also require their contractors and grantees to report programmatic data and information on program efficiency (outputs), quality, and effectiveness (outcomes), as well as financial data such as cost per output and cost per outcome. The only way that social service agencies can satisfy these reporting requirements is to have in place both a functional budgeting system and a program budgeting system.

To summarize:

- Government funding sources, as well as the United Way and some private foundations, frequently have standardized line-item budget formats that their contractors and grantees are required to utilize.
- Many government funding sources also require reporting on program outputs and outcomes and cost per output and cost per outcome. To provide these data, social service agencies must have in place both a functional budgeting system and a program budgeting system.

WHICH BUDGETING SYSTEM IS BEST?

In terms of the principal purposes of budgeting—control, management, and planning—it should be apparent at this point that no one budgeting system is optimum for all three purposes. To ensure that the control, management, and planning purposes of budgeting are all adequately addressed in a social service agency, the best solution is to have in place not only a line-item budgeting system but both functional and program budgeting systems as well.

It is really only convention that separates line-item, program, and functional budgeting systems. These three budgeting systems can just as easily be seen as components of one comprehensive budgeting system, with the parts building on and complementing one another. Program and functional budgeting systems both build on line-item budgeting. Extending a line-item budget system to incorporate the concepts needed for functional and program budgeting is well worth the effort and supports the effectiveness-based program planning model presented in this book.

In the next chapter, we conclude our presentation of effectiveness-based program planning by discussing performance measurement monitoring and program evaluation.

Chapter 11

PERFORMANCE MEASUREMENT, MONITORING, AND PROGRAM EVALUATION

Although the topics of performance measurement, monitoring, and program evaluation come at the end of this book, they are an integral part of effectiveness-based program planning. The material presented in the preceding chapters (including the discussion of needs assessment, planning, the establishment of goals and objectives, program design, budgeting, and management information) can all be seen as laying the groundwork for a discussion of performance measurement, monitoring, and program evaluation. Through the use of these assessment tools, social service agencies can determine if their programs are working as intended or are in need of refinement. In this chapter, we explore the use of performance measurement, monitoring, and program evaluation to assess the implementation, performance, results, and impacts of programs.

Historically, many social service agencies waited until a program had been in existence for some time before thinking about performance measurement, monitoring, and program evaluation. This approach virtually ensured that the data needed to assess the implementation, performance, results, and impacts of programs were not available when needed. Today, social service agencies realize that they must identify *up front,* at the beginning of a program, the type of performance measurement, monitoring, and program evaluation data and information that will be needed to conduct these assessments. In other words, thinking

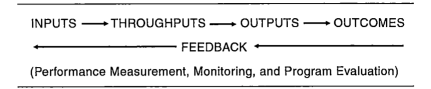

Figure 11.1. Feedback and Self-Learning Systems

about how programs will be assessed is an integral part of the planning process.

FEEDBACK AND SELF-LEARNING SYSTEMS

Throughout this book, we have used the systems framework as a model for thinking about effectiveness-based program planning. We return to it once more to assist us in thinking about performance measurement, monitoring, and program evaluation.

Self-learning systems, sometimes referred to as *heuristic systems,* learn by doing. Self-learning systems take data and information (*feedback*) about their operations, analyze it, and then use it to make adjustments in the way they function.

For example, a thermostat is a self-learning system. A thermostat monitors the temperature of a room and adjusts the air conditioning as needed to maintain a comfortable environment. If we think of a program as a self-learning system (see Figure 11.1), performance measurement, monitoring, and program evaluation provide feedback about the operations and functioning of a program. This feedback becomes new *input* into a program and can lead to changes, refinements, and improvements in how the program is designed and implemented.

PERFORMANCE MEASUREMENT

Performance measurement can be defined as the assessment of the efficiency, quality, and effectiveness of programs (Martin & Kettner, 1996). Performance measurement provides feedback on how well a program is performing in terms of outputs, quality outputs, outcomes, cost-efficiency, and cost-effectiveness.

Table 11.1

A Comparison of Performance Measurement,
Monitoring, and Program Evaluation

	Performance Measurement	*Monitoring*	*Program Evaluation*
Unit of analysis	Program	Program	Program
Primary purpose(s)	External reporting	Program management	Program and policy improvement
Perspective(s)	Financial/ managerial	Managerial	Policy/planning
Use of data	Feedback on program performance to external stakeholders	Feedback on program operations to agency managers	Feedback on program results (outcomes) and impacts to policymakers and planners

As Table 11.1 indicates, the principal purpose of performance measurement is external reporting. In terms of perspective, performance measurement has both a financial and a managerial orientation, but with emphasis on the financial, owing to its roots in accounting and performance auditing. The central idea behind what can be called the performance measurement movement is to have all government agencies and programs, including social service agencies and programs, collect and report feedback data and information on the efficiency, quality, and effectiveness of their programs to external stakeholders (i.e., funding sources, advocacy groups, citizens, clients, and others). A goal of the performance measurement movement is to make external stakeholders more knowledgeable about how government programs operate and how they help to improve the lives of citizens and clients. The hope is that increased understanding of government programs, and in particular social service programs, will lead to an increase in political support for their continuation and expansion.

More specifically, performance measurement is concerned with providing answers to such questions as these: How much product or service (intermediate outputs) did the program provide, and with what quality (quality outputs)? How many clients completed treatment or received a full complement of services (service completions)? What intermediate and final outcomes did the program achieve? And how cost-efficient and cost-effective is the program?

Performance measurement has become increasingly important in recent years. The provisions of the Government Performance and Results Act (GPRA) of 1993 (Pub. L. No. 103-62) require all federal agencies to collect and report performance measurement data and information about their various programs. The Governmental Accounting Standards Board (GASB), the organization that establishes what are called "generally accepted accounting principles" for state and local governments, wants these same governments to also report performance measurement data.

Due to the influence of GPRA and GASB, numerous state, city, and county governments already require, or are in the process of requiring, their various agencies and programs to collect and report performance measurement data. For example, at least 30 states today have legislation requiring state agencies and programs to report at least some types of performance measurement data and information (Melkers & Willoughby, 1998). Because government-funded social service programs are frequently provided under contracts and grants, many private non-profit agencies are also being required to collect and report performance measurement data and information (Martin, in press; Martin & Kettner, 1996).

It should be noted that performance measurement is concerned only with the collection and reporting of performance data and information. Performance measurement does not concern itself with such questions as: Was the program implemented as planned? Did the program achieve its intended results? And what was the program's impact? For feedback that addresses questions such as these, social service agencies must turn to monitoring and program evaluation.

MONITORING

Monitoring can be defined as an assessment of the extent to which a program is implemented as designed and serves its intended target group (Rossi & Freeman, 1993). Some program evaluation texts refer to monitoring as "formative evaluation" because it takes place during program implementation.

The word *monitoring* comes from the Latin *monere*, meaning "to warn." Monitoring can be compared to the navigation system on a commercial aircraft. When an airliner starts to stray off course, an alarm sounds in the cockpit, alerting the pilot, who then takes corrective action to return the plane to its proper course reading. In the same vein, monitoring feedback warns a social service administrator when the implementation of a program starts to deviate from its original design. The administrator can then take corrective action to bring the program back into line with its design.

The principal purpose (see Table 11.1) of monitoring is program management; consequently, monitoring has a managerial perspective. Monitoring provides social service administrators with feedback on the current status of a program in terms of such questions as these: Is the program being implemented as designed? What proportion of the community need is the program meeting? Are only eligible target group clients being served? Are subgeographical areas and subgroups (e.g., ethnic minorities, women, persons with disabilities, and others) being served in appropriate numbers? What products and services are being provided and in what amounts? And what results are being achieved in terms of outputs and outcomes? In terms of assessing program outputs and outcomes, monitoring and performance measurement overlap somewhat. Performance measurement and monitoring are both concerned with outputs, outcomes, and issues of cost-efficiency and cost-effectiveness. The difference between the two is that performance measurement is concerned with the reporting of feedback data and information to external stakeholders, whereas monitoring is concerned with using the feedback data and information to track the implementation of programs and to make changes and refinements as needed.

Monitoring also lays the groundwork for program evaluation by helping to ensure that a program is implemented as intended. No useful purpose is served in conducting a program evaluation if a program is not implemented as intended.

PROGRAM EVALUATION

Program evaluation can be defined as an assessment of the extent to which a program accomplishes its intended results (outcomes) and achieves measurable impacts (Fink, 1993; Mohr, 1992). *Impact* means an assessment of the outcomes achieved by a program that would not otherwise have occurred (Mohr, 1992). The assessment of program impact involves establishing cause-and-effect relationships: The program (the cause), and no other external factors, accounts for the achievement of the program outcomes (the effect). Because cause-and-effect relationships are difficult to establish, the assessment of program impact usually involves the use of social science research techniques and the application of statistics.

The primary purpose of program evaluation (see Table 11.1) is to provide feedback on program results (outcomes) and program impacts to inform policymakers and planners about the efficacy of programs and the appropriateness of the social intervention hypotheses that underline them. Program evaluation addresses such questions as: Did the program work as intended? What results (outcomes) did the program accomplish? What measurable impacts did the program achieve? And is the program cost-effective? Program evaluation can also lead to the discovery of positive as well as negative "unintended consequences" of social interventions (programs), thereby suggesting needed changes and refinements in social policy or program design.

In terms of the assessment of results (outcomes), program evaluation overlaps somewhat with both performance measurement and monitoring. The difference is that program evaluation is not concerned with the reporting of results data and information to external stakeholders (performance measurement) or with tracking a program's success in accomplishing results and impacts during implementation (monitoring) but, rather, is concerned with using program results and impact feedback data and information to improve policy and planning. Program evaluation also overlaps with monitoring in that both are concerned with ensuring that a program is implemented as intended. The difference is that monitoring assesses a program during implementation, whereas program evaluation makes the assessment after the fact.

PROGRAM IMPACT EVALUATION
AND HYPOTHESIS TESTING

The evaluation of program impact can produce one of three results, all of which are related to the intervention hypothesis that underpins a program (see Figure 11.2). In Chapter 5, we discussed program planning as a hypothesis-generating activity and program evaluation as a hypothesis-testing activity. A program hypothesis:

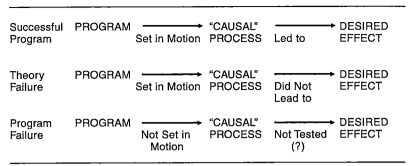

Figure 11.2. The Relationship Between Programs and Desired Effects

- Makes explicit the assumptions about program expectations.
- Establishes a framework to bring internal consistency to a program.
- Enables inputs, throughputs, outputs, and outcomes to be examined for internal consistency.

Program evaluation as a test of a hypothesis is concerned with determining and documenting the extent to which a program achieves its intended results (outcomes). For example, in Chapter 7 we offered a fairly detailed hypothesis related to single adolescent mothers and the goal of self-sufficiency. In essence, we argued that single adolescent mothers form a high-risk group (e.g., many drop out of school, become welfare dependent, and abuse their children). The suggestion was made that *if* we could identify the major problems/barriers (hypothesis) to single adolescent mothers becoming more self-sufficient and *if* we could successfully eliminate those barriers, *then* we would see positive changes leading to an increase in self-sufficiency. Now let us look at each of the three tracks depicted in Figure 11.2.

The first track, labeled "successful program," depicts an ideal situation. The hypothesis is that *if* child day care services and job training services are provided, *then* single adolescent mothers can get jobs and thereby become more self-sufficient. The program is implemented as designed (child day care and job training services are provided), and the desired results or outcomes are achieved (single adolescent mothers get jobs and become more self-sufficient). Given this finding, we conclude that the hypothesis is supported or validated. But programs can also fail to achieve their desired results (outcomes) due to flaws in either the theory or the program.

The second track in Figure 11.2, labeled "theory failure," describes a situation in which the program is implemented as designed but the anticipated results (outcomes) are not achieved. *Theory failure* refers to a flaw in the intervention hypothesis underlying the program: namely, that certain causal processes will lead directly to the desired results (outcomes). The hypothesis is the same: *If* child day care services and job training services are provided, *then* single adolescent mothers can get jobs and become more self-sufficient. The program is implemented as designed (child day care services and job training services are provided), but few single adolescent mothers get jobs and become more self-sufficient. Given this finding, we conclude that the hypothesis is not supported or validated.

The third track, labeled "program failure," describes a situation where the program is not implemented as designed. In such a case, we can say nothing about the achievement of program results (outcomes). Program results (outcomes) may or may not be achieved, but neither success nor failure can be attributed to the program. For example, the hypothesis is the same: *If* child day care services and job training services are provided, *then* single adolescent mothers can get jobs and become more self-sufficient. But let us say that due to funding reductions only job training services are provided; no child day care services are provided. The program hypothesis may or may not be correct; we will never know because it was not tested. Failure in this case is attributable not to flaws in theory but to deficiencies in program implementation.

To summarize:

- Performance measurement, monitoring, and program evaluation are three major approaches to assessing the implementation, performance, results, and impacts of programs.
- The data and information generated by performance measurement, monitoring, and program evaluation constitute feedback that can be used to improve programs.
- Performance measurement is principally concerned with using feedback on program efficiency, quality, and effectiveness for external reporting purposes.
- Monitoring is principally concerned with using feedback during program implementation for managerial purposes, including (a) ensuring that programs are delivered as intended and (b) assessing program efficiency, quality, effectiveness, cost-efficiency, and cost-effectiveness.

- Program evaluation is principally concerned with using feedback for policy and planning purposes, including the assessment of program results (outcomes) and the determination and measurement of program impact.

PROGRAM DATA REQUIREMENTS

At this point, the reader has probably already concluded that performance measurement, monitoring, and program evaluation are all important and necessary component parts of what might be called *program assessment*. With the availability of computer hardware and management information system (MIS) software, social service agencies only need ensure that they are collecting the necessary assessment data, and they should be able to report performance measurement data and information to external stakeholders, perform ongoing program monitoring, and conduct program evaluations.

The types of program data that social service agencies need to collect to satisfy the requirements of performance measurement, monitoring, and program evaluation include (a) coverage, (b) equity, (c) process, (d) effort, (e) cost-efficiency, (f) results, (g) cost-effectiveness, and (h) impact. These eight types do not constitute the entire universe of program data, but they are the ones that performance measurement, monitoring, and program evaluation are generally most concerned with. Each of these eight data types is discussed below, including the types of assessment questions the data are used to address (see Table 11.2).

Coverage Data

Coverage data provide feedback on the extent to which a program is (a) meeting the community need and (b) reaching its target population. Monitored during program implementation, coverage data can be used not only to determine the extent to which the target group is being reached but also to ensure that individuals ineligible for the program are not served. Conducted at the end of a program, or at some defined end point (e.g., the end of the fiscal year), coverage data can be used in a program evaluation mode to document that only eligible clients were served and to assess the adequacy, or inadequacy, of current program funding and service levels to meet the community need.

Table 11.2

Types of Program Data and Related Assessment Questions

Type of Program Data	Related Assessment Questions
Coverage	To what extent is the program meeting the community need?
Equity	To what extent is the program adequately serving subgeographical areas and subgroups (ethnic minorities, women, persons with disabilities, etc.)?
Process	To what extent is the program being implemented as intended in terms of a. Service definitions? b. Service tasks? c. Standards? d. Other service delivery requirements?
Effort (output)	To what extent is the program producing a. Products and services (intermediate outputs)? b. Quality products and services (quality outputs)? c. Service completions (final outputs)?
Cost-Efficiency	What is the a. Cost per intermediate output? b. Cost per quality output? c. Cost per service completion?
Results (outcome)	To what extent is the program achieving a. Intermediate outcomes? b. Final outcomes?
Cost-Effectiveness	What is the a. Cost per intermediate outcome? b. Cost per final outcome?
Impact	To what extent is the program achieving a measurable impact?

Equity Data

Equity data provide feedback on the extent to which specific sub-geographical areas of a community as well as specific subgroups (such as ethnic minorities, women, persons with disabilities, children, or the elderly) are being served by a program. Unless a program is targeted at a specific subgeographical area or specific subgroup of a community, all other things being equal, geographical subareas and subgroups should be served by a program in roughly the same proportion as their composition in the community. Equity data can be used to ensure adequate coverage of subgeographical areas and subgroups during implementation (monitoring) or at the end of a program (program evaluation) to document that a program is or is not reaching some geographical subarea or subgroup.

Process Data

Process data provide feedback on the extent to which a program is implemented as designed. During implementation (monitoring), process data can be used to compare actual service delivery to planned service design to ensure conformance with such items as service definitions, service tasks, service standards, work statements, service specifications, and other service requirements. At the end of a program, process data can be used to determine and document (program evaluation) that a program was implemented as intended.

Effort (Output) Data

Effort (output) data provide feedback on the amount of program: products and services (intermediate outputs) provided, the amount of quality products and services (quality outputs) provided, and the number of service completions (final outputs) achieved. Effort (output) data can be monitored during implementation to compare actual effort to planned effort and to take corrective action when actual effort fails to coincide with planned effort. Effort (output) data can be used at the end of a program year to document service delivery levels (program evaluation) and for purposes of performance measurement reporting. Effort (output) data are also used in determining a program's cost-efficiency.

Cost-Efficiency Data

Cost-efficiency data provide feedback on the costs of providing program products and services, including intermediate outputs, quality outputs, and final outputs (service completions). Cost-efficiency data are developed by computing costs per output: intermediate, quality, and final. During implementation, actual cost data can be compared with planned costs (monitoring). At the end of a program year, cost-efficiency data can be used to assess a program's productivity and are also required for purposes of performance measurement reporting.

Results (Outcome) Data

Results (outcome) data provide feedback on the extent to which a program achieves its intended results (outcomes), both intermediate and final. Results (outcome) data can be monitored during implementation to compare actual results (outcomes) achieved with planned results (outcomes). Used at the end of a program year, results (outcome) data document for policy and planning purposes the results (outcomes) achieved by a program. Results (outcome) data are also required for purposes of performance measurement reporting. Finally, results (outcome) data are used in determining a program's cost-effectiveness.

Cost-Effectiveness Data

Cost-effectiveness data provide feedback on the costs of achieving program results (outcomes), both intermediate and final. Cost-effectiveness data are developed by computing cost per intermediate outcome and cost per final outcome. Cost-effectiveness data are usually available only at the end of the program year (program evaluation) and are used to document the costs of achieving results (outcomes) for policy and planning purposes and for purposes of performance measurement reporting.

Impact Data

Impact data provide feedback on the most difficult assessment question of all: What happened to clients as a result of participation in a program that would not have happened in the program's absence? To address this question, impact data are usually generated using social science research techniques, including the creation of a control group for comparison purposes and the use of statistics to measure the magnitude of the impact. The development of impact data is a difficult undertaking. Nevertheless, limitations on program and agency resources make it imperative that available resources be put to the best use possible. Impact data can provide social service administrators with hard social science-based information that demonstrates the extent to which a program achieves measurable impacts with its clients.

Table 11.3

Performance Measurement, Monitoring,
Program Evaluation, and Type of Program Data

Type of Assessment Data	Performance Measurement	Monitoring	Program Evaluation
Coverage		X	X
Equity		X	X
Process		X	X
Effort	X	X	
Cost-Efficiency	X	X	
Results	X	X	X
Cost-Effectiveness	X		X
Impact			X

PERFORMANCE MEASUREMENT, MONITORING, PROGRAM EVALUATION, AND PROGRAM DATA

As Table 11.3 shows, performance measurement, monitoring, and program evaluation overlap in terms of their use of program data. In particular, considerable program data overlap exists between monitoring and program evaluation, and performance measurement overlaps somewhat with both monitoring and program evaluation.

The overlap in terms of types of program data leads to an important observation: To a great extent, the differences between performance measurement, monitoring, and program evaluation are not so much differences in the types of program data used as differences in when and how program data are used. Performance measurement uses program data for *external reporting purposes.* Monitoring uses program data during implementation for *management purposes.* Program evaluation uses program data after implementation for *policy and planning purposes.* The Palmdale Job Training Center case study demonstrates these points.

A CASE STUDY OF A JOB TRAINING PROGRAM

Let us assume that you are the executive director of the Palmdale Job Training Program. The program provides job training services to unem-

Table 11.4
The Palmdale Job Training Program Objectives
for Program (Fiscal) Year 20XX

Coverage Objective 1	To serve at least 1,000 clients and meet at least 10% of the community need during program year 20XX.
Coverage Objective 2	To ensure that 100% of all 1,000 clients served meet all U.S. Department of Labor eligibility criteria for participation in Joint Training˙ Partnership Act (JTPA) funded job training.
Equity Objective 1	To serve a minimum of 300 clients (30%) who are Hispanic or African American.
Equity Objective 2	To ensure that no more than 600 clients (60%) come from either of the agency's two geographical service areas.
Process Objective 1	To ensure that each of the four 12-week training programs is delivered in accordance with the City of Palmdale's contract work statement, including service definitions, service tasks, standards, instructor qualifications and certifications, and total number of classroom instruction hours.
Effort Objective 1	To provide a minimum of 30,000 hours of classroom instruction (intermediate output). Definition: one client attending training for 1 hour.
Effort Objective 2	To provide a minimum of 28,800 quality hours of classroom instruction (conducted with planned instructor), with an error rate of no more than 5.0%.
Effort Objective 3	To ensure that at least 870 clients (87%) complete the program (service completions).
Cost-Efficiency Objective 1	To achieve a unit cost per intermediate output of no more than $300.
Cost-Efficiency Objective 2	To achieve a unit cost per quality output of no more than $312.
Cost-Efficiency Objective 3	To achieve a unit cost per final output (service completion) of no more than $10,345.
Results (Outcome) Objective 1	To place a minimum of 750 graduates in unsubsidized jobs paying at least 115% of the minimum wage (intermediate outcome).

Table 11.4

Continued

Results (Outcome) Objective 2	To have a minimum of 650 graduates working in unsubsidized jobs paying at least 115% of the minimum wage for at least 6 months following completion of the program (final outcome).
Cost-Effectiveness Objective 1	To achieve a unit cost per intermediate outcome of not more than $12,000.
Cost-Effectiveness Objective 2	To achieve a unit cost per final outcome of not more than $13,800.

ployed and underemployed adults and youth. The program's annual operating budget (line-item budget) is $9 million. Let us further assume that you are involved in implementing effectiveness-based program planning as outlined in the previous chapters of this book. By combining what you have learned about establishing goals and objectives and creating functional and program budgeting systems, you created a program plan at the beginning of the fiscal year (January 1) that includes the measurable objectives identified in Table 11.4. You also took steps to ensure that the program's MIS would collect these data.

The program objectives identified in Table 11.4 cover all eight types of program data. For example, the program has a coverage objective of serving 1,000 clients, which represents 10% of the community need. The program also has equity, process, effort (output), cost-efficiency, results (outcomes), and cost-effectiveness objectives. The only type of program data missing is impact data. More will be said about impact data and the assessment of program impact following this case study.

By collecting the program data identified in Table 11.4 as part of your agency's MIS, you anticipate collecting all the requisite data needed during the program (fiscal) year to report performance measurement data, conduct ongoing monitoring, and perform program evaluations. Let us now assume that it is April 1 and you have just received the monthly MIS report for March (see Table 11.5). The monthly MIS report includes the annual objectives, monthly data for the last 3 months (January, February, and March), and year-to-date totals.

As you review the March MIS report, you are *engaging in monitoring*. You are comparing actual program data to planned program data (objectives) to determine if any corrective action needs to be taken. You

Table 11.5

April MIS Program Data Report

Program Data	January Results	February Results	March Results	Year-to-Date Totals	Annual Objective	% of Objective
Clients served (no.)	75	110	125	310	1,000	31
Eligibility (%)	100	100	100	100	100	100
Need (%)	.8	1.0	1.3	1.3	10	13
Minority clients (%)	25	27	30	27	30	90
Clients from Service Area 1 (%)	45	52	60	53	55	53
Implementation (yes/no)	Yes	Yes	Yes	Yes	Yes	Yes
Training hours (no.)	2,300	2,400	2,600	7,300	30,000	24
Quality training hours (no.)	2,300	2,300	2,400	7,000	28,800	24
Service completions (no.)	0	0	75	75	870	9
Job placements (no.) (intermediate outcome)	0	0	50	50	750	7
Job placements (no.) long term (6 months) (final outcome)	0	0	0	0	650	0

	January Results	February Results	March Results	Year-to-Date Totals	Annual Objective	Variance (+ or −)
Cost ($) per unit of service (intermediate output)	315	310	305	310	312	−
Cost ($) per quality unit of service (quality output)	318	315	315	316	312	+
Cost ($) per service completion				11,000	11,000	0
Cost ($) per placement			18,000	18,000	12,000	+
Cost ($) per long-term placement	0	0	0	0	13,800	0

conclude that after 3 months of operations the program is in "good shape." No implementation problems have arisen, and actual program data are in keeping with the annual objectives. You make this determination by noting that after 3 months of operations, the program should have accomplished about one fourth of its objectives—which it has, with the exception of final outputs (service completions), intermediate outcomes, final outcomes, and their cost-related objectives. The job training program takes 12 weeks to complete, so clients from the first class are just now (March/April) graduating (final outputs) and finding jobs (intermediate outcomes). You also note that most of the program data (with the exception of outcomes) is trending upwards, which is a good sign, and that cost-efficiency and cost-effectiveness data are again in keeping with annual objectives, except for intermediate and final outcomes. Your conclusion (that the program is operating smoothly) is based on monitoring program data and is not just a "gut feeling."

Now let us jump ahead to early January of the next program (fiscal) year. You have just received the December MIS report, which is also the end-of-the-year MIS report. As you review the MIS report (see Table 11.6) for the previous year, you note that the program accomplished or exceeded its objectives in some instances (clients served, service completions, and job placements) but fell somewhat short in other instances (need, minority clients, quality hours, long-term placements, cost per service completion, and cost per long-term placement). Your overall assessment is that the program was quite "successful" but that you definitely need to make some policy and planning changes. For example, more client outreach is needed to recruit more ethnic minorities to the program. You are *engaging in program evaluation.*

Now you take the data from the end-of-the-year MIS report and begin developing the program's annual performance measurement report (see Table 11.7). You are *engaging in performance measurement.* In preparing the annual performance measurement report, you try to avoid using terms such as *intermediate outputs* and *final outcomes* that external stakeholders might not understand. Instead, you use terms that will be more meaningful to the average person: *Final outputs* become "clients graduating from the program" and *intermediate outcomes* become "graduates hired."

IMPACT PERFORMANCE EVALUATIONS

Now let us return to the discussion of impact data and impact program evaluation that we placed on hold while we reviewed the Palmdale Job Training Program case study. The essence of impact

Table 11.6
End-of-Year MIS Program Data Report

Program Data	October Results	November Results	December Results	Year-to-Date Totals	Annual Objective	% of Objective
Clients served (no.)	125	125	125	1,050	1,000	105
Eligibility (%)	100	100	100	100	100	100
Need (%)	9.2	9.4	9.6	9.6	10	96
Minority clients (%)	25	25	25	25	30	83
Clients from Service Area 1 (%)	45	55	50	53	55	100
Implementation (yes/no)	Yes	Yes	Yes	Yes	Yes	Yes
Training hours (no.)	2,500	2,500	2,500	30,000	30,000	100
Quality training hours (no.)	2,300	2,400	2,300	28,000	28,800	97
Service completions (no.)	75	85	80	880	870	101
Job placements (no.) (intermediate outcome)	50	45	55	755	750	101
Job placements (no.) long term (6 months) (final outcome)	500	550	625	625	650	96

						Variance (+ or −)
Cost ($) per unit of service (intermediate output)	305	302	300	300	300	0
Cost ($) per quality unit of service (quality output)	312	312	312	312	312	0
Cost ($) per service completion	12,000	11,500	11,200	11,200	11,000	−
Cost ($) per placement	12,800	12,500	12,000	12,000	12,000	0
Cost ($) per long-term placement	14,500	14,300	14,000	14,000	13,800	+

program evaluation is comparison. What is is compared with what was or probably would have been in the absence of a particular program. Typically, comparisons are based on observations of different groups at

Table 11.7

Palmdale Job Training Program

20XX Annual Performance Report

Performance Measure	Total
1. Clients served[a]	1,050
2. Hours of training provided	30,000
3. Hours of quality training (training hours conducted by regular full-time staff)	28,800
4. No. of graduates	880
5. No. of placements (graduates hired)	755
6. No. of long-term placements (graduates still employed 6 months after completing training)	625
7. Cost per hour of training	$ 300
8. Cost per graduate	$11,200
9. Cost per placement	$12,000
10. Cost per long-term placement	$14,000

a. Not required by most performance measurement systems but useful in putting performance data into perspective.

the same time or of the same group at different points over time. Impact evaluation seeks to measure and compare these observations with one another in such a way as to be able to attribute any differences that may exist to the influence of the program.

A variety of impact evaluation designs are available for use depending on the particular environmental situation and the resources available. These research designs vary in complexity, timeliness, cost, feasibility, and potential usefulness. Impact evaluation is a complicated, demanding, and difficult undertaking that, to be successful, must be approached with realism, commitment, and considerable knowledge.

Table 11.8 presents three basic impact evaluation designs: (a) pre-experimental designs, (b) quasi-experimental designs, and (c) experimental designs. Each "X" in the table represents a program provided to a defined client group. Each "O" refers to an observation—the actual measurement of defined client characteristics or conditions that are intended to be influenced by the program. Random assignment of clients (the process of selecting individuals in such a way that each client has an equal chance of being included in either the control or the treatment group) is indicated by an R preceding the row; rows not preceded by R indicate that the groups to be compared are not formed by random assignment. Letters in the same row horizontally indicate that the same

Table 11.8

Types of Program Impact Evaluation Designs

Type 1: Preexperimental Designs				
One-shot case study			X	0
Single-group pretest/posttest		01	X	02
Type 2: Quasi-Experimental Designs				
Nonequivalent comparison group		01	X	02
		03		04
Type 3—Experimental Designs				
Pretest/posttest control group	R	01	X	02
	R	03		04

group is participating in the program and being observed. Vertical alignment of letters with the same design indicate events occurring at the same time. Temporal order is left to right.

With the exception of the one-shot case study, each design is based on either (a) a comparison of observations before participation in the program and again after completion of the program or the receipt of a full complement of services or (b) a comparison of observations of a group that participated in the program and a similar group that did not. These basic comparisons are elaborated or combined in the more complex designs to allow for a comparison of the impacts of different programs. True experimental designs include random assignment of clients to ensure that no selection bias (e.g., screening for those clients most likely to benefit) influences the measurement of the program's impact. (Readers who would like more complete listings and critiques of experimental and quasi-experimental designs are referred to Gabor, Unrau, & Grinnel, 1998, and Rossi & Freeman, 1993).

Preexperimental Impact Evaluation Designs

The first impact evaluation design to be discussed, the *one-shot case study,* is quite common in the social services but is really not an impact evaluation design at all. After clients have completed a program or received a full complement of services, data are collected on the results (outcomes) achieved. For example, adolescent mothers are provided parent training. After completion of the program, their parenting knowledge is tested. The test scores are assumed to reflect knowledge gained from the program. However, because the young women were not tested before they started the program (to create a baseline for comparison purposes), it is impossible to tell if parenting knowledge increased or not.

The second impact evaluation design, the *one-group pretest/posttest design,* creates a baseline for comparison purposes. Each young mother is tested on her parenting knowledge before she enters the program and again after she completes the program or receives a full complement of services. Diagrammatically, we can depict the results as follows:

$$\text{Change} = O2 - O1$$

Program impact is determined by subtracting the pretest score from the posttest score; the difference is attributable to the program. For example, if a young mother scores 50 on the pretest and 75 on the posttest, we can conclude that there was an improvement of 25 points in her case. For confidentiality purposes, we would of course not talk about individual clients but about aggregate client data. In this instance, we might compare the means (the arithmetic average) of the pretest and posttest scores for all the young mothers in the parent training class.

$$\text{Change} = \overline{X}O2 - \overline{X}O1$$

Although this design resolves the problem (lack of a baseline) raised in the one-shot case study design, it fails to deal with another important problem. Granted, we did observe improvement in the parenting skills of the young mothers as measured by changes after participation in the program, but we still cannot conclude that these changes were produced by the program. This problem, known as the *competing hypothesis dilemma,* asserts that although changes were observed, factors other than the program might have produced them. These "other factors" might range from the young women's being exposed to television shows or school programs dealing with parenting knowledge to the young women's "learning" how to take the test (i.e., being taught, by the first test, how to respond to the second test).

The third impact evaluation design, the *nonequivalent comparison group design,* begins to deal with the competing hypothesis dilemma and falls under the umbrella of those designs called "quasi-experimental." In this design, a comparison group is created of individuals who are "statistically similar" to the clients in the program. *Statistically similar* means that the comparison group is the same on all characteristics hypothesized to be relevant to achieving the program's results (outcomes). For example, subjects for the comparison group could be (a) people who are eligible for the program, who apply, but who are denied access because demand exceeds supply; (b) people who are eligible for the program but are unaware of its existence; or (c) people who are technically eligible for the program and would like to participate but who are not residents of the community or target area. The comparison (or nontreated) group usually receives some other type of program rather than no program at all. This practice avoids the ethical problem of withholding services from some clients for the purposes of experimentation. With the nonequivalent comparison group design, the potential problem of competing hypotheses is minimized in that factors outside the program are likely to affect both groups, and the effect of testing (the pretest effect) is minimized in that both groups are exposed to the same tests. The impact analysis consists of subtracting the pretest scores from the posttest scores for the control group and for the experimental group and then determining if the results differ.

$$\text{Change (treatment)} \quad = \overline{X}O2 - \overline{X}O1$$

$$\text{Change (comparison)} = \overline{X}O4 - \overline{X}O3$$

If any difference exists between the control group and the program participants, that difference is said to be the program's impact, provided the difference is statistically significant (i.e., there is little probability that the difference is due to chance).

The final impact evaluation design, the *experimental design,* is the strongest design in that randomization is used to assign participants, or subjects, either to the control group or to participation in the program. *Random assignment* means that each participant, or subject, has an equal chance of being assigned to the control group or to participation in the program. Random assignment ensures that the two groups are likely to be similar on all characteristics and that any differences between the two groups are likely to be due to the program and not to external factors. Once random assignment has occurred, the process and analysis are the same as for the quasi-experimental design. Although this design holds the promise for producing data that clearly and unequivocally demonstrate the impact of a program, if randomization were the sine qua non for evaluating the impact of social programs (as some authors argue) few impact evaluations would ever be conducted. Beyond the ethical issues involved in withholding participation in a program from clients, it is legally difficult to withhold services from any individual who meets the eligibility criteria for public programs and for private programs supported by public funds. For these reasons, social service administrators tend to rely more on quasi-experimental and other less rigorous designs when attempting to evaluate program impact.

THE UTILITY OF PERFORMANCE MEASUREMENT, MONITORING, AND PROGRAM EVALUATION

The test of any feedback system is the usefulness of the resulting data and information. As we have repeatedly stressed in earlier chapters, the critical questions to effectiveness-based program planning are these:

- What types of clients?
- With what types of problems?
- Receive what types of services?
- With what results?
- At what cost?

The program feedback data and information produced by the answers to the above questions are useful for a number of purposes. The first and most important use is to satisfy the program data and information needs of social service administrators and front-line managers. These are the individuals most immediately responsible for implementing programs, and it is critical that they have current data and information on which to base decisions.

A second purpose is to meet reporting requirements such as those of funding sources and regulatory agencies as well as to generate performance measurement reports. Much of the same program data, perhaps aggregated in different ways, can be used for a variety of purposes, including performance measurement, depending on the needs of the funding sources and regulatory agencies.

A third purpose is in dealing with the political environment, including the media. The political environment of the social services today is often turbulent, irrational, demanding, and frustrating. Every social service administrator has experienced the helpless feeling of not being able to respond to questions about why his or her agency is, or is not, doing something that a particular politician, reporter, or interest group favors or opposes. Program assessment data and information represent tools that can be used by social service administrators to respond to inquiries about their programs. Data and information, of course, do not guarantee that all community and political interests will be satisfied, but at least they provide a sound, data-based response. Data and information can also be used to sell a program and to enlarge its support base in a community.

A CONCLUDING COMMENT

The underlying thrust of this book has been to outline a process that encourages mutual respect between direct service practitioners and social service administrators and managers, a process that assumes a partnership relationship between or among administrators, managers, practitioners, and clients through the development of a supportive and open problem-solving environment. Although effectiveness-based program planning may appear to be linear—that is, problem analysis precedes the development of the program hypothesis, which in turn precedes the development of goals and objectives, and so forth—it is, in reality, more of an iterative process. Our belief is that all problem solving should be viewed as a process of social learning through social transactions and not just as adherence to a set of cookbook-type rules. We recognize the reality of the ever-changing and nonstable environments in which social services administration is conducted, and it is this reality that has guided our development of this effectiveness-based program planning model.

APPENDIX
Line-Item, Functional, and Program Budgeting Systems: A Case Example

The Centerville Child and Family Treatment Center (CCFTC) is a social service agency that provides individual, family, and group counseling as well as a number of other activities that fall under the general heading of parent support services. CCFTC is attempting to move from a line-item budgeting system to a combined functional and program budgeting system.

The first step in developing a combined functional and program budgeting system is the creation of a line-item budget. A simplified version of CCFTC's line-item budget for the coming fiscal year is shown in Table A.1. As can be seen, CCFTC's line-item budget is balanced: Anticipated revenues are equal to or greater than proposed expenses.

IMPLEMENTING A COMBINED FUNCTIONAL AND PROGRAM BUDGETING SYSTEM

The second step in developing a combined functional and program budgeting system is the determination of the agency's program structure. CCFTC has determined that it operates two programs: the Family Counseling Program and the Teen Parenting Program.

The third step involves the creation of a cost allocation plan format (see Table A.2). The expense items that appear in CCFTC's line-item budget appear as rows on the cost allocation plan format. The three columns across the top are for CCFTC's two programs (the Family Counseling Program and the Teen Parenting Program) and the indirect

Table A.1
CCFTC Line-Item Budget

Revenues			
Contributions		$	250,000
United Way allocation		$	400,000
Government contracts and grants		$	285,000
Client fees		$	100,000
			$1,035,000
Expenses			
Salaries		$	760,000
Executive director	$ 75,000		
Program manager			
(Family Counseling)	$ 55,000		
Program manager (Teen Parenting)	$ 60,000		
Family counselors (5 @ $45,000)	$225,000		
Teen parenting counselors			
(4 @ $50,000)	$200,000		
Parenting trainers (2 @ $35,000)	$ 70,000		
Secretaries (3 @ $25,000)	$ 75,000		
Employee-related expenses (@ 20%)		$	152,000
Supplies		$	20,000
Telephone		$	12,000
Postage and shipping		$	5,000
Rent		$	27,000
Utilities		$	15,000
Equipment		$	10,000
Travel		$	14,000
Printing and duplicating		$	20,000
			$1,035,000

cost pool. (*Note*: The reader may wish to make a photocopy of this page to use as a worksheet.)

The fourth step involves examining each cost item and determining whether it is a direct cost or an indirect cost. If a cost item benefits only the Family Counseling Program or only the Teen Parenting Program, it is identified as a direct cost (DC). If a cost item benefits both programs,

Table A.2
CCFTC Cost Allocation Plan

Budget Line Item	Family Counseling Program	Teen Parenting Program	Indirect Cost Pool
Salaries and Wages			
Executive director			
Program manager (Family Counseling)			
Program manager (Teen Parenting)			
Family counselors			
Teen parenting counselors			
Parenting trainers			
Secretaries			
Total Salaries and Wages			
Employee-Related Expenses (@ 20%)			
Other Operating			
Supplies			
Telephone			
Postage and shipping			
Rent			
Utilities			
Equipment			
Travel			
Printing and duplicating			
Column Totals			
Allocate Indirect Costs			
Total Program Costs			

it is identified as an indirect cost (IC). Table A.3 identifies each cost item, except for employee-related expenses (ERE), as either a direct cost (DC) or an indirect cost (IC). The assignment of ERE costs follows the assignment or allocation of salary and wage costs. (*Note*: Before reviewing Table A.3, the reader may want to try identifying the costs in Table A.2 as direct or indirect.)

The fifth step involves assigning all direct costs to either the Family Counseling Program or the Teen Parenting Program. If a cost item is identified as a direct cost to the Family Counseling Program, it is placed under that column heading. Likewise, if a cost item is identified as a

Table A.3

CCFTC Cost Allocation Plan,, With Identification of

Direct Costs (DC) and Indirect Costs (IC)

Budget Line Item	Family Counseling Program	Teen Parenting Program	Indirect Cost Pool
Salaries and Wages			
Executive director (IC)			
Program manager (DC) (Family Counseling)			
Program manager (DC) (Teen Parenting)			
Family counselors (DC)			
Teen parenting counselors (DC)			
Parenting trainers (DC)			
Secretaries (IC)			
Total Salaries and Wages			
Employee-Related Expenses (@ 20%)			
Other Operating			
Supplies (IC)			
Telephone (IC)			
Postage and shipping (IC)			
Rent (IC)			
Utilities (IC)			
Equipment (IC)			
Travel (IC)			
Printing and duplicating (IC)			
Column Totals			
Allocate Indirect Costs			
Total Program Costs			

direct cost to the Teen Parenting Program, it is placed under that column heading. Table A.4 shows the assignment of direct costs to the two CCFTC programs. (*Note*: Before reviewing Table A.4, the reader may want to try assigning direct costs to the two programs using the photocopy of Table A.2 as a worksheet.)

The sixth step involves assigning all indirect costs to the indirect cost pool and determining total program costs. When all costs have been assigned to either the two programs or the indirect cost pool, all columns

Table A.4
Assignment of Direct Costs to Programs

Budget Line Item	Family Counseling Program	Teen Parenting Program	Indirect Cost Pool
Salaries and Wages			
Executive director (IC)			
Program manager (DC) (Family Counseling)	$ 55,000		
Program manager (DC) (Teen Parenting)		$ 60,000	
Family counselors (DC)	$225,000		
Teen parenting counselors (DC)		$200,000	
Parenting trainers (DC)		$ 70,000	
Secretaries (IC)			
Total Salaries and Wages	$280,000	$330,000	
ERE (@ 20%)	$ 56,000	$ 66,000	
Other Operating			
Supplies (IC)			
Telephone (IC)			
Postage and shipping (IC)			
Rent (IC)			
Utilities (IC)			
Equipment (IC)			
Travel (IC)			
Printing and duplicating (IC)			
Column Totals			
Allocate Indirect Costs			
Total Program Costs			

are totaled. Then the indirect cost pool must be allocated to the two programs using some base; we will use total direct labor costs (total direct salaries and wages plus total direct ERE). The indirect cost rate is determined by placing the amount in the indirect cost pool in the numerator and the combined total direct salaries, wages, and ERE of both the Family Counseling Program and the Teen Parenting Program in the denominator. The resulting indirect cost rate is then applied to the total direct labor costs (total salaries, wages, and ERE) of the Family Counseling Program and the Teen Parenting Program.

Table A.5 shows the completed cost allocation plan, including (a) the total direct costs of the Family Counseling Program, (b) the total direct costs of the Teen Parenting Program, (c) the total indirect costs in the indirect cost pool, (d) the allocation of the indirect cost pool to the Family Counseling Program and the Teen Parenting Program, and (e) the computation of total program costs (direct plus indirect) for the Family Counseling Program and the Teen Parenting Program. When the total costs of both programs are added together, the result ($1,035,000) is the total amount of CCFTC line-item budget (see Table A.1). (*Note*: Before reviewing Table A.5, the reader may want to try completing the cost allocation plan and the various activities associated with (a) through (e) above, using the photocopy of Table A.2 as a worksheet.)

Determining the total costs of the Family Counseling Program and the Teen Parenting Program completes the first six steps in moving from a line-item budget system to a combined functional and program budgeting system. Three additional steps are required to complete the process.

The seventh step involves the selection of performance measures for each program, including an intermediate output (unit of service), a final output (service completion), a quality output, an intermediate outcome, and a final outcome. (*Note*: Before reviewing the following section, the reader may want to try developing output, quality and outcome performance measures for the two programs. Remember that the measures appearing below are not necessarily the only ones that could be used, or even the best ones. They are just examples.)

After consultation with their stakeholders (clients, funding sources, advocacy groups, etc.), CCFTC has identified the following performance measures (outputs, quality, outcome) for its two programs:

Family Counseling Program

- *Intermediate Output (Unit of Service)*: 1 hour of face-to-face counseling

- *Quality Output*: 1 hour of face-to-face counseling with counselor of record

- *Final Output (Service Completion)*: One family completing at least 8 of 10 scheduled counseling sessions

- *Intermediate Outcome*: One family demonstrating improvement of at least 25% on the Family Assessment Scale (administered on completion of treatment)

Table A.5

Assignment of Direct Costs to Programs

Budget Line Item	Family Counseling Program	Teen Parenting Program	Indirect Cost Pool
Salaries and Wages			
Executive director (IC)			$ 75,000
Program manager (DC) (Family Counseling)	$ 55,000		
Program manager (DC) (Teen Parenting)		$ 60,000	
Family counselors (DC)	$225,000		
Teen parenting counselors (DC)		$200,000	
Parenting trainers (DC)		$ 70,000	
Secretaries (IC)			$ 75,000
Total Salaries and Wages	$280,000	$330,000	$150,000
Employee-Related Expenses (@ 20%)	$ 56,000	$ 66,000	$ 30,000
Other Operating			
Supplies (IC)			$ 20,000
Telephone (IC)			$ 12,000
Postage and shipping (IC)			$ 5,000
Rent (IC)			$ 27,000
Utilities (IC)			$ 15,000
Equipment (IC)			$ 10,000
Travel (IC)			$ 14,000
Printing and duplicating (IC)			$ 20,000
Column Totals	$336,000	$396,000	$303,000
Allocate Indirect Costs	$139,082	$163,918	
Total Program Costs	$475,082	$559,918	

NOTE: Direct labor costs for the Family Counseling Program = $336,000 ($280,000 + $56,000); direct labor costs for the Teen Parenting Program = $396,000 ($330,000 + $66,000). Total direct labor costs for both CCFTC programs = $732,000 ($336,000 + $396,000). $303,000 (indirect cost pool)/$732,000 = 41.393% = indirect cost rate.

- *Final Outcome*: One family maintaining its improvement level of at least 25% on the Family Assessment Scale (administered 6 months following treatment)

Teen Parenting Program
- *Intermediate Output (Unit of Service)*: One teen parent training session
- *Quality Output*: One teen parent training session conducted by trainer/ counselor of record

Table A.6

CCFTC Combined Functional and

Performance Budgeting System and Format

Family Counseling Program
(Total Program Cost = $475,082)

1. Outputs
    (a) Intermediate Output (Units of Service)
         Provide 6,250 hours of service at a unit cost of $76.

    (b) Quality Output
         Provide 5,938 quality hours of service at a unit cost of $80.

    (b) Final Output (Service Completions)
         Achieve 500 service completions at a unit cost of $950.

2. Outcomes
    (a) Intermediate Outcome
         Improve the level of functioning of 350 families at a unit cost of $1,357.

    (b) Final Outcome
         Maintain long term the improved level of functioning of 300 families at a
         unit cost of $1,584.

Teen Parenting Program
(Total Program Cost = $559,918)

1. Outputs
    (a) Intermediate Output (Units of Service)
         Provide 550 training sessions at a unit cost of $1,018.

    (b) Quality Output
         Provide 500 quality training sessions at a unit cost of $1,120.

    (b) Final Output (Service Completions)
         Achieve 350 service completions at a unit cost of $1,600.

2. Outcomes
    (a) Intermediate Outcome
         Improve the parenting skills of 300 teen parents at a unit cost of $1,866.

    (b) Final Outcomes
         Maintain long term the improved parenting skills of 250 teen parents at a
         unit cost of $2,240.

- *Final Output (Service Completion)*: One teen parent completing a
  written and agreed-on treatment plan
- *Intermediate Outcome*: One teen parent demonstrating at least a 50%
  improvement on the Parenting Skills Assessment Scale (administered
  on completion of treatment)

- *Final Outcome*: One teen parent accomplishing short-term career objectives on time as stated in the written career plan (assessed 1 year following treatment)

The eighth step involves determining quantifiable objectives for each of the performance measures identified in Step 7. After much deliberation, the management and staff of CCFTC formally adopted the following performance measure objectives for the coming fiscal year:

Family Counseling Program

- *Intermediate Output (Unit-of-Service) Objective*: A minimum of 6,250 hours of service
- *Quality Output Objective*: A minimum of 5,938 hours of service (95% quality rate) with counselor of record
- *Final Output (Service Completion) Objective*: A minimum of 500 families completing treatment
- *Intermediate Outcome Objective*: A minimum of 350 families demonstrating at least a 25% improvement on the Family Assessment Scale (on completion of treatment)
- *Final Outcome Objective*: A minimum of 300 families maintaining their improvement level of at least 25% on the Family Assessment Scale (at 1-year follow-up)

Teen Parenting Program

- *Intermediate Output (Unit-of-Service) Objective*: A minimum of 550 training sessions
- *Quality Output Objective*: A minimum of 500 training sessions conducted by instructors/counselors of record (90% quality rate)
- *Final Output (Service Completion) Objective*: A minimum of 350 teen parents completing treatment
- *Intermediate Outcome Objective*: A minimum of 300 teen parents demonstrating at least a 50% improvement on Parenting Skills Assessment Scale (on completion of treatment)
- *Final Outcome Objective*: A minimum of 250 teen parents maintaining their 50% improvement level on the Parenting Skills Assessment Scale (at 1-year follow-up)

The ninth step in developing a combined functional and program budgeting system for the CCFTC is the computation of unit costs for each of the performance measures (outputs, quality, and outcomes) identified above. Unit costs are determined by dividing total program costs (numerator) by the units to be provided (denominator). For example, the unit cost per intermediate output (unit of service) for the Family Counseling Program is $76. This figure is derived by dividing the total cost of the Family Counseling Program ($475,082) by the number of intermediate outputs (units of service) to be provided (6,250). Table A.6 shows the end result of this case study: a combined functional/program budgeting system and format for both the Family Counseling Program and the Teen Parenting Program. It should be noted that the format itself is only one of several that could be used to present the resulting data. (*Note*: Before reviewing Table A.6, the reader may want to try computing the various unit costs identified above and then compare answers.)

At least initially, some of the unit cost figures may be rather crude in terms of the degree of precision. Nevertheless, unit cost data provide valuable insights into the operation of programs. For example, unit costs are needed to calculate break-even points and to determine client fees. Funding sources may also require unit cost data for purposes of grants and contracts. Unit costs also enable agencies to calculate the effects on agency services and clients created by funding increases and decreases. Finally, unit costs provide social service agencies with "bottom-line" information about the efficiency, quality, and effectiveness of their programs.

This case example has illustrated the following:

- All budgeting systems begin with the development of a line-item budget.
- Both functional and program budgeting systems require the identification of a program structure and calculation of total program costs.
- Calculating unit costs requires defining output, quality, and outcomes measures, developing measurable output, quality, and outcome objectives, and determining the cost to provide one unit.

REFERENCES

Babbie, B. (1983). *The practice of social research.* Belmont, CA: Wadsworth.

Bell, W. (1955). Economic, family and ethnic status: An empirical test. *American Sociological Review, 20,* 45-52.

Berry, B. (1972). *City classification handbook: Methods and classifications.* New York: John Wiley.

Bradshaw, J. (1972). The concept of social need. *New Society, 30,* 640-643.

Cloward, R., Ohlin, L., & Piven, F. (1959). *Delinquency and opportunity.* New York: Free Press.

Cohen, N. (1964). *Social work and social problems.* New York: National Association of Social Workers.

Crosby, P. (1980). *Quality is free.* New York: Mentor.

Crosby, P. (1985). *Quality without tears: The art of hassle-free management.* New York: Plume.

Cross, T. (1989). *Towards a culturally competent system of care.* Washington, DC: Georgetown University, CASSP Technical Assistance Center.

Delbecq, A., Vandeven, A., & Gustafson, D. (1975). *Group techniques for program planning: A guide to nominal group and Delphi processes.* Glenview, IL: Scott, Foresman.

Deming, W. (1986). *Out of the crisis.* Cambridge: MIT Center for Advanced Engineering Study.

Department of Economic Security. (1995). *Arizona dictionary and taxonomy of human services* [Photocopy]. Phoenix, AZ: Author.

Department of Human Services. (1978). *Physically abused women and their families: The need for community services.* Trenton, NJ: State of New Jersey.

Eggers, W., & Ng, R. (1993). *Social and health services privatization: A survey of state and county governments.* Los Angeles: Reason Foundation.

Fink, A. (1993). *Evaluation fundamentals.* Newbury Park, CA: Sage.

Fischer, J. (1973). Is casework effective? A review. *Social Work, 18,* 5-20.

Fischer, J., & Corcoran, K. (1994). *Measures for clinical practice: Vol. 1. Couples, families, and children.* New York: Free Press.

249

Gabor, P., Unrau, Y., & Grinnel, R. (1998). *Evaluation for social workers.* Needham Heights, MA: Allyn & Bacon.

Gundersdorf, J. (1977). Management and financial controls. In W. F. Anderson, B. J. Frieden, & M. J. Murphy (Eds.), *Managing human services.* Washington, DC: International City Management Association.

Gurin, G. (1960). *Americans view their mental health.* New York: Basic Books.

Harris, A. (1971). *Handicapped and impaired in Great Britain.* London: HMSO.

Hay, L., & Wilson, E. (1995). *Accounting for governmental and nonprofit entities.* Chicago: Irwin.

Hobbs, N. (1975). *The futures of children.* San Francisco: Jossey-Bass.

Horngren, C., Foster, G., & Datar, S. (1997). *Cost accounting: A managerial emphasis.* Englewood Cliffs, NJ: Prentice Hall.

Hudson, W. W. (1982). *The clinical measurement package: A field manual.* Chicago: Dorsey.

Juran, J. (1988). *Juran's quality control handbook* (4th ed.). New York: McGraw-Hill.

Juran, J. (1989). *Juran on leadership for quality: An executive handbook.* New York: Free Press.

Kane, R., & Kane, R. L. (1981). *Assessing the elderly: A practical guide to measurement.* Lexington, MA: Lexington.

Kettner, P. M., Daley, J. M., & Nichols, A. (1985). *Initiating change in organizations and communities.* Monterey, CA: Brooks/Cole.

Kettner, P. M., & Martin, L. L. (1987). *Purchase of service contracting.* Newbury Park, CA: Sage.

Kuechler, C. F., Velasquez, J. S., & White, M. S. (1988). An assessment of human services program outcome measures: Are they credible, feasible, useful? *Administration in Social Work, 12,* 71-89.

Lee, R. D., & Johnson, R. W. (1973). *Public budgeting systems.* Baltimore: University Park Press.

Lourie, N. (1964). Poverty. In N. Cohen (Ed.), *Social work and social problems* (pp. 201-240). New York: National Association of Social Workers.

Lynch, T. D. (1995). *Public budgeting in America.* Englewood Cliffs, NJ: Prentice Hall.

MacMahon, B., Pugh, T., & Ipsen, J. (1960). *Epidemiologic methods.* Boston: Little, Brown.

Martin, L. L. (1988, November). *Consumer satisfaction surveys: Are they valid measures of program performance?* Paper presented at the Eleventh National Conference on Specialized Transportation, Sarasota, FL.

Martin, L. (1993). *Total quality management in human service organizations.* Newbury Park, CA: Sage.

Martin, L. (1997). Outcome budgeting: A new entrepreneurial approach to budgeting. *Journal of Public Budgeting, Accounting and Financial Management, 9,* 108-126.

Martin, L. (in press). Performance contracting: A comparative analysis of selected state practices. *Administration in Social Work.*

Martin, L., & Kettner, P. (1996). *Measuring the performance of human service programs.* Newbury Park, CA: Sage.

Maslow, A. (1954). *Motivation and personality.* New York: Harper & Row.

McMurtry, S., Netting, F., & Kettner, P. (1990). How non-profits adapt to a stringent environment. *Non-Profit Management and Leadership, 1,* 235-252.

Melkers, J., & Willoughby, K. (1998). The state of the states: Performance-based budgeting requirements in 47 out of 50 states. *Public Administration Review, 58,* 66-73.

Millar, A., Hatry, H., & Koss, M. (1977). *Monitoring the outcomes of social services: Vol. 1. Preliminary suggestions.* Washington, DC: Urban Institute.

Mohr, L. (1992). *Impact analysis for program evaluation.* Newbury Park, CA: Sage.

Morales, A., & Salcido, R. (1989). Social work with Mexican-Americans. In A. Morales & B. Sheafor (Eds.), *Social work: A profession of many faces* (pp. 543-566). Boston: Allyn & Bacon.

Moroney, R. (1973). Utilization of small area analysis for evaluation. In R. Yaffe & D. Zalkind (Eds.), *Evaluation in health services delivery.* Washington, DC: Engineering Foundation.

Moroney, R. (1976). The uses of small area analysis in community health planning. *Inquiry, 13,* 145-151.

Moroney, R. (1986). *Shared responsibility.* New York: Aldine.

Morris, R., & Zweig, F. (1966). The social planning design guide: Process and proposal. *Social Work, 11,* 13-21.

National Center for Child Abuse and Neglect. (1981). *Child sexual abuse: Incest, assault and exploitation* (DHHS Pub. No. 81-30166). Washington, DC: Government Printing Office.

Netting, F., Kettner, P., & McMurty, S. (1998). *Social work macro practice* (2nd ed.). New York: Longman.

Osborne, D., & Gaebler, T. (1992). *Reinventing government.* New York: Plume.

Patti, R. (1985). In search of purpose for social welfare administration. *Administration in Social Work, 9,* 1-14.

Phyrr, P. A. (1973). *Zero based budgeting: A practical management tool for evaluating expenses.* New York: John Wiley.

Ponsioen, J. (1962). *Social welfare policy: Contributions to theory.* The Hague: Mouton.

Rauch, J. (1989). Gender as a factor in practice. In A. Morales & B. Sheafor (Eds.), *Social work: A profession of many faces* (pp. 335-350). Boston: Allyn & Bacon.

Redich, R., & Goldsmith, H. (1971). *Census data used to indicate areas with different potentials for mental health and related problems* (DHEW Pub. No. 72-9051). Washington, DC: Government Printing Office.

Rosenberg, M., & Brody, R. (1974). *Systems serving people.* Cleveland, OH: Case Western Reserve School of Applied Social Sciences.

Rossi, P. H., & Freeman, H. E. (1993). *Evaluation: A systematic approach* (5th ed.). Newbury Park, CA: Sage.

Rubin, A. (1985). Practice effectiveness: More grounds for optimism. *Social Work, 30,* 469-476.

Schick, A. (1966). The road to PPB: The stages of budget reform. *Public Administration Review, 26,* 243-258.

Shanas, E., Townsend, P., & Streib, G. (1968). *Old people in three industrial societies.* London: Routledge & Kegan Paul.

Solomon, B. (1989). Social work with Afro-Americans. In A. Morales & B. Sheafor (Eds.), *Social work: A profession of many faces* (pp. 567-587). Boston: Allyn & Bacon.

Srole, L., Rennie, T., & Cumming, A. (1962). *Mental health in the metropolis.* New York: McGraw-Hill.

U.S. Bureau of the Census. (1971). *Health information system, Part 2* (Census Report Study No. 2012). Washington, DC: Government Printing Office.

U.S. Department of Health and Human Services. (1995). *Performance measurement in selected public health programs.* Washington, DC: Public Health Service.

United Way of America. (1976). *UWASIS II: A taxonomy of social goals and human service programs.* Alexandria, VA: Author.

Wallace, H., Gold, E., & Dooley, S. (1967). Availability and usefulness of selected health and socio-economic data for community planning. *American Journal of Public Health, 57,* 762-771.

INDEX

ABOUT THE AUTHORS

Peter M. Kettner is Professor of Social Work at Arizona State University. He is the author of six books and over 50 articles and book chapters on the topics of purchase-of-service contracting, privatization, macro practice in social work, human services planning, and social work administration. He has served as consultant to several state and local human service agencies in the design and implementation of effectiveness-based planning systems.

Robert M. Moroney is Professor of Social Policy and Planning at the School of Social Work at Arizona State University. He is the author of eight books and over 60 articles and book chapters on various aspects of policy, planning, and program evaluation. He has been associated with a number of policy centers, including the Bush Institute at the University of North Carolina and the Vanderbilt Institute of Public Policy Institutes. He recently was a Senior Fulbright Fellow with the Department of Social Policy and Social Work, University College Dublin. He currently serves as a board member of the Rosalyn Carter Institute for Human Development. He does extensive consultation with numerous national, state, and local human service organizations.

Lawrence L. Martin (PhD, Arizona State University, Tempe) is Associate Professor of Social Work and Director of the Social Administration Program at the Columbia University School of Social Work. He has published five books and more than 60 articles and book chapters dealing with such topics as social services administration, privatization, purchase-of-service contracting, performance measurement, budgeting and financial management, and state and local government.